CW01305278

INDIGO GREENS
KITCHEN COOK BOOK
PATTI BULLOCK

INDIGO GREENS

THIS BOOK DOES NOT PROVIDE MEDICAL ADVICE.

All material contained in this book is for informational purposes only. Always seek medical advice from your healthcare provider or dietician with any questions you may have regarding medical conditions or treatment before undertaking any new health care regime, supplements and/or lifestyle changes.

AUTHOR –	Patti Bullock
EDITOR–	Mark Aston
EDITOR/BOOK DESIGN -	Mary Turner Thomson
PHOTOGRAPHERS –	Laura Hardman, Craig Dowd
FOOD STYLIST –	Patti Bullock
PROP STYLIST –	Patti Bullock, Laura Hardman, Craig Dowd

Copyright © Patti Bullock

First published in Great Britain November 2021

All rights reserved. No part of this publication may be reproduced, distributed, stored, or transmitted in any form or by any means, including recording, photocopying, or other electronic or mechanical methods, without the prior written permission of the author of publisher, except in the case of brief quotations embodied in critical reviews and certain other non-commercial uses permitted by copyright law.

DEDICATION

This book is dedicated to my dear mother who has guided me on this path through both life and death, her love for cooking lives on through me.

APPRECIATIONS

A note of gratitude to all the people who made this book possible ... especially Mark, my soul mate, my best friend, my business partner, and my life teacher. Thank you for believing in me every step of the way, for all your wise words, your love, compassion, kindness and of course your continuous support that showed me there are no limits, I am truly grateful for all the healing and growth we have both experienced together since the day the universe aligned us on this path. Your courage and devotion to help others heal is a true expression of pure love and selflessness.

Thank you to all the lightworkers, medicine carriers, space holders, teachers and holistic practitioners who have helped heal us on our own journeys, while aligning us and guiding us on this path, it's clear to see this is our true calling, by healing ourselves we were able to heal others and raise the vibration of our city and beyond through plant-based education.

Thank you to all our loyal customers who have confided in us and trusted in us over the years, I am truly grateful to have been in service for you, knowing how much of an impact our food has had on the lives of many, genuinely fills my heart with so much love! Thank you for your continuous support!

I am also grateful to all the wonderful talented staff of Indigo Greens, past and present, for your loyalty, hard work and beautiful input which made us who we are today, I'd like to name you all but there really has been too many, and to those of you who just passed through as part of your own healing journeys, it's been magical to see so many of you blossom and step onto your own path.

I am thankful for our small support network who has been there since day one, the circle of trust who dedicated their lives to us daily to ensure our vision was brought to life, Jamie Robinson, Old Joe and of course Lord Kai, Mark's son who gave up many of his childhood days to be part of our vision at Indigo Greens, your passion and drive to see us succeed is an honour and it's been amazing to watch you grow into a polite, hardworking and very talented young man who will definitely go far In life.

Thank you to Laura and Craig from RFM Media for capturing all our beautiful dishes here throughout the book and to Emma Durney, our apprentice, who spent weeks on end re-typing all the recipes, so they can be enjoyed in family size portions at home. Thank you again to my beloved Mark, who carefully went through every single word and corrected my lazy grammar and awful spelling. Thank you to Dr Hayley Tait author of 'Health on The Hob' for inspiring me to finally fulfil my dream and write a recipe book, thank you for helping me make this happen and thank you to Rayner Jordan, from 'The Plant Based Directory' for being an instrumental figure on our journey with Indigo Greens.

Thank you to all our kind customers who tested our recipes at home, your feedback was well and truly appreciated.

Thankful to all my old head chefs for teaching me culinary professionalism, while I'm here, I'd also like to apologise for the lack of discipline I had as a young chef, your teachings came later in life when karma came back round and bit me on my bottom, now I know what I put your through!

And finally, so much gratitude to my late nan, grandad, and dear mother, who all taught me how to cook from the moment I could stand on a chair and hold a utensil in my hand. Writing this book has taken me down memory lane over and over, a reminiscence I will cherish forever.

Thank you, thank you, thank you.

I love and appreciate you all!

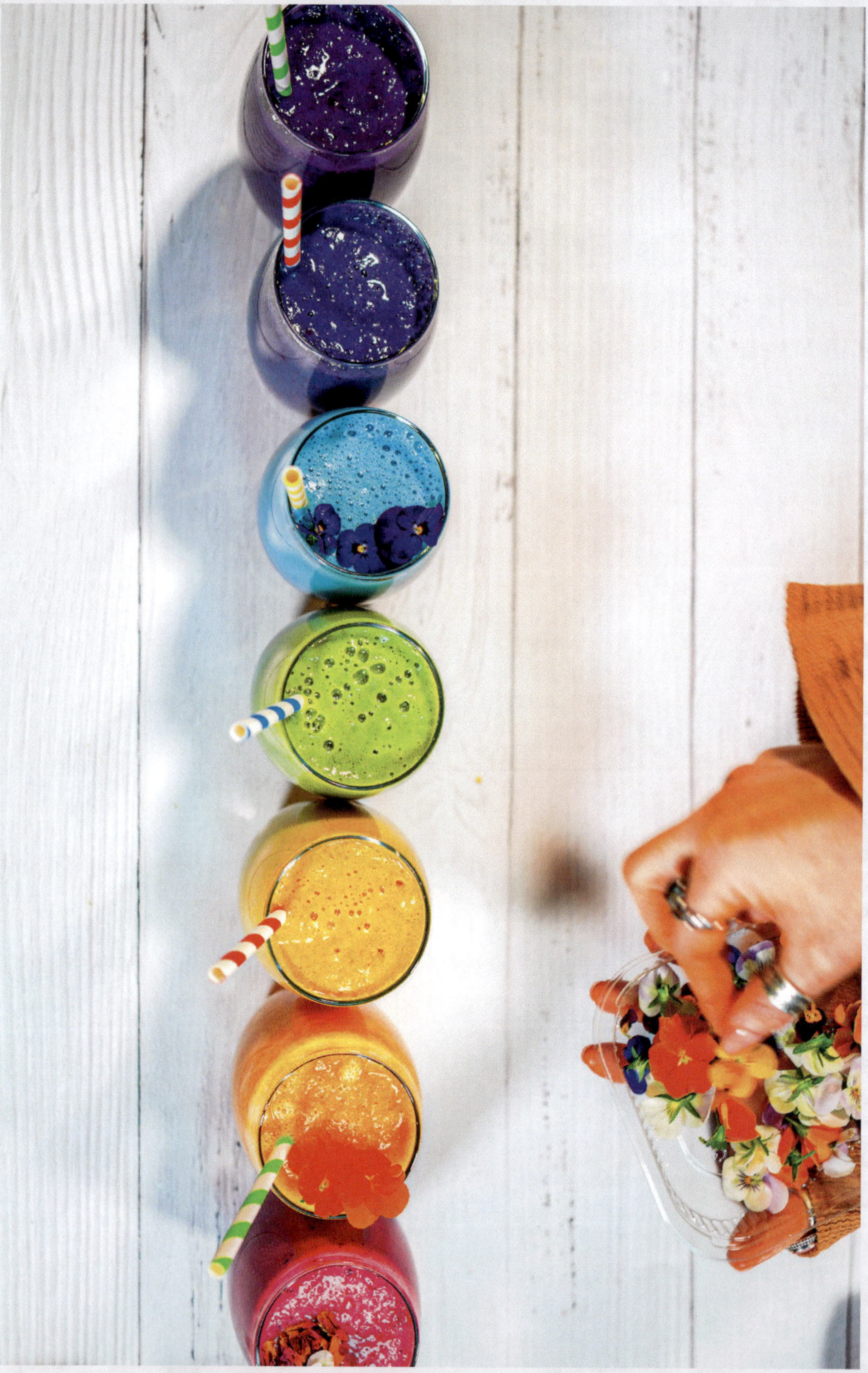

CONTENTS

OUR STORY — 1

WHY PLANT BASED? — 7

CONSCIOUS COOKING — 14
- KITCHEN EQUIPMENT — 15
- OVENS — 15
- BLENDERS AND FOOD PROCESSORS — 15
- WEIGHING AND MEASURING — 15
- COOKING — 16
- PREPPING — 16
- STORING — 16
- UTENSILS — 16

STOCKING AND SHOPPING — 17
- SHOPPING LIST — 18

THE BENEFITS OF SOAKING — 20
- HOW TO CREATE THE RIGHT CONDITIONS FOR SOAKING? — 20
- SOAKING NUTS — 20
- SOAKING SEEDS — 21
- SOAKING AND COOKING GRAINS, BEANS AND PULSES — 21

SUPERFOODS & SUPPLEMENT BENEFITS — 22

RAW AND CHILLED BREAKFAST — 25
- SUPER FOOD MUESLI – RAW OR TOASTED — 26
- SWEET APPLE AND SULTANA BIRCHER MUESLI — 28
- NUTTY KETO COCONUT GRANOLA — 30
- FRUIT AND CRUNCHY NUT GRANOLA — 32
- CULTURED CASHEW YOGHURT WITH BAOBAB — 34
- PASSION FOR PROTEIN CHIA SEED PUDDING — 36
- BANANA BREAD — 38
- CHIA BERRY PROTEIN JAM — 40
- DEEP ROASTED PEANUT BUTTER — 40
- QUINOA AND CHIA LOAF WITH SUNFLOWER SEEDS — 42

I AM: CHAKRA HEALING SMOOTHIES   45

- VIOLET CROWN SMOOTHIE — 46
- INDIGO THIRD EYE SMOOTHIE — 46
- BLUE THROAT SMOOTHIE — 46
- GREEN HEART SMOOTHIE — 46
- YELLOW SOLAR PLEXUS SMOOTHIE — 47
- ORANGE SACRAL SMOOTHIE — 47
- RED ROOT SMOOTHIE — 47

ON TOASTS   49

- PUMPKIN SEED PESTO AND POMEGRANATE HUMMUS — 50
- GRILLED CASHEW CHEESE, CHIVE AND CARAMELISED ONION CHUTNEY — 52
- MASHED AVOCADO ON TOAST WITH LIME, CHILLI AND CORIANDER — 54
- TOAST 3 WAYS — 56
- MUSHROOM BRUSCHETTA WITH PUMPKIN SEED PESTO — 58
- SAUSAGE ON — 60
- TERRACOTTA BEANS — 62
- TLT - TOFU, LETTUCE, TOMATO ON TOAST — 64

BIG BREAKFASTS   67

- THE FULL INDIGO GRILL — 68
- HERBY SAUSAGES — 70
- GRILLED HASH BROWNS — 72
- SMOKEY BREAKFAST BEANS — 74
- ROSEMARY AND GARLIC MUSHROOMS — 76
- BALSAMIC GLAZED BABY VINE TOMATOES — 78
- GOLDEN TURMERIC SCRAMBLED TOFU — 80
- BUTTERED SPINACH — 80
- THE GREEN GRILL — 82

SAUCES AND DIPS   85

- CARAMELISED ONION CHUTNEY — 86
- TAHINI WHIP — 88
- CHUNKY PUMPKIN SEED PESTO — 90
- CREAMY SMOOTH TRADITIONAL HUMMUS — 92
- BALSAMIC GLAZE — 94
- MAPLE AND MUSTARD DRESSING — 94
- IG BURGER SAUCE — 95
- SPICY CHIPOTLE SAUCE — 95
- TOMATO CHUTNEY — 98
- GUACAMOLE — 99
- STICKY KUNG PAO SAUCE — 100
- SMOKED CASHEW CHEESE — 101
- PINEAPPLE AND MINT SALSA — 102

INDIGO FAVOURITES — 105

- BLIND BUT AWAKE SCOUSE — 106
- PERUVIAN QUINOA AND VEGETABLE STEW — 108
- CHUNKY PEA NO HAM STEW — 110
- RAINBOW EARTH BOWL — 112
- SPICY VEGETABLE STIR-FRY — 114
- JENS MEXICAN 3 BEAN CHILLI WITH LIME AND CORIANDER — 116
- PEA AND MINT FRITTERS — 118
- THE ULTIMATE BEYOND BURGER — 120

SIDES AND SMALL PLATES — 123

- CRISPY SALT AND PEPPER TOFU — 124
- SALT AND PEPPER SWEET POTATO WEDGES — 126
- CHINESE SALT AND PEPPER SEASONING — 128
- GOLDEN BATTER INGREDIENTS — 129
- DUSTING FLOUR INGREDIENTS — 129
- LOADED SWEET POTATO WEDGES — 130
- CRISPY KUNG PAO CAULI WINGS — 132
- CASHEW MAC AND CHEESE — 134
- SWEET PICKLED CABBAGE — 136
- SPICY KALE SLAW — 138

RAINBOW ROAST DINNER — 141

- LENTIL, CRANBERRY AND ORANGE NUT-LESS ROAST — 142
- GARLIC, LEMON AND HERB ROAST POTATOES — 144
- BUTTERY CARROT AND SWEDE MASH — 146
- SWEET CUMIN ROASTED PARSNIPS — 150
- SWEET BRAISED RED CABBAGE — 152
- MINTED MUSHY PEAS — 154
- TRADITIONAL RICH GRAVY — 156

DESSERTS — 159

- CHOCOLATE ORANGE COOKIE DOUGH SLABS - THE NAKERY RECIPE — 160
- TAHINI ENERGY BALLS – HI VIBE NUTRITION RECIPE — 162
- POWER HEALING BALLS – CELL FUEL RECIPE — 164

SUPERFOOD LATTE BLENDS — 167

- TURMERIC LATTE BLEND — 168
- MUSHY MACA CHOCO LATTE BLEND — 168
- BEETROOT AND GINGER LATTE BLEND — 168
- SPICED CHAI LATTE BLEND — 168

RESOURCES — 170

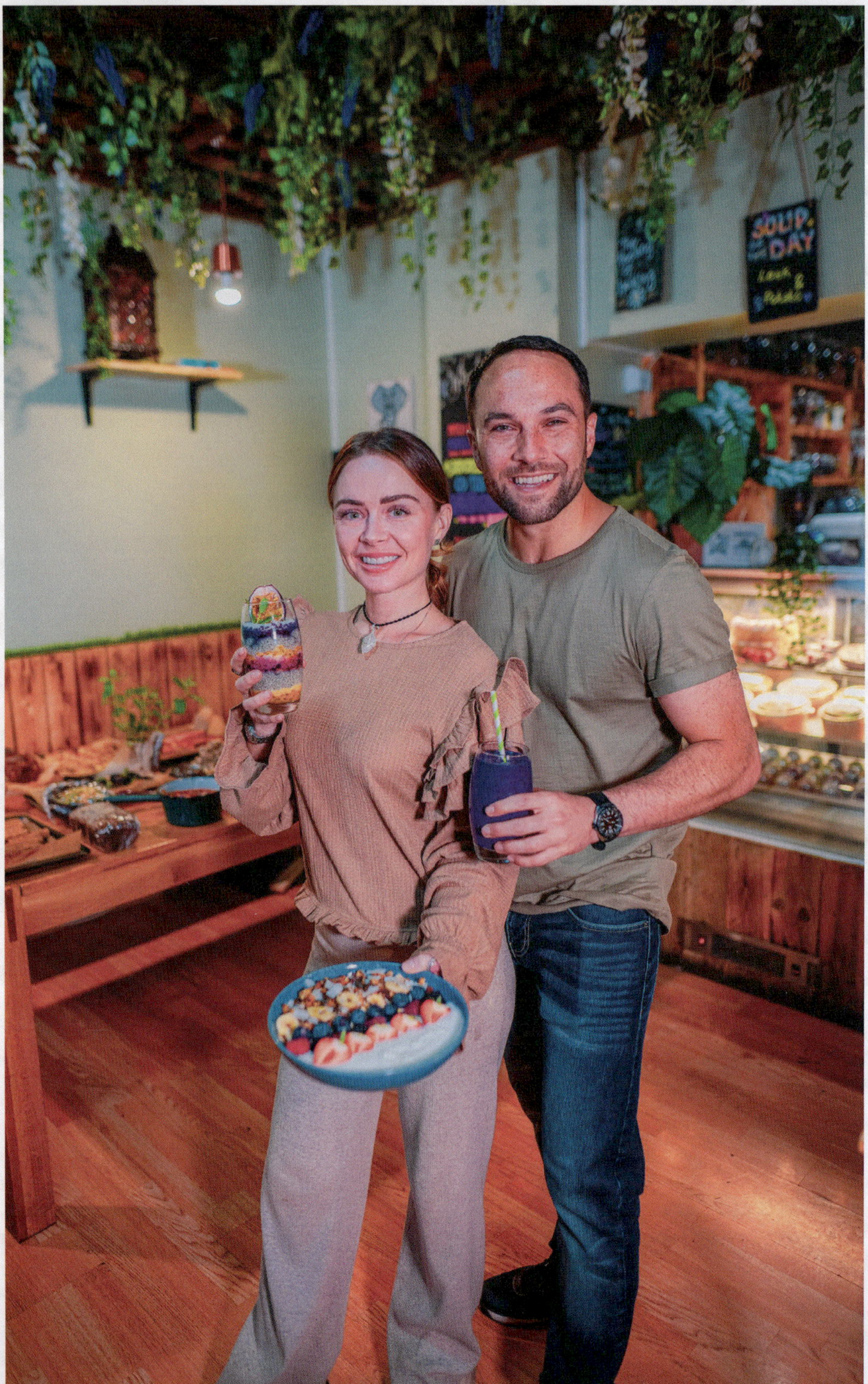
SOUP DAY

OUR STORY

Our mission at Indigo Greens has always been to educate people by feeding people, showcasing that a plant-based diet does not have to be boring, tasteless, or "extreme" as some have said in the past.

In 2017 when myself and Mark transitioned from vegetarian to vegan, it highlighted the lack of whole food options available in the city which opened me up to a whole new world of cooking, it inspired me, and triggered something deep within making me look at food in a different light. Food was no longer something that just filled us, food was medicine that had the power to heal us.

We both always loved being in the kitchen together, cooking and eating home-made food each night, but once we removed all animal products and started working only with plants our love for food got stronger and I started creating new and exciting dishes with health food ingredients we had never even heard of before, never mind used. The more we experimented the more diverse our ideas became, taking old classical favourites that we grew up loving and re-inventing them with a guilt-free and karma-free stance, everyday got more and more exciting as we kept finding new ways to work with new super food ingredients.

Cooking has been a part of my life since I can remember, it has been deeply embedded into my heart since childhood and developing new dishes was just always a part of growing up in a home that loved to cook. My connection with food has always been very intimate, which ultimately aligned me later in life to alchemical cookery and food as a philosophy.

I developed my love for cooking at home in my early years, from my mum, where her style was very Mediterranean and European, but it was when I left Liverpool later in life that I really started connecting with ingredients on a deeper level. I moved to Australia in my early 20s and the lifestyle there was just incomparable to Liverpool, health and wellness was on everyone's agenda. There were fresh food cafes, superfood salad, smoothie and juice bars on every corner. The dishes were filled with rainbow foods, unbelievably colourful, bursting with utter goodness and fresh flavours that radiated pure health on plate, even the fast-food establishments were packed with nutrient dense superfood options. Travelling and working around Australia is what definitely defined the way I utilise ingredients and infuse flavours in our dishes today, I just remember thinking "this is exactly what Liverpool is lacking"

I then went on and travelled to many parts of the Far East including India, Thailand, Bahrain and Bali, visiting some pretty rural places which opened my eyes and of course my heart to world-wide flavours and multicultural cuisines even more.

During my lifetime I have become well equipped with a lot of knowledge and tools from experience, self-education, study and research, so in 2017 when I decided to go plant-based, I didn't see it so much as a challenge, more so a mission, and that mission was to help raise the vibration of humanity by offering food as a medicine.

Mark's love for food, interest in health and passion for conscious cooking is what brought us together. When he left school he qualified as a personal trainer, sports coach, and nutritionist - he always had his interest in health and wellness. Later he went on to gain his teaching qualifications which led him to working with young people aged 14–19 all over the northwest, mentoring them in sports and personal social development which helped them into employment.

Mark and I crossed paths in 2015 through a multitude of synchronicities but when we finally connected on a deeper level and actually started speaking, we realised we shared the same vision which ultimately led to the birth of Indigo Greens. We shared conversations for months on end - before we had even met - of a whole food plant-based eatery that would change the eating habits of our beloved city of Liverpool. We both envisioned the idea of creating a space for healing, an all-encompassing centre for spiritual growth and development, a place where conscious communities could unite and raise their vibration together, supported by good food, conscious music, and desire to bring change to the world. The name Indigo Greens came to Mark as a download during a shamanic meditation years before we met, then the pieces fell into place and our community healing hub had its name, it couldn't have been anything else. The symbolism of the respective chakras and how our personalities, attributes and traits complement each other, it was a perfect fit - 'Food from a Higher Consciousness' became our motto.

Over the course of the next 2 years, I left my full-time job as an offshore chef to teach yoga. I opened my own yoga school and aligned myself to living holistically through teaching yoga and meditation - although it didn't have space for a café. What it did was give me so much more time to spend at home retraining myself as a plant-based chef, but it was when we began working intensively with Plant Medicines that the path began to unfold, which then gave us a push from above to begin our project.

In 2017 after lots of persuading by Mark, I finally started to believe my food was good enough to help others transition too, to open them up to a whole new way of living and show people that eating a whole food diet can ultimately change the vibration we live in. We started out in a production kitchen, which was based in an old school and was surrounded by offices. They generously gave us 3 months' rent free to get our feet off the ground and we began by delivering freshly made meal prep with dishes from around the world, 3 different meals a day, 6 days a week.

We then started popping up at festivals, health and wellness events, and yoga retreats, as well as doing buffets and banquets for weddings and parties, we even held kitchen takeovers where we offered a fine dining experience from other restaurants as we didn't have one of our own, at this point it was plain to see that was just what we were missing.

As our brand grew and our message spread, we became well known in the city and Indigo Greens was nominated for an award at 'The Liverpool Lifestyles' where we were "inundated with votes" and won 'The Best Healthy Lifestyle Business Award' in March 2018

In September 2018 we opened our Queens Drive Eatery, opening as the first 100% Plant Based Eatery in the city. Our breakfast and brunch menu, a huge hit with both vegans and carnivores alike. Our menu was created around well-known favourites, the kind of foods that everyday people could relate to, we designed it in a way that it helped people transition or at least incorporate more plant-based foods without missing out on flavours they love. We have seen all walks of life enter our sacred little healing hub in the heart of Liverpool, a place so unique that you would not usually find on a local parade of shops in a small Liverpool suburb. We were told if we were located in the city centre or in south Liverpool, we would have been even more successful. It was not about success though, it was about helping change the lives of people in need and north Liverpool was where we were needed most - with greasy cafes, Chinese take outs, pizza houses and kebab shops on every corner. It was time to elevate our end of the city with our high vibe food, and that is what we did!

We built a community and became the bridging gap between the north and south of Liverpool, we have seen friendships form, relationships flourish and children born into our community over the years and we have helped thousands of people change their lifestyle by giving up meat or dairy first and then seen people fully transition - some overnight some over time - all through sharing our vision and educating people by feeding them.

During these early years we travelled the globe as a couple, taking inspiration from some of the finest Plant Based Eateries in Metropolises in the world including London, New York and Los Angeles. It was in LA that we observed a number of growing progressive health food trends that inspired us to educate ourselves more on Gluten Free options, Keto and Paleo food groups. We made the decision to split our business in order to cater for more diverse diets. All our meal prep would now be Gluten Free with a number of Keto options available all courtesy of The Vegan Meal Prep Company who would now stock their meals in Indigo Greens as we all as some of the other health food stores, gyms, and coffee shops in the North West.

Then In 2019 we were invited to open a new restaurant in Duke Street Food Market, - which had been launching with critical acclaim after winners of the BBC show 'Million Pound Menu' were awarded kitchen space for winning the show - lining up alongside some of the leading names in the city's hospitality industry. It was an honour for us to be recognised and to be able to showcase our vegan cuisine from around the world in such an exciting new venue in the city centre. Our menu at Duke Street Market was adventurous, we stepped it up to fit with the classy up-market venue and the rapid expansion of Indigo Greens was followed by a second award nomination, this time for 'The Best Vegan Restaurant 2019', by VegfestUK. We literally couldn't believe it; we were now being recognised nationally for our plant-based creations and in October 2019 we won 'The Best Vegan Restaurant UK' award.

In 2020 we decided it was time to open our doors for the evening customers, with a 'sense-teasing / small-plates' dining experience which proved a huge hit, people just couldn't get enough of it, but unfortunately, 2020 was a year of great change. The entire world came to standstill. Restaurants were forced to close their doors and our safe-haven was no longer accessible for our community.

This was a time when our plant-based food was needed the most and amongst the fear mongering while everyone closed their doors, we chose to stay open and serve the whole city with high quality plant based whole food introducing speciality takeaway & delivery menus. We adapted to the times and made sure that no-one In the city went without wholesome plant based whole food. We extended our opening hours and opened up our delivery radius to every "L" postcode in the city, leading us to be nominated for yet another award, 'The Healthy Eating Business of the Year' by 'Fit Pro' and in November 2020 we scored a hat-trick, 3 years in a row, 3 awards won! Our dream for serving the community was well and truly being recognised.

Which brings us to the year of 2021, the pandemic over the previous year really had an impact on the way people lived. People's priorities changed and food as medicine was brought to light and we saw so many people turn to plant-based living, food consciousness was on the rise, health, fitness, and vitality was the new sanctuary for people now and this in turn made Indigo Green the go-to for all. We became so busy with meal prep and home deliveries that we decided not to return to our second home at Duke Street Market. Our focus and priority was with people of our community, who needed guidance and direction to live a more wholesome and sustainable lifestyle through plant-based eating.

This year saw no let-up in recognition, being awarded a lucrative TripAdvisor Travellers Choice 'Best of The Best' Rosette, awarded to only 1% of restaurants in the world. THE WORLD ... We were now being recognised world-wide, from city recognition to national recognition, to global recognition. We feel now we can say we've made an impact and changed the eating habits of a whole lot of people and we thank all our loyal customers who are now friends and part of the Indigo family for all your support, and if you're new we welcome you too. ... wherever you are in the world.

Love

Patti and Mark

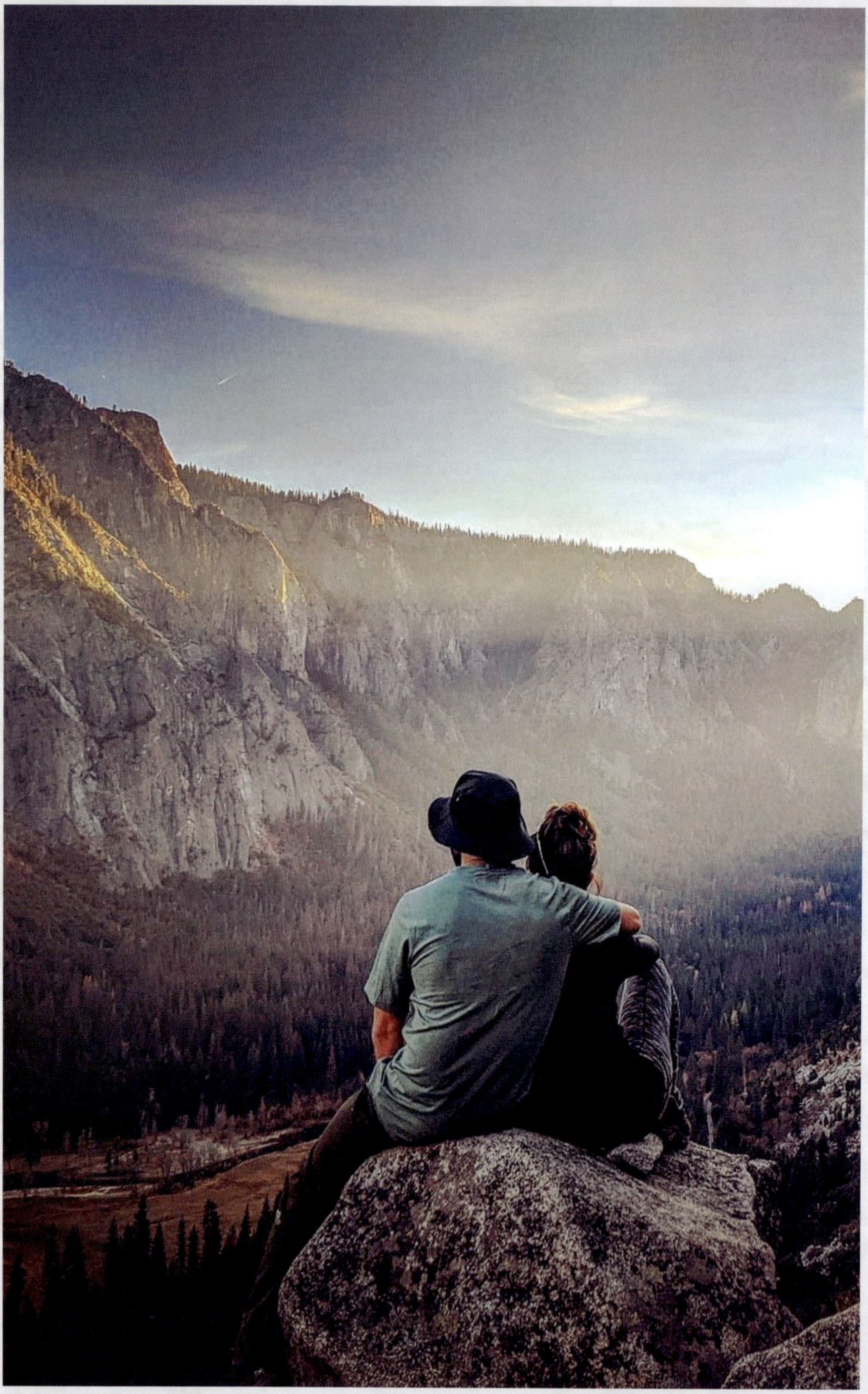

WHY PLANT BASED?

Veganism has slowly been on the rise for many years but just in the last year alone the surge has spiked by over 40%, people are becoming a lot more conscious, not only because plant-based living is constantly being proven to improve human health, but because it also promises a more sustainable future for us and the planet, stopping endless animal cruelty, deforestation, ocean pollution and global warming.

When I first went vegan nearly 5 years ago it was purely for health benefits, myself and Mark had no idea how cruel, brutal and inhumane commercial farming actually was, and how much of an impact animal agriculture was having on the planet as well as human health. We were astounded by this insanity and needed to take action, the saying "ignorance is bliss" comes to mind, but we couldn't be part of a society that consciously chose to turn a blind eye, we knew the truth and there was no turning back, we couldn't live with ourselves knowing that we could have done something to raise awareness on this worldwide catastrophe.

PLANT BASED FOR HEALTH

The plant protein, amino acids, fibre, vitamins, minerals, antioxidants, flavonoids, carotenoids, and phytonutrients we consume from the plant kingdom is what genetically and biologically supports every micro-organism of the body, providing the foundations for a healthy gut, brain and strong immune system. The immune system is the body's first line of defence, which fights off infection, short and long-term illnesses, deadly diseases, viruses and pathogens, and what we eat directly affects the efficiency of this mechanism as 70-80% of the immune system is housed in the gut. The gut is also in direct contact with the brain via the Vagus Nerve, which is a channel that sends signals back and forth, meaning the food we eat is also having an impact on the way we think and the decisions we make. Adapting to a more whole food, fibre rich diet will not only help improve healing on a physical level, but will also enhance mental and emotional well-being by stabilising hormones, and strengthening/supporting the neurological pathways which reduce stress and mental illnesses such as depression and anxiety.

The key to thriving on a plant-based diet is to ensure you're eating a variety of different plants - fruits, vegetables, wholegrains, legumes, lentils, pulses, fresh herbs, and spices. If your diet is plant based but primarily processed- store bought, fast or factory food that is sanitised, full of harmful chemicals, dead and lifeless, then you will not only be starving yourself of essential nutrients you will be feeding disease instead of fighting disease. The body needs fresh foods that are in their most natural state, the closer they are to 'whole', the wider the range of healing properties they contain. They are called 'Whole Foods' because they are closest to their natural whole food state without interference from processes. Plants are perfectly formulated compounds created by nature that give the entire body what it needs to thrive.

When first transitioning to a fully plant-based diet and cutting out heavily processed foods, hidden sugars, animal hormones and disease-ridden flesh, your body will go into detox mode - and depending on how "distorted from nature" your diet was before, will depend on how heavy your detox symptoms may be. Many people claim to feel nausea and weakness, stomach upset, mind fog, headaches, and flu like symptoms as the body goes into withdrawal, years of embedded toxins will start to be released. As the body works sternly to flush out built up toxins, it will be pulling water from anywhere it can to help expel the toxicity so drinking plenty of warm lemon water to rehydrate is key during detoxification. You may also notice a lot more gas and bowel movement than usual, this is all the fibre clearing the pathways, breaking down years of built-up foods that have become dredged in parts of your body that was not able to process full digestion, but don't worry this a natural occurrence and the bodies way of healing, these symptoms won't last forever, just stay steadfast with the cleansing and as the body is getting what it needs to heal, you will feel more alive than you ever have in no time.

Another reason which is becoming prevalent in modern society and is perhaps the most concerning of our lifetime is the immunity humans are building up to antibiotics (previously viewed as a wonder drug for the impact they've had on human health) only around for the last century antibiotics revolutionised healthcare and greatly reduced the number of fatalities from infections. However, it is estimated that nowadays antibiotic use is 4 times greater in farmed animals than in humans, which means this usage is being passed on to humans who consume animal produce. This over consumption gives cause to the fear that the next pandemic may well be microbial in nature and humans would not have the immunity or the medication to combat this. Swine Fever, Bird Flu, E.Coli and Foot-and-Mouth disease have all been caused from consuming dead animals. You only have to visit a local farm to see that pigs are kept in conditions that are rife for bacteria and disease to enter into the human food chain. This is at a farm so can you think about how a slaughterhouse which no one is allowed to enter may look?

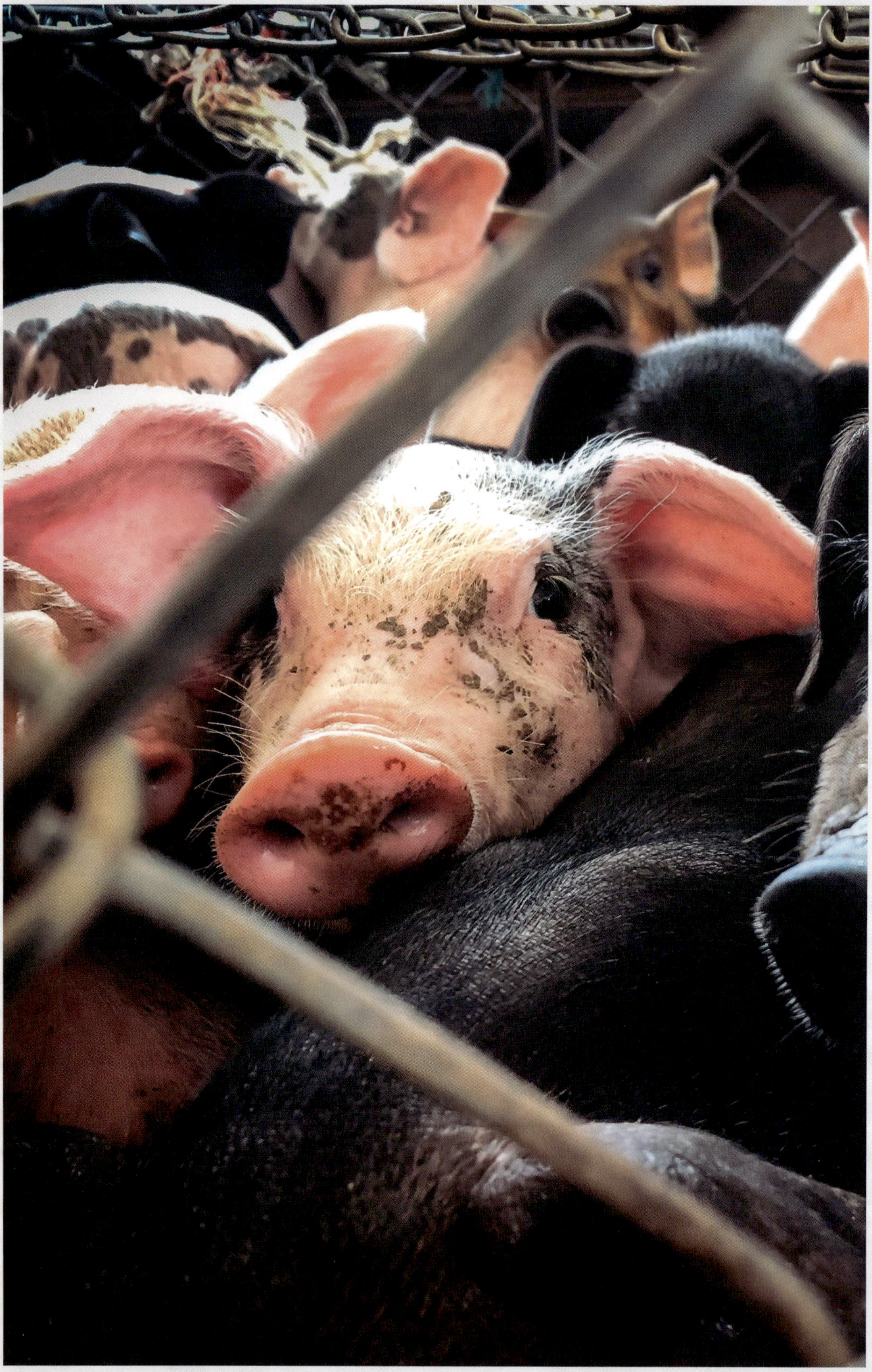

PLANT BASED FOR ANIMALS

The most obvious and logical reasoning for going plant based is one that is genetically ingrained in us from birth – do not kill other beings, whilst there is no doubt that over the past 400,000 years of evolution there will have been times that humans had to kill to survive (which is why we have a fight or flight capability built into our nervous system). However, this is not something that is needed any more and especially regarding animals. We have no known predators and therefore do not need to kill in order to survive. We have also come a long way from the days of our hunter-gatherer ancestors who would continually have to relocate and find food sources to maintain their energy levels.

Animal agriculture has also come a long way over the last 50 years, with the exponential rise in population and demand for dead animals (meat) also rising, farmers have transitioned from local landowners to large scale profit driven corporations and mass-producing slaughterhouses. As with many things that have led to decline on our planet the greed for more profit has come at the expense of human welfare but of course also to the decline of animal welfare.

Animals which once roamed green pastures and ate a natural diet on the farm are now bred for mass slaughter, never seeing daylight, eating poor nutrient deficient GMO products which are cheaper to maximise profits, living in below standard facilities in conditions that are so poor, you're not allowed to see them. How many people would choose this as their staple food if we were taken to slaughterhouses as children to show where "meat" really comes from. Instead, though we are fed images and propaganda from every source of media, watch out for happy cows and smiling pigs often mistakenly used to portray cruelty free imagery of farm life.

One thing we know is no living being wants to die, and none of them/us want to experience pain. Just because we speak different languages it doesn't mean animals don't feel pain. Their screams and squeals before slaughter are sure fire ways of knowing they are scared and traumatised. When they are in this state, they release toxins which are then taken on by all those who consume. Trust me there is no such thing as humane murder and if there were, people would be allowed to visit slaughterhouses. Many people do not realise the extent of this chain of command as they buy their products packed in supermarkets without a care for the whole process, but as discussed in conscious cooking we really need to be mindful to the energy we consume and be under no illusion when you "buy meat" you are basically funding contract killers to mass murder innocent beings, whether you're Vegan or not I'm sure you don't want to be responsible for this needless genocide.

Being Vegan has been termed as extreme but that's total conditioning from our environment and the supply chain of these products. Tell me what's more extreme, eating fresh, natural ripe and abundant fruits and veggies provided by the Earth? Or slaughtering innocent animals and chewing the flesh off their bones?

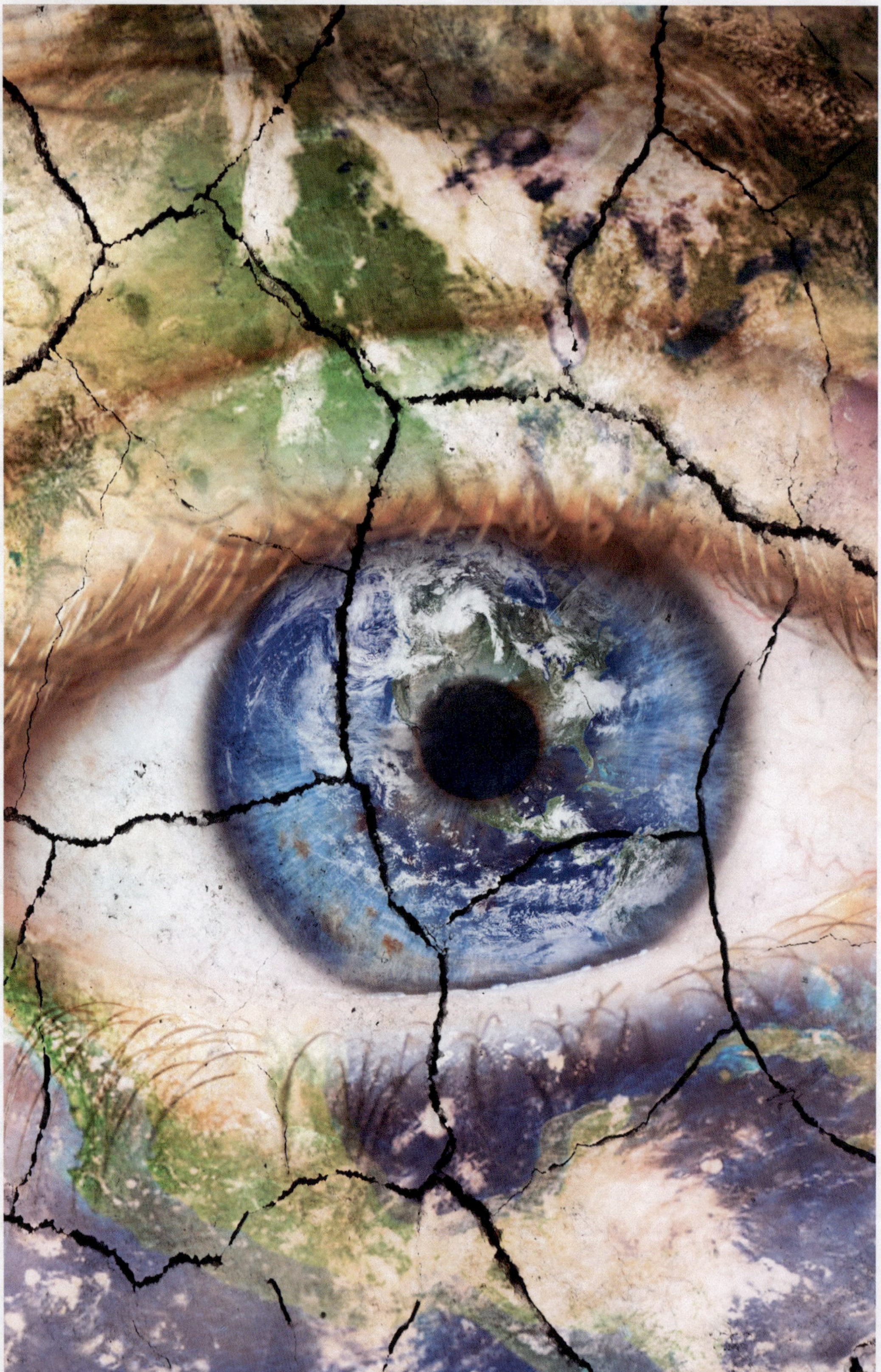

PLANT BASED FOR THE PLANET

Not only is human demand to blame for all destruction on land, but we are also accountable for emptying the oceans too. Overfishing, bottom trawling, Illegal fishing, whale and dolphin slaughtering, plastic pollution, oil spills and illegal dumping all play a part in the decline of marine life. Oceans host 80% of the planet's biodiversity and are the largest ecosystems on the earth, often referred to as a "carbon sink" which absorbs 90% of heat caused by human activity, if the ecosystem of the ocean continues to weaken, the whole planet will fall into great collapse, already the temperature of waters are rising and becoming more acidic causing coral bleaching, turning what was once a wonderland of living breathing organisms, marine life and sea plants, into a skeleton graveyard and an ocean of blood on the hands of humankind.

Our planet is at a point of no return, we are currently in a global crisis and need to act now. There are so many documentaries, studies, and articles available with the touch of a button nowadays that the evidence is overwhelming. There is no excuse to not want to make a change. Over the last 50 years alone, our oxygen producing rainforests have declined by half. They too are one of the biggest ecosystems we have on the planet, which stabilize the world's climate by absorbing CO_2 from the atmosphere. If 7.8 billion people chose to eat a mainly plant based diet, then 80% of global farmland used for livestock would reduce to half, which contributes to up to 33% of greenhouse gas emissions.

We could start to rewild the wild and reinstall the biodiversity of the earth, rehome thousands of species of plants, birds, mammals, fish, and insects that all play a part in keeping our planet alive. Every single living organism within the ecosystem works in synergy. Us humans are a single race, the only species that live apart from nature have completely turned what was once a thriving planet into a dying planet through the last 100 years of a 200,000-year-old civilisation

CONSCIOUS COOKING

Society has come so far away from nature and unfortunately, we as a race have mostly lost touch with one the most magical gifts we have to offer - we live in a world where time is more important than food, and eating for convenience comes before eating for health, but ultimately the quality of food we eat now will decide how much time we have later in life. Yes, we live in a fast-paced world, but slowing down to feed and nourish every single mechanism of the body will either be the catalyst of vitality or destruction.

Most of the western world sees cooking as a chore but it's a sacred offering to oneself and those around us, which forms a deep connection with the earth, and the medicinal ingredients she has to offer. Cooking should not be rushed, or made with resentment, this isn't to say you need to spend hours on end in the kitchen, but to be present and honour this gift, experiencing food made with love, devotion and with intention to nourish, hydrate and heal those that consume it is something kind of special.

Next time you are cooking or are being cooked for, just take a moment to observe the energy of the room, or the people in it, what is your mood or their mood, what's the vibration? Be mindful of the words spoken over the food you are preparing, are the conversations light-hearted or heavy and daunting? What background noise is coming from the radio, TV? Is the negative news on, spitting out fear?

The energy we put into something is undoubtable and noticeable, everyone vibrates at a unique frequency which resonates with the words they speak, thoughts they think, and actions they carry out. If you are stressed in the kitchen, this will no doubt show in the food you produce. Does the phrase "food made with love" come to mind here? Well, it should, because you can also certainly tell when someone has put all their loving thoughts and positive energy into a meal. A phrase we use a lot at Indigo is "words carry vibrations". We relay this daily to our staff as the offering of food is a sacred act and both negative and positive vibrations around food can change the vibration in which the food resonates. The atmosphere will also change to that vibe and people within the energy field will sync into it too, like a domino effect throughout the space. This is why at Indigo, we recite mantra and medicine music through our speakers, light sage throughout the day and have crystals in and around the restaurant to keep the vibration high no matter what is happening in the outside world, we know our place is safe and free from negative and low vibrational frequencies.

Conscious cooking is a spiritual experience that can bring so much stillness, joy and creativity out in you, if you allow it. You just have to change your mind set about cooking, rewire your train of thought, set the tone, clear the space, put on some relaxing meditative music, let go of the day, forget about work and any problem that may have arisen and just be grateful for the fresh and vibrantly ripe fruits of the earth you have in front of you, that are going nourish your mind, body and soul. Build a relationship with these foods, look at their fibrous structures, smell them, taste them, get to know them and most of all say thank you to them!

One thing I will say is that reading an entire recipe first, from start to finish, will really help you understand the method and the process each dish undergoes before just rolling with it step by step, lots of unnecessary mistakes can be made when limited understanding of a recipe is followed, leading to confusion, stress and mess in the kitchen. So, get prepared, set an intention and flow, no stress necessary!!

KITCHEN EQUIPMENT

When it comes to cooking from scratch you will find the tools you use will really have an impact on your overall experience in the kitchen and the quality of the food you make. Having useful tools will help make life so much easier and efficient, as you start to spend more time in the kitchen you will slowly need to invest in more equipment if you want to experiment with plant-based cooking. In this section I have added all the equipment you will need to follow these recipes.

OVENS

I know most people in the world will have some kind of oven in their kitchen, but I thought it would be worth noting, from one home to another, that everyone's oven will differ in temperature, meaning the timing of our recipes are only guidelines and may need adjusting according to the personality of your oven.

BLENDERS AND FOOD PROCESSORS

Investing in a good quality food processor and blender is a great move to become a plant-based cook as they are used in so many recipes. They can be expensive but will last a lifetime if you invest, the better brands always have 10 – 15-year warranty. Depending on what blender or part of a food processor you are using, the time and speed will differ and the results you achieve. Throughout this book we use a Vitamix and MagiMix which are both high speed and high powered for best results.

- Blenders - Vitamix or Nutri-bullet – Soups, Smoothies, Cheeses, Flours, Nut Butters & Milks
- Food Processor – Magimix – Raw Desserts, Breads, Prepping Veg, Sauces

WEIGHING AND MEASURING

Weighing and measuring can sometimes put people off cooking as it can be quite time consuming, especially for people who work intuitively. Throughout this book I have used mainly cups for measuring as it's much more convenient. Not everyone has a set of cups, but they are essential in this book and cost a couple of pounds online.

- A Set of Measuring Cups (essential)
- Measuring Jugs
- Electric Scales
- 5cm Ice Cream Scoop with trigger

COOKING

When it comes to cook-wear it's important to pay attention to the material they are made of, this is something probably not a lot of people think of as you would presume cook-wear is safe. But many brands of cook-wear contain heavy metals, toxins and chemicals which seep into food when cooking. Ceramic, Clay or Cast Iron are always a good choice but always check the labels to see if they are eco-friendly.

- xtra Large Casserole Pan
- Small and Medium Saucepans
- Non-Stick Frying Pans
- Baking Trays
- Bread Tins
- Sieve
- Colander

PREPPING

A good set of knives is definitely a must for better quality cuts, saving you time and making prep a lot easier. Having useful gadgets like a mandolin aren't essential but will help you achieve those fine slices. One thing to remember when preparing vegetables that need cooking, is that they always come in variety of different shapes and sizes, depending on season and location, some may be more ripe, juicy or sweeter than others, and not one person is ever going to cut the same as another, which means cooking times and cutting preferences may need adjusting slightly depending on the size of each vegetable. All times stated in this book are guidelines so presence is key when getting to know your vegetables.

- Chef's Knife
- Bread Knife
- Knife Sharpener or Steel
- Chopping board
- Garlic Crusher (not necessary, can always use the fine side of the grater)
- Mandolin
- Box Grater
- Peeler

STORING

Look for BPA free when buying food storage containers, most hard plastics contain a chemical called BPA (Bisphenol) which seeps into food. When using foil, always make sure the food is covered with greaseproof paper to avoid leaching of aluminium into food. Look for non-plastic and non-aluminium alternatives, and use baking paper and brown bags to keep food covered. Storing food in airtight glass jars will expand shelf life as well as keep food fresher with less oxidation.

- Glass Tupperware and Mixing Bowls
- Food Grade Metal Storage
- Silicone Food Covers
- Airtight Jars
- Grease-Proof Paper
- Foil

UTENSILS

A good range of utensils is always useful to have in the kitchen, always use a wooden spoon or spatula when cooking, never use metal on metal to avoid scraping of the pan.

- Wooden Spoons
- Spatulas
- Potato Masher
- Mixing Bowls
- Whisk

STOCKING AND SHOPPING

The first excuse when it comes to eating more plant-based food is "not knowing where to start" and it's right, if you don't know where to start, then how can you even begin. The foundation of any healthy lifestyle starts with knowing what to stock and that's always the first challenge, set yourself up for success and go to the markets well prepared, with a list, and never go shopping on an empty stomach, this will lead to temptation.

I've created a full shopping list of everything you need to start your Indigo cooking adventure with a few extra ingredients you may find useful in home-cooking. Many of our dishes require multiple recipes to make another recipe, so I thought adding this section in may come in handy, especially with the dried goods as these foods are long life and are always worth having on hand when you feel like getting in the kitchen. Root Vegetables will also last a while so it's worth stocking up on them too, basically anything that is not kept in the fridge at the supermarket means it's got a long shelf life and if you store them in the fridge, they will often last twice as long stated on any packaging. Dates on fresh ingredients are often so misleading and create so much waste in the world, once you get to know your ingredients you will know when it's really time to pop them in the food waste. It's the more delicate items like salad ingredients, fruit, and fresh herbs that you will want to pick up fresh as these can wilt quickly and lose quality quite rapidly.

Opting for non-GMO (genetically modified organisms) and organic produce wherever possible should be on the top of everyone's priority list. The chemicals sprayed on non-organic agriculture can cause adverse health effects causing short term and long-term illnesses. I know it may seem more expensive at the time, but when it comes to one's personal health there shouldn't be anything more important, start looking at ways you can save money in other areas of your life and put it to good health, because you will pay in one way or another. If buying organic really isn't an option for whatever reason, whether that be climate or cost, then try bathing your fresh produce in a cold water, bicarbonate soda solution, this will remove surface pesticides and chemical residue.

Use 1-2 tbsp of bicarb to every litre of water and let soak for 10-15minuites and rinse well.

SHOPPING LIST

HEALTHY FATS AND COOKING OILS
Virgin Olive Oil
Coconut Oil, cold pressed
Avocado Oil
Naturli's Block Butter
Sesame Oil

LENTILS, LEGUMES & BEANS
Dried Puy Lentils
Dried Red Lentils
Dried Yellow Split peas
Dried Marrowfat peas
Canned Chickpeas
Canned Haricot Beans
Canned Kidney Beans
Canned Black Beans
Canned Cannellini Beans

CANNED VEGETABLES
Chipotle Peppers in Abode Sauce
Roasted Red Peppers
Chopped Tomatoes
Tomato Puree

FROZEN VEGETABLES
Garden Peas
Sweet Corn

WHOLE GRAINS
Brown Rice
Red/ White Quinoa
Amaranth (Ancient Grain)
Whole Grain Pasta
Buckwheat Pasta
Whole Wheat or Gluten free Macaroni Pasta
Gluten Free Rolled Oats

FLOURS
Gluten Free Self-Raising Flour
Corn Flour
Arrowroot
Gluten Free Baking Powder

NON–DAIRY ITEMS
Coconut Milk
Almond Milk
Block Butter
Koko Coconut Yoghurt
Vegan Mayonnaise

HERBS AND SPICES
Smoked Paprika
Cumin Powder
Mild Chilli Powder
Chinese 5 Spice
Nutmeg Powder
Cinnamon Powder
Cracked Black Pepper
Bay Leaves
Garlic Powder
Ground White Pepper
Oregano
Cumin Seeds
Crushed Chilli Flakes
Ginger Powder
Cardamom Powder
Fennel seeds
Mustard Seeds
Peppercorns

VINEGARS AND SAUCES
Pickled Gherkins
Wholegrain Mustard
Frenchies American Mustard
Dijon Mustard
Wholegrain Mustard
Sriracha Chilli Sauce
Balsamic Vinegar
White Wine Vinegar
Rice Wine Vinegar
Tahini Sauce

SWEETENERS AND SUGARS
Maple Syrup or Agave
Raw Cane sugar
Molasses

NUTS AND SEEDS
Cashew Nuts
Peanuts
Walnuts
Almonds
Brazil Nuts
Pecan Nuts
Chia Seeds
Sunflower Seeds
Pumpkin Seeds
Hemp Seeds (shelled)
Black Sesame
White Sesame

PLANT PROTEINS
Firm Tofu
Tempeh
Sos Mix
Beyond Meat Burgers

ROOT VEGETABLES
White Onions
Red Onions
Garlic Bulbs
Ginger
Turmeric
Carrots
Swede
Red Cabbage
Parsnips
Red Rooster Potatoes
Sweet Potatoes
Beetroot

FRESH FRUIT
Avocado
Lime
Lemons
Oranges
Pineapple
Bananas
Red/Green apples
Blueberries
Raspberries
Strawberries
Red Grapes
Mango
Passion Fruit
Plumbs
Pomegranates
Kiwis
Beef Tomatoes
Baby Vine Tomatoes

FRESH HERBS
Basil
Coriander
Thyme
Rosemary
Mint
Chives

SALAD VEGETABLES AND LEAF
Baby Spinach
Baby Gem Leaf
Mixed Peppers
Baby Cucumbers
Spring Onions
Red Chillies
Bean Sprouts
Bok Choy
Tender stem
Cauliflower
Flat Mushrooms
Celery
Kale
Courgettes

DRIED FRUIT
Medjool Dates
Sultanas or Raisins
Goji Berries
Cranberries
Apricots
Mango
Mulberries
Banana Chips
Desiccated Coconut
Coconut Flakes

JUICE
Orange Juice
Apple Juice

SUPERFOOD POWDERS
Cacao
Beetroot powder
Spirulina powder

FLAVOUR ENHANCES
(Most of these can be found in health food or international stores)
Nutritional Yeast B12
Gravy Salt (Compton's)
Kallo Stock Cubes
Nori Sheets
Sea Salt or Himalayan Salt
Mushroom Stock

THE BENEFITS OF SOAKING

Nuts, seeds, grains, lentils and peas are full of powerful antioxidants, nutrients, minerals, and vitamins are all essential ingredients in a plant-based diet for protein, dietary fibre and heart healthy fats like omega 3. What a lot of people don't know is that these foods have a protective barrier of inhibitors known as anti-nutrients (phytates) which when consumed, bind to minerals like calcium, magnesium, and iron, negatively impacting the absorption rate of nutrients, compromising digestion and health. Hence their name – anti-nutrients. Foods like lentils and peas also contain a sugar called oligosaccharide that the body doesn't have the enzymes to break down, causing them to ferment in the lower intestinal tract creating bloat and gas. Suffering with bloating, cramps, and gas after eating certain foods could well and truly be a result of consuming too many phytate containing foods leading to poor digestion.

Soaking neutralizes these harmful inhibitors and activates the nutrient profile releasing a much more potent source of life force energy. Live enzymes, vitamins and minerals are awakened, and proteins become more bioavailable. It also reduces the cooking and preparation time as it breaks down the hard fibres making them much easier to work with. For instance, soaking nuts and seeds result in a much silkier, smoother consistency if blending into soups, desserts or making cheeses, while soaking brown, wild and black rice fluffs up the texture as well as speeding up the cooking time, beans and peas are much harder and dense, soaking them with a little bicarb helps breaks down their tough coating and can reduce the cooking time by half.

HOW TO CREATE THE RIGHT CONDITIONS FOR SOAKING?

Using a room temp, acidic, salt water recreates the perfect moist environment for nuts seeds and grains tricking them into germinating by recreating the conditions they wait round in nature for.

- Always soak different varieties of nuts, seeds, beans & legumes in separate bowls
- Soak with a 2:1 ratio of warm water
- Add 1-2tbs lemon juice or vinegar, ¼ tsp sea salt
- Cover the bowl with a muslin cloth so it can breathe
- Allow to soak at room temperature for the required time being precautious not to over soak as it can adjust flavours, textures and reduce the nutritional profile (See charts below)
- Rinse well and wash until all the water runs clear

SOAKING NUTS

Almonds, Pistachios, Hazelnuts, Peanuts	8 hours to overnight
Pecans, Brazil Nuts	4-8 hours
Cashews, Macadamias, Pine Nuts, Walnuts	2-3 hours

Soaking Seeds

	Pumpkin Seeds	Chia Seeds	Sunflower Seeds	Hemp Seeds	Sesame Seeds
Soaking Time	8-12 hours overnight	15-30 minutes	2-4 Hours	Don't soak	8-12 hours overnight

If you choose to soak your nuts and seeds, drying them out for certain recipes may be required. You can either dehydrate them if you have a dehydrator or slow roast them until they are completely dried out. Any moisture left inside will result in them going rancid much faster and becoming a breeding ground for mould, ruining anything else they are mixed with.

Soaking and Cooking Grains, Beans and Pulses

As soaking grains, lentils and pulses reduces the time of cooking, below I have offered some extra cooking guidelines per cup as packet foods will only give instructions for non-soaked ingredients. In general, soaking grains usually requires 25% less water and 20% less cooking time than stated on dried.

Grains Per Cup	Quinoa	Brown	Basmati Rice	Amarnath
Soaking time	8-12 hours overnight	8-12 hours overnight	8-12 hours overnight	8-12 hours overnight
Cooking Time	12-15 minutes	20-25 minutes	12-15 minutes	12-15 minutes
Water per cup	2 cups water	2.5 cups water	2 cups water	2 cups
Resting Time	15 mins	15 mins	15 mins	15 mins

Beans and Pulses per cup	Red Lentils	Brown, Green, Puy	Yellow Split Peas	Marrowfat peas	Chickpeas
Soaking Time	30 mins-1hour	2-3 hours	8-12 hours overnight	8-12 hours overnight	8-12 hours overnight
Cooking Time	15-20 minutes	15-20 minutes	30-45 minutes	30-45 minutes	90-180 minutes

SUPERFOODS & SUPPLEMENT BENEFITS

Adding superfoods to smoothies is a great way to squeeze even more vitality into your diet, most superfoods are now easily accessible online and are available in concentrated powders which is sometimes all that is available due to the climate we live in, but they are often just as effective as having them fresh. Do some research on the suppliers and always check the ingredient list on any pre-packed superfoods and make sure they are 100% what they say they are.

CBD: Is a chemical substance found in cannabis, it's been studied for its pro-active use in helping ease anxiety, depression, PTSD, insomnia, improve memory and cognitive functioning, acne, eczema, psoriasis, anti-ageing, maintains healthy cells, lowers the risk of diabetes and heart disease, improves seizures and for those with cancer it provides a natural and safe alternative for pain relief and inflammation.

MACA ROOT POWDER: Maca is widely known in the health world for its ability to improve libido and sexual drive in both men and women, while increasing and strengthening fertility rates in men and improving symptoms of menopause in woman including hot flushes, insomnia, osteoporosis, anxiety and depression. It also helps boost sports performance and energy levels with claims of muscle gain, increased strength, stamina, and overall performance, a great pre and post work out supplement. It's also known to help improve memory, learning capabilities and overall mood. It's important that the "gelatinised" form of Maca is used as the root itself can be extremely hard to digest and can limit the nutrient intake.

SEA MOSS: Irish moss or algae also known as wild foraged chondus crispus, an edible sea plant found at the bottom of the ocean and is one of the most nutrient dense foods on the planet. It contains 92 of the bodies 102 essential minerals meaning it's a powerhouse for all symptoms and a preventative for all dis-eases. It's a direct source of omega 3 essential fatty acids improving heart, gut, brain, and immune functions by reducing inflammation and the ability to increase nutritional intake. It also regulates appetite by improving metabolism.

SPIRULINA POWDER: Spirulina is a now well-known powerhouse in the superfood category and is extensively rich in vitamins and minerals essential for maintaining a healthy immune system, like vitamins E, C, and B6. Research finds that spirulina also boosts the production of white blood cells and antibodies that fight viruses and bacteria in your body. Spirulina is an organism that grows in both fresh and salt water.

BUTTERFLY PEA POWDER: Butterfly Pea Powder is a powerful superfood tea which is rich in antioxidants. It's bright blue in colour and has an earthy flavour that offers mood enhancing and stress-busting benefits, reducing symptoms of anxiety and depression. It is also known to maximise energy, stamina, productivity and promote positive emotions.

VITAMIN C: Also known as ascorbic acid plays an essential role in many bodily functioning's and is key to maintaining a strong immune system. Vitamin C promotes growth and repair in all parts of the body, contributes to skin, cartilage, tendons, formational collogen, bones and teeth. It also assists the body in the absorption of iron.

TURMERIC: A highly regarded spice used far and wide in the East for its medicinal properties. Turmeric contains an active ingredient called Curcumin, a compound that naturally fights inflammation linked to health conditions such as heart disease, cancer, metabolic syndrome, Alzheimer's disease and other various degenerative and chronic conditions.

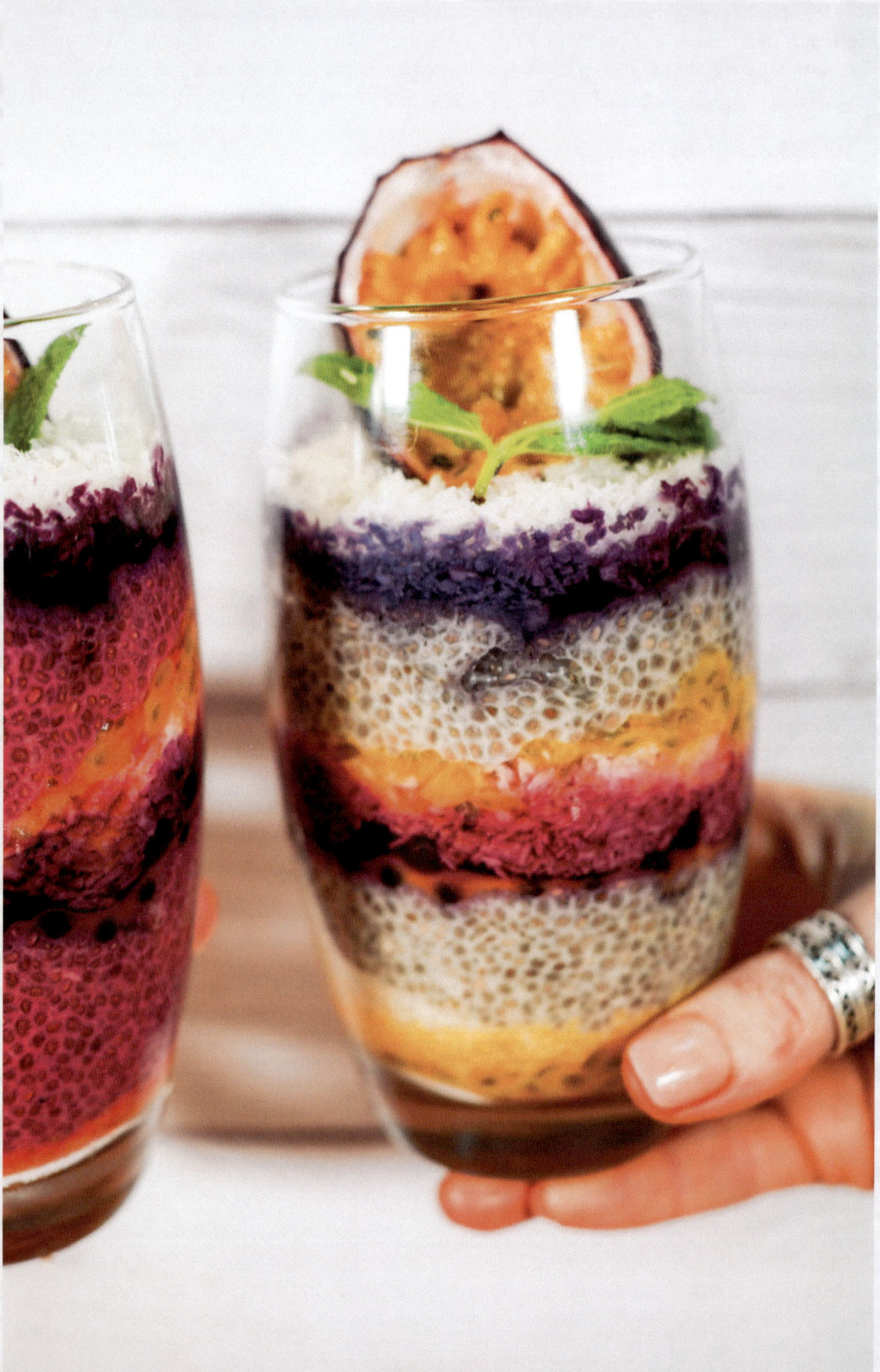

RAW AND CHILLED BREAKFAST

Said to be the most important meal of the day, and rightly so. 'Breakfast' means to 'break the fast' after a long night of resting and repairing, and this is why it's important when you awaken to rehydrate, replenish and reward all of those wonderful cells and organs that have been working all night long. While your mind may have been sleeping it's safe to say those vital organisms have been doing the night shift. For optimal energy try some of these recipes that contain raw living enzymes, slow-release carbs and juicy ripe fruits to keep you satiated and fully nourished throughout the morning.

SUPER FOOD MUESLI – RAW OR TOASTED

SOY FREE · GLUTEN FREE · REFINED SUGAR FREE

A bowl full of whole food delights, topped with whatever fresh and local fruit is in season. This quick and simple breakfast recipe can be made in advance and can be stored for several weeks making your mornings on the go even more efficient. It's packed with antioxidants, fibre, protein and the healthy fats including those brain boosting omega 3s. Muesli recipes are super versatile, both in how you make it and how you eat it, you can literally chop and change this entire recipe if you wish, as long as you have a good ratio of nuts, seeds and fruits to oats, you can go wild and get as creative as you like with whatever you have lurking about in your kitchen. This recipe has all our favourite ingredients, its nutty, chewy, and truly satiating with just the right amount of natural sweetness.

8-10 Servings

EQUIPMENT NEEDED:

A set of measuring cups, chopping board, strong, sharp knife, food processor (Optional), large baking tray, bowls for soaking, a colander, large airtight jar for storing.

INGREDIENTS:

4 Cups Rolled Oats, Gluten Free
1 Cup Hemp Hearts, Shelled
1 Cup Raw Pecan, Rough Chopped
1 Cup Raw Almonds, Rough Chopped
7 Cup Medjool Dates, Pitted, Chopped
1 Cup Mango, Sliced
1/2 Cup Apricot, Sliced
1/2 Cup Pumpkin Seeds
¼ Cup Milled Flax Seed
½ Cup Chia Seeds
1 Cup Coconut, Desiccated
½ Cup Raisins

If you have allergies to nuts or certain grains don't worry you can easily swap them out for other similar ingredients.

Store in an airtight jar and keep in a cool dry place for up to one month.

Pre-soak all the nuts and pumpkin seeds for 8 hours overnight. (This step is optional but advised - see page 20 for details - and/or TIP below.)

Pre heat the oven on 170c / 325f / gas mark 3.

Once the nuts and seeds are soaked, rinse well and drain. Set aside on a clean cloth or kitchen roll to soak up any excess moisture, roughly chop or add to a food processor and pulse 5-8 times to break down into chunks.

Place in the oven for 60-75 minutes on the middle shelf, flipping over halfway until golden brown and crunchy, or If you didn't soak your nuts place in the oven for less time, 20-30 minutes until golden brown and crunchy.

Meanwhile measure out the rest of the ingredients and begin to chop the mango, dates and apricots.

Place into a bowl along with the coconut, raisins, chia seeds, milled flax seeds, hemp hearts and oats.

Once the nuts are fully dried and roasted, allow to cool, and add to the bowl with the rest of the ingredients.

Serve with plant milk or our Cultured Cashew Yoghurt (see page 34) and some seasonal fresh fruit, or try making it into a Bircher Muesli (see page 28).

TIP:

If you choose to soak your nuts and seeds you will have to roast or dehydrate them afterwards - to remove all moisture before adding them to the rest of the dried muesli mix. If they contain any moisture they will decay after a couple of days.

If you choose not to soak, you can lightly toast to deepen the flavours or keep it simple and just toss them in the mix raw.

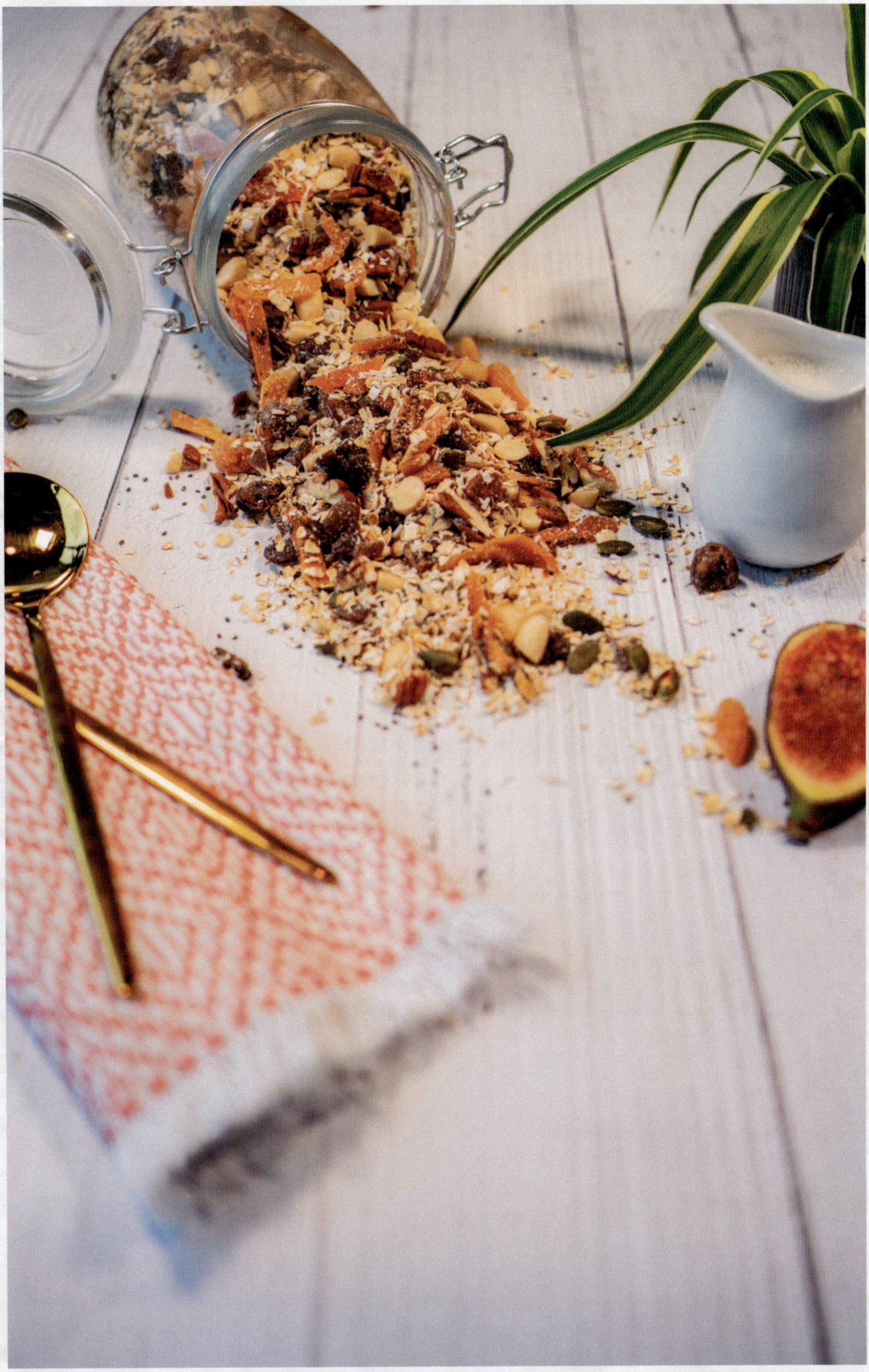

SWEET APPLE AND SULTANA BIRCHER MUESLI

SOY FREE · GLUTEN FREE · REFINED SUGAR FREE

It's creamy and fruity, chewy, soft, crunchy, crisp, sweet, and savoury all at the same time. This combination of flavours is a tropical paradise that can be enjoyed morning, noon, or night. Using our Superfood Muesli along with our Cashew Yoghurt will give you a bowl full of gut-feeding and gut-healing bacteria due to the lacto-fermentation process in our own yoghurt. This little breakfast combo is super simple to make and bursting with living, breathing, micro-organisms - keeping the good bacteria in the gut growing while feeding them with all the fibre they need to stay strong.

NOTE: You can skip making the yoghurt and add store bought if you wish but just be sure it has live cultures. I would personally use the Koko brand as they add their live cultures in the final stages of making their yoghurt, they also feed them some natural sugars to ensure they thrive.

4 Servings

EQUIPMENT NEEDED:

A set of measuring cups, chopping board, knife, bowl, medium size glasses or jars for serving, mixing bowl.

INGREDIENTS:

3 Cups Superfood Muesli (see page 26)
1 Cup Fresh Apple Juice
1 Cup Plant Yoghurt Or Cultured Cashew Yoghurt, (see page 34)
1 Cup Almond Milk, Unsweetened

To Garnish:

Coconut, Desiccated
Sultanas, Soaked
3-4 Small Red Apples, Small Diced
Poppy Seeds

Store in an airtight jar and keep in a cool dry place for up to one month.

Mix muesli, apple juice, milk, and yoghurt in bowl, cover and place in the fridge to set, allow 15-30 minutes. Alternatively prepare the night before, cover and leave in the fridge overnight. You may need add a drop more liquid the longer its left.

Soak the sultanas by submerging them under the water in an airtight container for a couple of hours until they expand.

Cut the apple into small cubes (keep in lemon water if preparing for later).

When ready, check that the consistency of the oats, they should be like a loose porridge. If you're happy with your oats, it's time to get creative and layer away.

Add 1tbsp of soaked sultana to a jar or glass, be sure to add some of the sugar syrup juices, then add a layer of chopped apples, a sprinkle of poppy seeds and a thin layer of coconut around the edge of the glass or jar, now spoon in 2-3 tbsp of Bircher mix, repeating this until you fill it a 3rd of the way up.

To decorate the top, garnish with more chopped apple, sultanas and sultana syrup, coconut, and seeds.

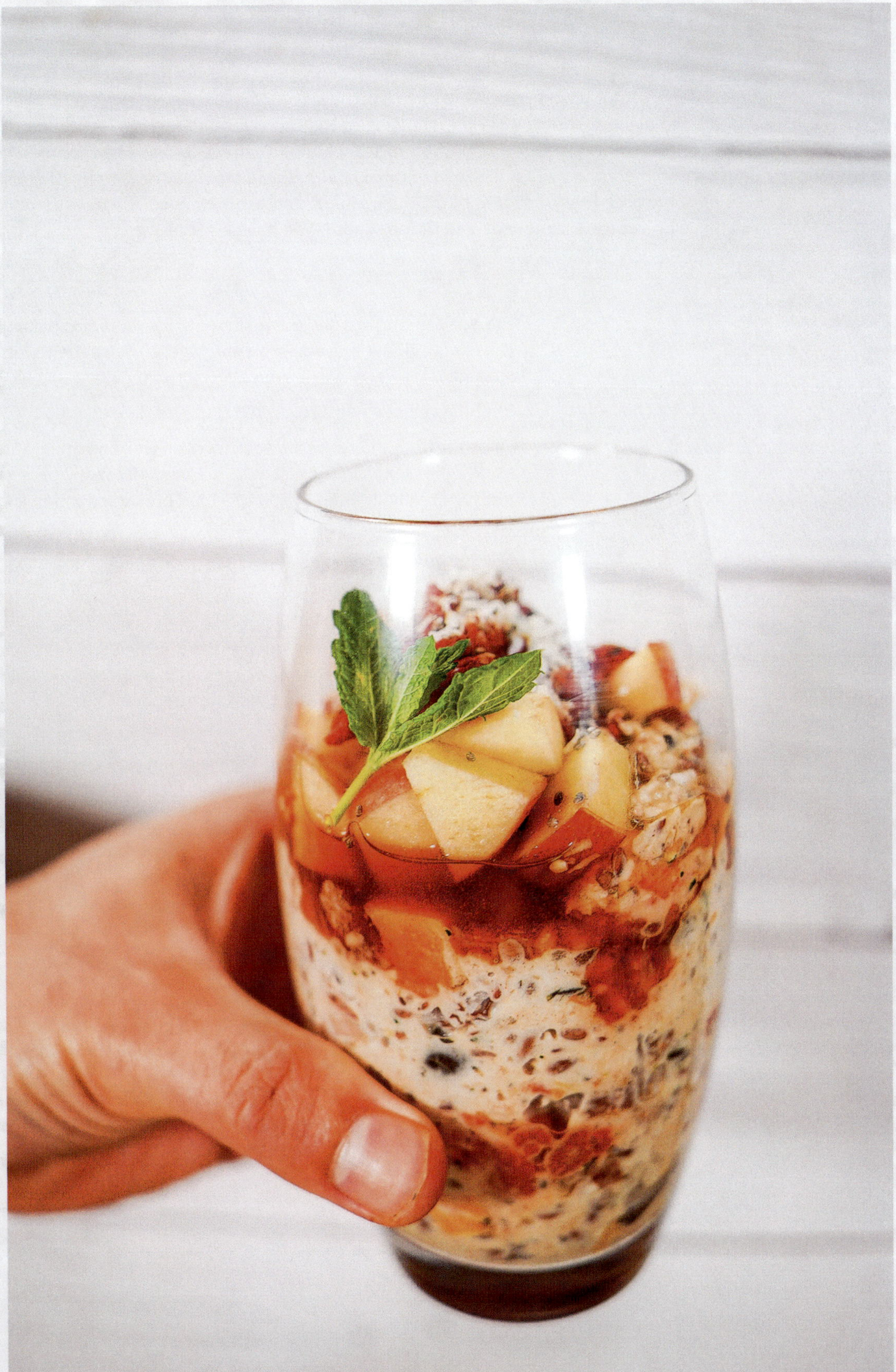

NUTTY KETO COCONUT GRANOLA

SOY FREE · GLUTEN FREE · REFINED SUGAR FREE

This grain free granola is perfect for anyone following a low carb, low sugar diet such as the ketogenic diet, due to its high protein and high fat count. But isn't indulging in too much fat bad for you? Well, that's all down to the types of fats you eat! There is common misconception that ALL fats are bad for us but consuming the right fats from nuts and seeds is key to optimal health, these are mainly made-up of good fats the body relies on for proper brain, cell and bodily functioning. You can switch up the nuts to your own personal preference or just use a variety of super food seeds if you have a nut allergy.

8-10 Servings

EQUIPMENT NEEDED:

A set of measuring cups, chopping board, strong, sharp knife or food processor, large baking tray, bowls for soaking, a colander, a large airtight jar for storing, mixing bowl, whisk.

INGREDIENTS:

Molasses Mix

2 Tbs Black Strap Molasses
2 Tbs Coconut Oil, Melted
¼ Cup Poppy Seed
2 Tbs Pure Vanilla Essence

Granola Mix

1 Cup Almonds
1 Cup Brazil Nuts
1 Cup Peanuts
1 Cup Walnuts
1 Cup Pecan Nuts
1 Cup Pumpkin Seeds
2 Cups Coconut, Shavings

Store in an airtight jar and keep in a cool dry place for up to one month, or portion into smaller batches and freeze for up to 3 months.

Pre-soak all the nuts and pumpkin seeds for required soaking times – Optional but advised (see page 20 for benefits on soaking).

Pre heat the oven on 170 c / 325 f/ gas mark 3.

Once the nuts and seeds are soaked, rinse well and drain. Set aside on a clean cloth or kitchen roll to soak up any excess moisture, roughly chop or add to a food processor and pulse 5-8 times to break down into chunks.

Mix the coconut oil, vanilla essence, poppy seeds, and black strap molasses together.

If you chose not to soak the nut mix, then place in the oven for 25-35 minutes on the middle shelf, until golden brown and crunchy, adding the molasses mix halfway to avoid burning, make-sure all the nuts and seeds are coated and glossy.

When removing the mix from the oven, check the liquid has dried into the nuts, they should now be slightly tacky and glossy, this tacky coating will dry and harden as they cool.

If you pre-soaked the nut mix, they will take much longer to dry out, slightly lower the oven and bake for 60-75 minutes until golden brown and crunchy, mixing halfway, and adding the molasses mix for the last 20 minutes

Allow to cool and add the coconut shavings, store in an airtight jar for up to one month.

Serve with our Cultured Cashew Yoghurt (page 34) or your choice of plant-based milk along with some seasonal fruits.

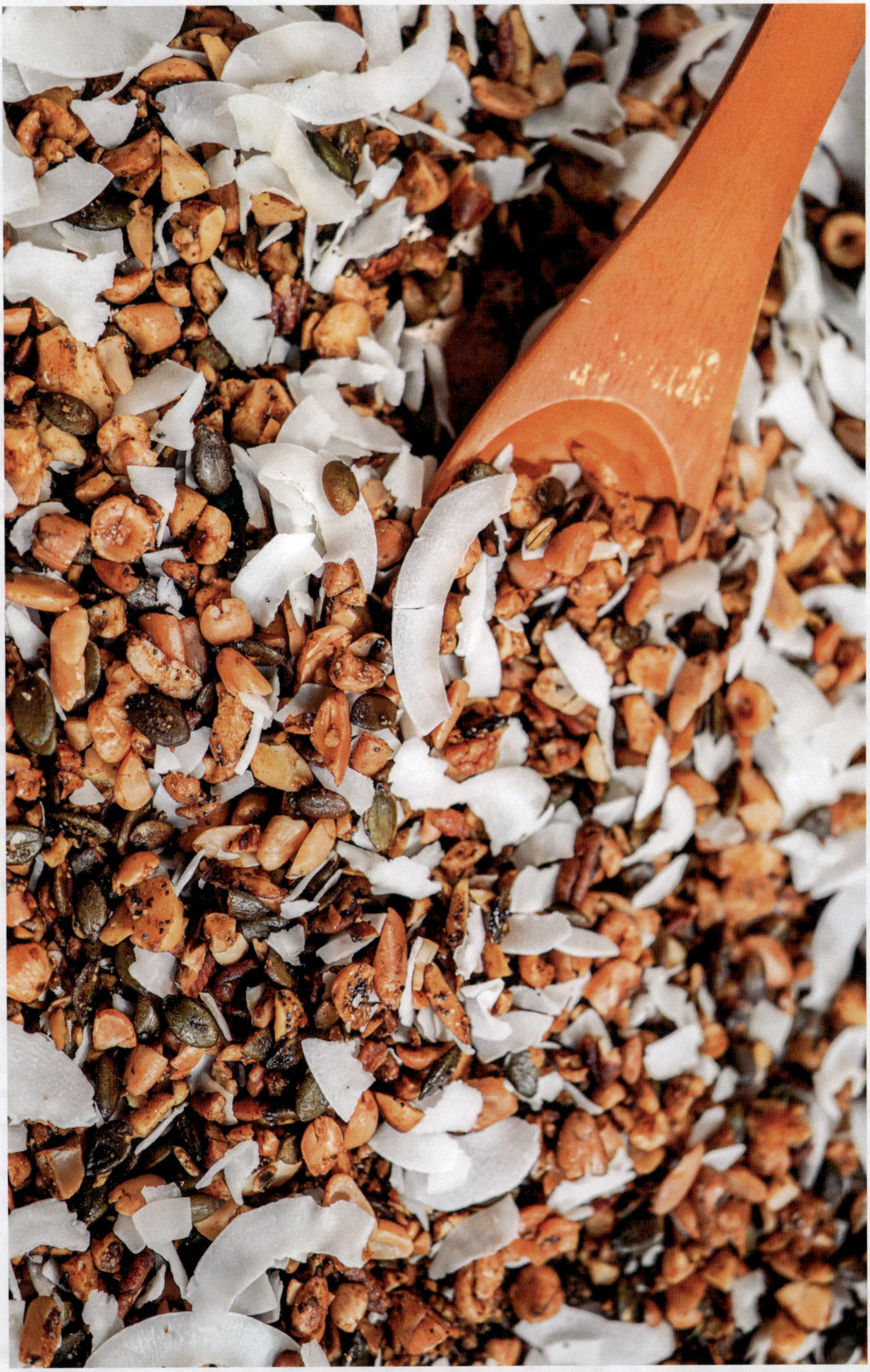

FRUIT AND CRUNCHY NUT GRANOLA

You can't beat the smell of sweet, spiced oats, slow roasting in the oven. This combination of ingredients is far healthier than any store bought, it is made with gluten free, whole grains, unrefined oils, and sweetened by nature. Our granola is also loaded with an array of super food ingredients, filled with fibre, omega 3s and plant proteins. Once you try this recipe you will wonder why you ever bought it from a store.

6-8 Servings

EQUIPMENT NEEDED:

a set of measuring cups, large baking tray, large mixing bowl, large airtight jar for storing

INGREDIENTS:

Toasted Oats Recipe

3 Cups Rolled Oats, Gluten Free

½ Cup Unrefined Coconut Oil, Melted

½ Cup Natural Maple Syrup

¼ tsp Spiced Chai Blend (see page 168) Or Mixed Spice

1 tsp Pure Vanilla Extract

Pinch Of Himalayan Salt

Granola Recipe

1 Cup Paleo Keto Granola (Or Mixed Nuts Of Your Choice Roasted)

1/3 Cup White Mulberry's

1/3 Cup Cranberries/ Sultanas

1/3 Cup Banana Chips

½ Cup Coconut Flakes

Toasted Oats Recipe (above)

Store in an airtight jar at room temperature for up to 1 month, or portion into smaller batches and freeze for up to 3 months.

Pre heat the oven at 170c/325/gas mark 3.

In a large mixing bowl combine the oats, coconut oil, maple syrup, salt, vanilla, Spiced Chai Blend or all spice, and a pinch of salt. Mix well until every oat is all coated. It should be nice and shiny.

Lay out the mixture in a large, lined baking tray, using a large spoon or spatula to create an even layer, the oats need to be quite crowded to stick together but not so much they don't cook evenly.

Place in the oven and bake for 12 minutes, you will see the outer edges and the top layer of oats starting to brown.

Carefully remove from the oven and give the oats a mix, pulling outer layer into the middle so they don't overcook and go bitter, press the mix back down firmly to stick back together and bake for a further 12-15 minutes until oats are evenly baked and golden brown.

Take from the oven and allow to completely cool, undisturbed before touching.

After it's completely cooled add the rest of the ingredients and break the mix gently with your hands to retain big chunks of clusters.

Serve with our Cultured Cashew Yoghurt (see page 34) or a plant milk of your choice, season fruit and enjoy!

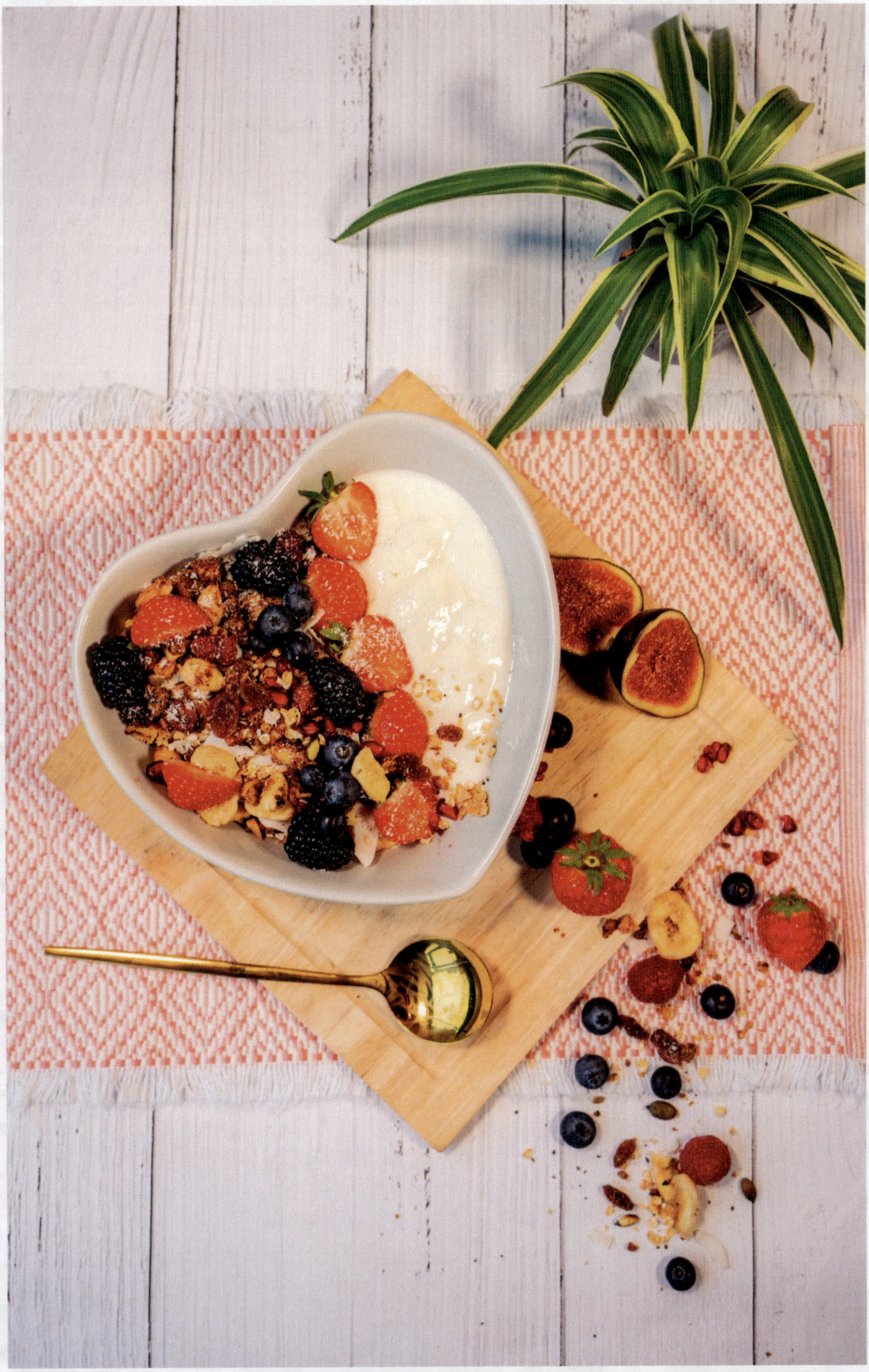

CULTURED CASHEW YOGHURT WITH BAOBAB

SOY FREE · GLUTEN FREE · REFINED SUGAR FREE

I just absolutely love how easy it is to make yoghurt at home that isn't full of preservatives, sweeteners, and artificial flavours, with a final product that contains live and active micro-organisms. Most store-bought yoghurts don't contain any gut flora feeding bacteria in their final product due to the heat treatment it undergoes to extend shelf life and they usually contain lots of refined sugars too, which have the opposing effect on gut healing. Luckily our Cultured Cashew Yoghurt is super simple to make, and is much more luxurious than shop bought yoghurt, its tangy, its silky smooth and filled with all the probiotic cultures one needs to have a healthy happy gut with all the beneficial prebiotic the live bacteria need to grow strong. While probiotic and prebiotic sound the same, they play different roles, a probiotic is the living micro-organisms, while the prebiotic is the carb substance they feed off like fibre and sugars found in natural foods. Baobab is an amazing source of prebiotic.

8-10 Servings

EQUIPMENT NEEDED:
A set of measuring cups, bowl foe soaking, colander, high speed blender, whisk, a large airtight jar for storing, lemon juicer, measuring jug.

INGREDIENTS:
2 Cups of Soaked Cashews
650ml Water
4 Tbsp Maple Syrup or To Taste, Needed for Fermentation
2tbsp Lemon Juice, Fresh
2 Probiotics Caps, ½ TSP
1/2tbsp Baobab Powder
1 Tsp Vanilla Extract, Pure

Keep refrigerated in an airtight jar for up to 1 week, or portion into smaller batches and freeze for up to 3 months.

TIP: To sterilise your jar, use boiling hot water only. Never sanitise your equipment using harsh chemicals.

Pre-soak cashew nuts for 2 hours (see page 20 for benefits on soaking).

Once soaked, give your cashews a good rinse and pop them in a high-powered blender, we use a Vitamix.

Add the maple, baobab, vanilla and water to the blender and blend. After a couple of minutes, turn off the machine and scrape down the sides. Blend again until thick and creamy. Depending on what blender you are using will depend on the time it takes, but ours takes around 5 minutes. There should be no grainy bits in the mix at all, however various blenders will produce a range of results.

Add the pro-biotic powder out of the capsules to the mix and discard of the casing, pulse the machine once or twice until completely dissolved.

Pour the mix into a clean sterilized jar to avoid the growth of bad bacteria, cover with a clean muslin cloth so it can breathe and secure it with a rubber band (to sterilize use boiling hot water not chemicals).

Keep in a warm place on top of the fridge or somewhere toasty in the house, if your house is cold, it may take longer so wrap it in a blanket to keep warm.

Allow the mix to ferment for 24 hours, you should see little bubbles starting to appear after a few hours. This is the start of the fermentation.

After 24 hours your yoghurt will be ready, when you open the lid, the yoghurt should smell sour and pungent, but in a nice way. It will be extremely thick and look unpleasant, this is the curdling effect that takes place and is completely normal.

Empty the yoghurt into a mixing bowl and gently whisk in the rest of the ingredients, adding a little more water slowly until you reach a desired consistency.

You can add more maple if you like, the good bacteria thrive off it and have probably consumed all of what was previously added.

Make sure the yoghurt is stored back in the fridge or it will keep fermenting, and always ensure to use a clean spoon every time you take a portion to avoid contaminating.

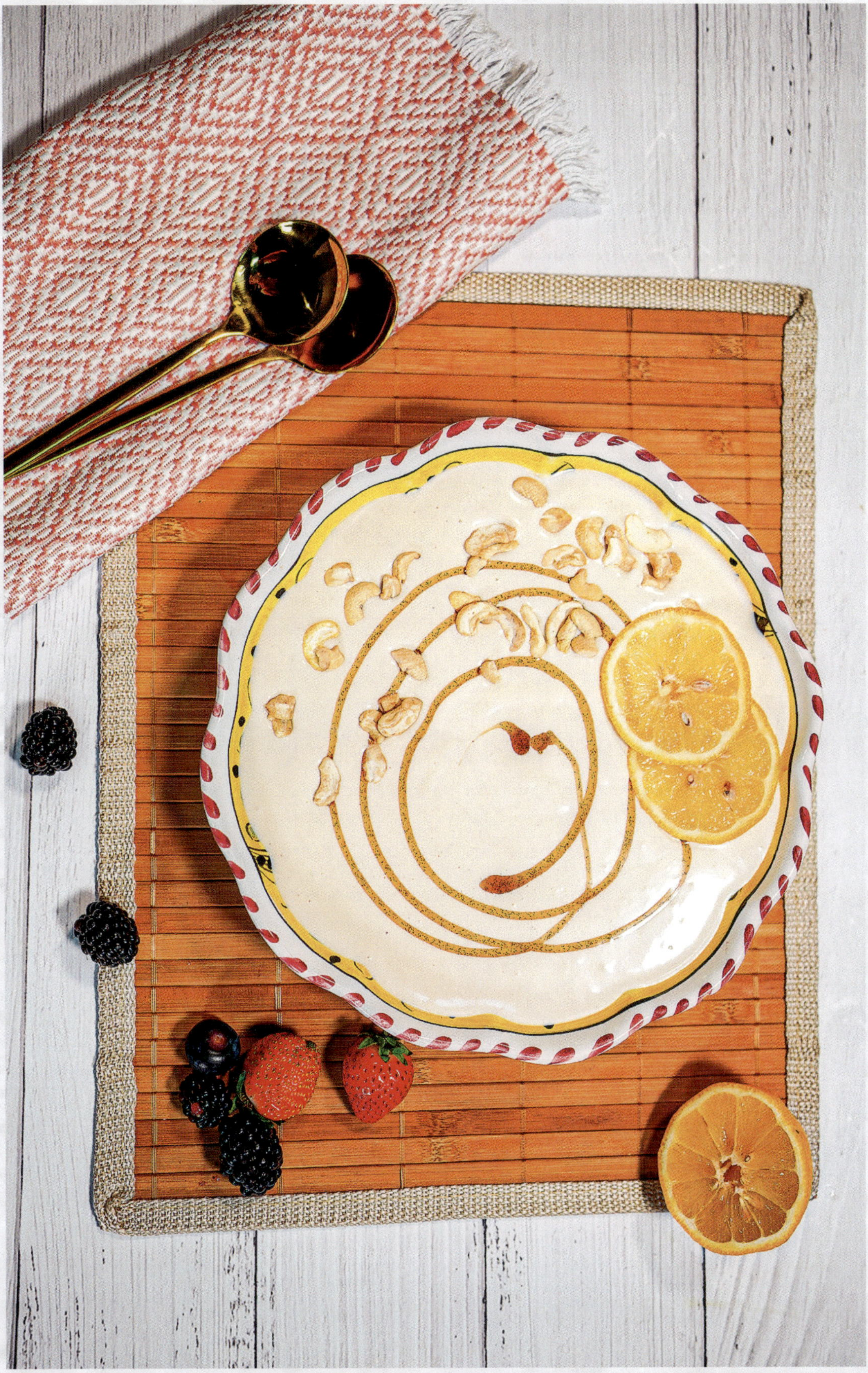

PASSION FOR PROTEIN CHIA SEED PUDDING

NUTS FREE · SOY FREE · GLUTEN FREE · REFINED SUGAR FREE

Protein, where do you get your protein from? A common misconception that we need so much protein to survive, but pretty much everyone in the west is over consuming protein in one way or another, whether it's derived from the flesh of an animal or from of a factory-made protein powder. Over consumption of protein becomes acidic in the body as it cannot be broken down or processed in excess amounts. The perfect proteins in the right ratio for the human diet comes from fruits, dark leafy greens, herbs, and seeds. Especially chia seeds, which are around 14% protein with a good balance of essential amino acids which help break down protein. The word "Chia" in the ancient Mayan language means strength and these tiny seeds do truly live up to their name.

4-6 Servings

EQUIPMENT NEEDED:

A set of measuring cups, chopping board, sharp knife, medium mixing bowl, whisk, medium glasses, or jars to serve in.

INGREDIENTS:

Chia Pudding Mix

1.2 Cups Chia Seeds
1litre Of Oat Milk, Unsweetened
1-2 Tbs Beetroot Powder Or Butterfly Pea Powder
1-2 Tbs Maple Syrup, Optional

To Garnish:

6-8 Large Passionfruit
Mint, Fresh
Frozen Blueberries, Thawed
Fresh Blueberry's
Fresh Raspberries
Coconut, Desiccated

Keep refrigerated in an airtight jar for 4-5 days.

Mix all the ingredients for the chia mix in a bowl and set aside for an 30 minutes until they have fully absorbed all the milk, or you may want to prepare the chis mix in the evening, so they are ready to go in the morning.

Once this chia mix is ready you will need a jar or a glass to layer and get creative, alternatively you can just dish it out in serving bowls and add the nest of the ingredients as toppings if you're in a rush.

For the layered effect:

Start by slicing a passion fruit in half and scooping out the seeds into a glass or jar, and spread around the edge of the glass, next sprinkle in some coconut around the edges of the glass to create layered affect and spoon in the thawed blueberries and juices.

Add 2-3 tbsp of spoons of chia and repeat the steps above until all the glass or jar is full.

Top the glass with half a passion fruit, fresh blueberries, more coconut, a sprig of mint and enjoy.

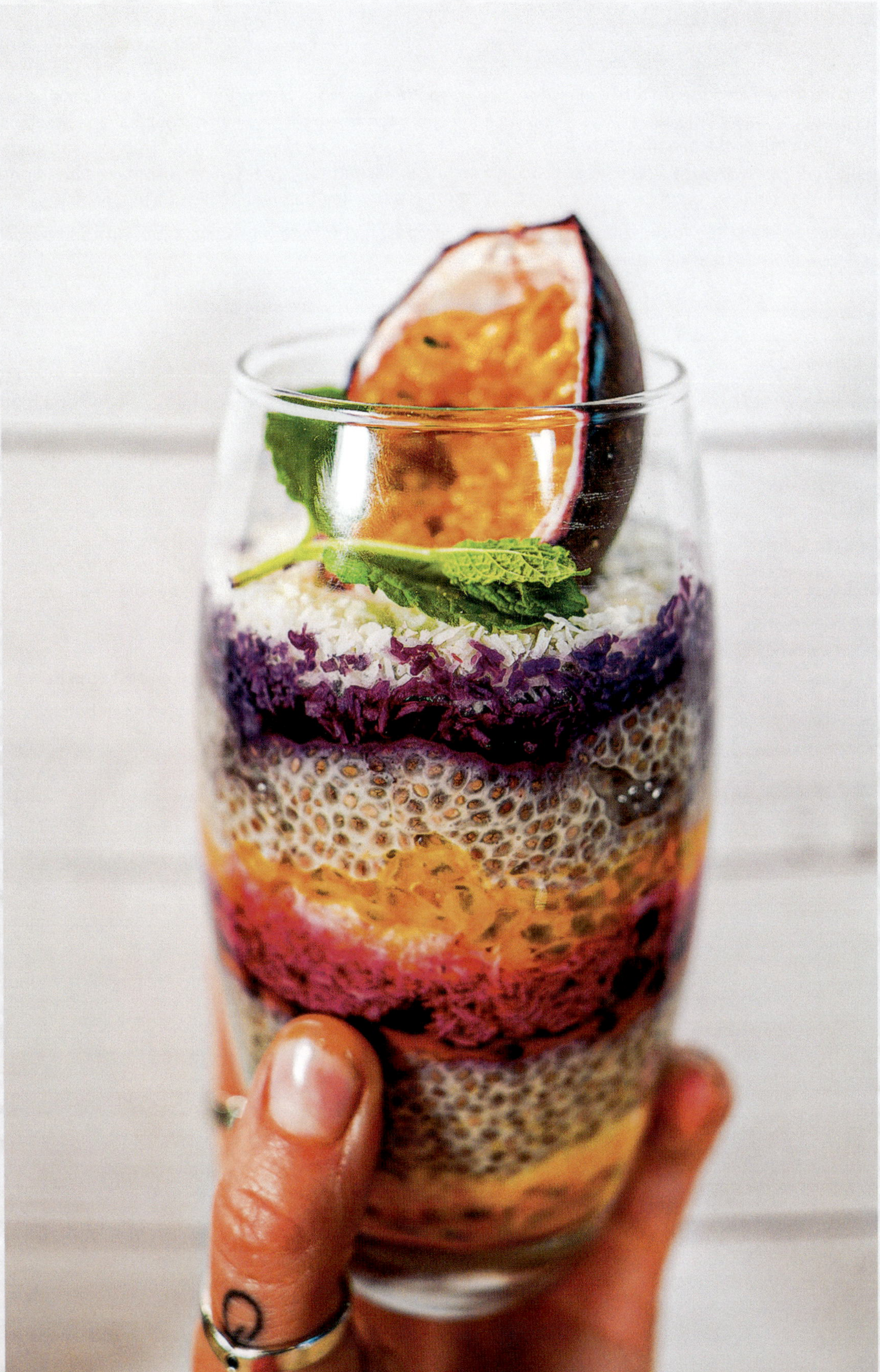

BANANA BREAD

NUTS FREE · SOY FREE · GLUTEN FREE · REFINED SUGAR FREE

Looking for ways to use up those over ripe, brown spotted bananas wasting away in the fruit bowl, well, let us let you into a little secret, there's no such thing as a too ripe banana when making banana bread, in fact the browner the banana the better the bread. As bananas ripen the starch in the fruit turns to sugar which ultimately give the bread great taste and texture while naturally sweetening. Just make sure to pop the bananas in the freezer before they go black, there is a fine line between really ripe and rotting.

This recipe is just the foundation recipe of all our breads, feel free to add some extra nuts and seeds, spices, and fruits to mix it up.

6-8 Servings

EQUIPMENT NEEDED:
A set of measuring cups, a food processor, a bread tin, chopping board, small knife.

INGREDIENTS:
5 Medium Bananas, Brown Spotted
1.5 Cups Self-Raising Flour, Gluten Free
1 Cup Medjool Dates, Pitted
3 tsp Baking Powder, Gluten Free
½ Cup Coconut Oil, Melted
½ Tsp Ginger, Ground
½ Tsp Cinnamon, Ground

Store at room temp for 3-4 days or in the freezer for up to 3 months.

Pre heat oven to 180 c / 350 f/ gas mark 4

Chop up 4 of the bananas and add into the bowl of a food processor with the rest of the ingredients, pulse until all the ingredients are mixed and a couple of small chunks of banana are remaining, 30-45 seconds.

Tip: If you do not have a food processor you will have to chop up all the dates until they form into a paste, and then mash them together with the bananas using a fork. Mix together all the wet ingredients first, then gently fold in all the dry ingredients.

Line a bread tin with parchment paper using some coconut oil on the tin to hold the paper in place and add the mix.

Slice the other banana in half-length ways and sit both pieces on top of the bread mix.

Place on the middle shelf of the oven and bake for 45- 55 mins.

Use skewers to check if it is fully cooked, if the skewer comes out clean its done, if it's still gooey place back in the oven for a further 10-15 minutes and lower the heat slightly.

Allow to cool before slicing, if fully chilled then toast under the grill to soften again.

Serve with some of our Chia Seed Jam (see page 40), Peanut Butter (see page 40) and fresh fruit.

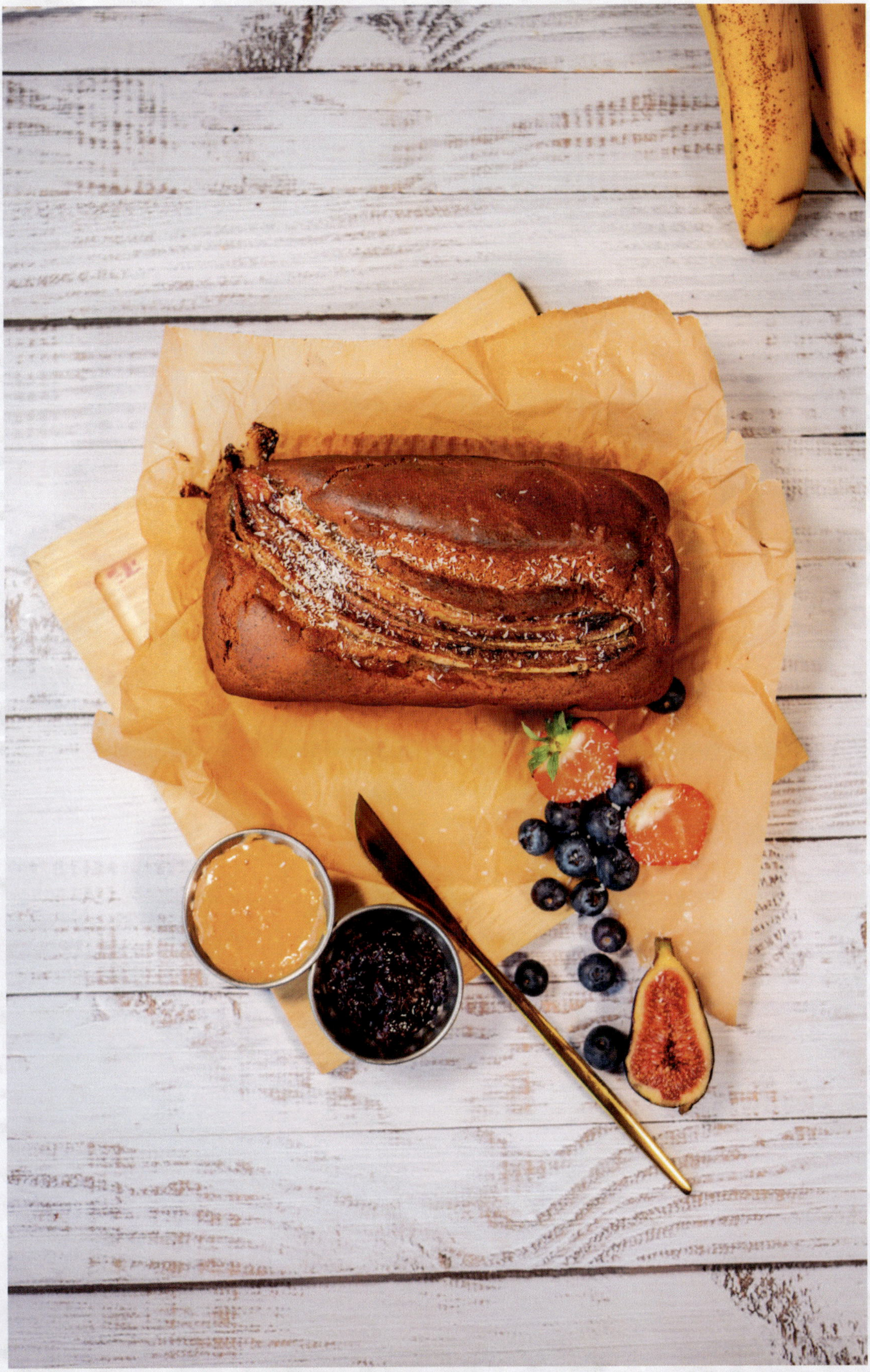

CHIA BERRY PROTEIN JAM

NUTS FREE · SOY FREE · GLUTEN FREE · REFINED SUGAR FREE

Jam usually consists of heaps of refined sugars to get its jelly like consistency, but instead of adding so much sugar to our already naturally sweetened fruits, we achieve its consistency by adding chia seeds which create a jelly like texture, that sugar usually provides. These minute seeds are excellent binding and thickening agents, which can be added to a variety of dishes to thicken. These tiny little powerhouses are also full of protein, fibre, and an unbeatable source of omega 3 fatty acids.

Quantity 300g

EQUIPMENT NEEDED:

A set of measuring cups, a medium heavy based saucepan, airtight jar for storing.

INGREDIENTS:

2 cups Frozen Mixed Berries
¼ Cup Pure Maple Syrup
¼ Cup Water
1 Sprig of Fresh Rosemary
2 Slices Fresh Lemon
2 tbs Chia Seeds

Place all the ingredients, except the chia seeds in a thick based saucepan on a medium heat and slowly simmer for around 20 minutes until most of fruits have stewed down, mash up with a fork if needed.

Add the chia seeds and allow them to soak up any excess liquid.

Once done, allow to cool fully before storing.

Store in an airtight container for up to 10 days in the fridge, or portion into smaller batches and freeze for up to 3 months.

DEEP ROASTED PEANUT BUTTER

SOY FREE · GLUTEN FREE · REFINED SUGAR FREE

This recipe is a one ingredient wonder with just the hit of a button. Peanuts are high in fat, protein, and fibre while low in carbs making this nut butter perfect for anyone following the ketogenic diet.

Quantity 500g

EQUIPMENT NEEDED:

A set of measuring cups, large baking tray, airtight mason jar, food processor or high-speed blender, a colander.

INGREDIENTS:

2 Cups Raw Peanuts
Pinch Of Sea Salt (optional)
A drop of oil (optional to help brake the nuts down)

Store in an airtight container at room temperature for up to one month.

Pre- soak the peanuts for a minimum of 8 hours or simply over night before starting this recipe - Optional but advised (see page 20 for benefits on soaking).

Once the nuts are ready, rinse well and drain, set aside on some kitchen paper to soak up any excess moisture.

Pre heat the oven on 180 c / 350 f/ gas mark 4.

Place the peanuts in a shallow baking tray and roast peanuts for 25 minutes until golden brown, if you soaked the nuts, they would need another 20minuits or so until completely dried out.

Add the peanuts and a pinch of salt to a high-speed blender and blend until smooth, scraping down the sides when necessary.

Allow to cool before storing.

TIP: At first you may not believe this mixture in the blender will turn into a lovely smooth peanut butter, but just let the blender do the work and as the natural oils start to release from the nuts you will eventually see a liquid like peanut butter develop. Depending on your blender this can take up to 30 minutes. If you dont mind a crunchy peanut butter, save some time and just blend until its the butter has reached your desired consistency

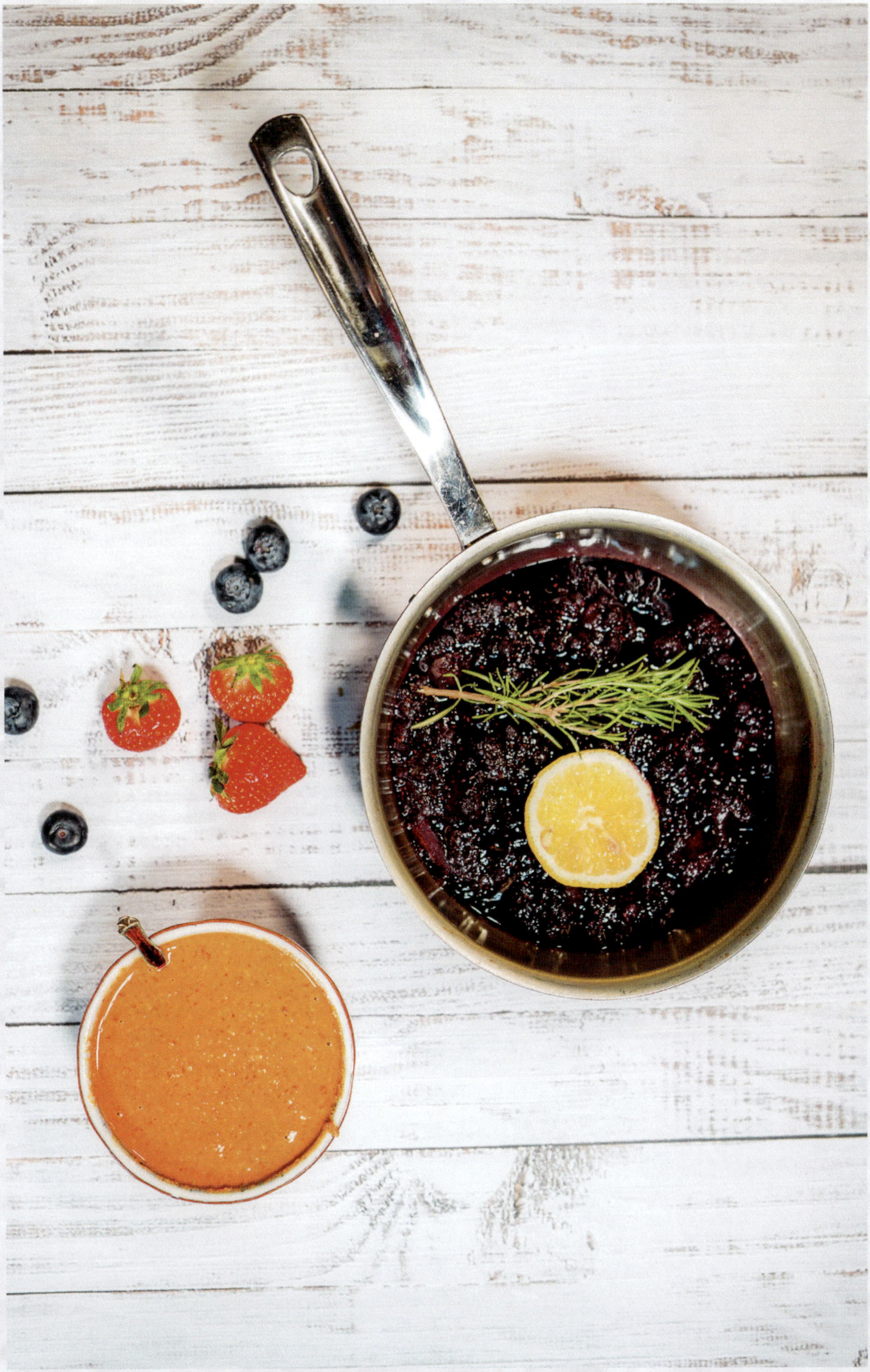

QUINOA AND CHIA LOAF WITH SUNFLOWER SEEDS

NUTS FREE · SOY FREE · GLUTEN FREE · REFINED SUGAR FREE

This loaf was introduced to Indigo Greens through our 100% gluten free meal prep company, its super easy to make and a great alternative for anyone who suffers with intolerances or allergies to gluten and wheat. It binds together with gelatinous fibre which acts as a broom, sweeping its way through the digestive tract, moving along any stubborn waste that could be lodged causing inflammation. This recipe is made up of superfood wholegrains and seeds which are also high in protein and healthy fats like omega 3 which is essential for brain health. It's not the typical texture to regular bread, but its moist, crunchy slices of utter goodness toasted with your favourite toppings curbs the cravings for carbs.

Note: A high-speed blender like a Vitamix or really good food processor is needed for this recipe to break down the quinoa

6-8 Servings

EQUIPMENT NEEDED:

A set of measuring cups, a high-speed blender or food processor, a bread tin, small mixing bowls, a colander.

INGREDIENTS:

1.5 Cups Red Quinoa, Pre-Soaked
1 Cup Chia Seed, Soaked 1.5cups Water
1/3 cup Olive Oil
1 Tsp Baking Powder
¼ Tsp Garlic Powder
½ Tsp Fresh Rosemary, Chopped
2 Tsp Maple Syrup (Optional)
½ Cup Sunflower Seeds
1tsp Sea Salt

Store in the fridge for up to 1 week or in the freezer for up to 3 months.

Pre-soak the quinoa for 8 hours or overnight to soften the grain for blending.

Pre- soak the sunflower seeds for 2 hours– Optional but advised (see page 20 for benefits on soaking).

Mix the chia seeds and water together to form the binding gel.

Rinse the sunflower seeds and set aside on a clean cloth/ kitchen roll.

Preheat the oven at 180c/350f/gas mark 4.

Grease the loaf tin with a a drop of oil and line with baking paper.

Drain the soaked quinoa and rinse well, then pop half the quinoa into the blender with the soaked chia seeds, bicarbonate of soda, maple, oil, garlic, and rosemary and blend until the mixture is almost smooth and then stir in the other half of the quinoa for added texture.

Pour the mixture into the loaf tin and scatter the mixed seeds over the top.

Pop in the oven on the middle shelf and bake for 65-75 minutes, or until you can stick a skewer or sharp knife into the middle of the loaf, and it comes out clean, if its still moist lower the oven slightly and cook for a further 10-15 minutes.

Allow to cool before slicing and try toasting the bread before serving for extra flavour and crunch.

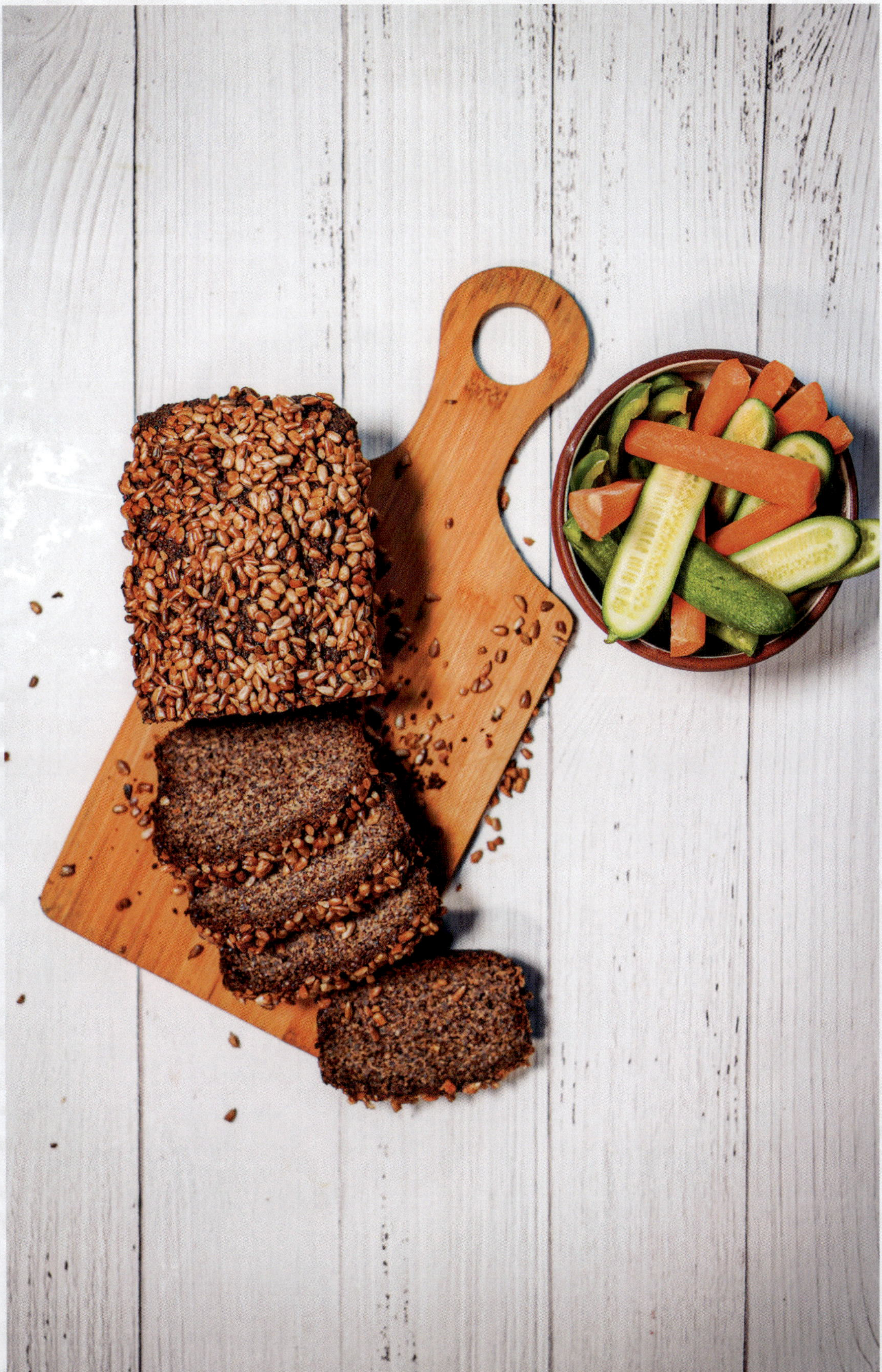

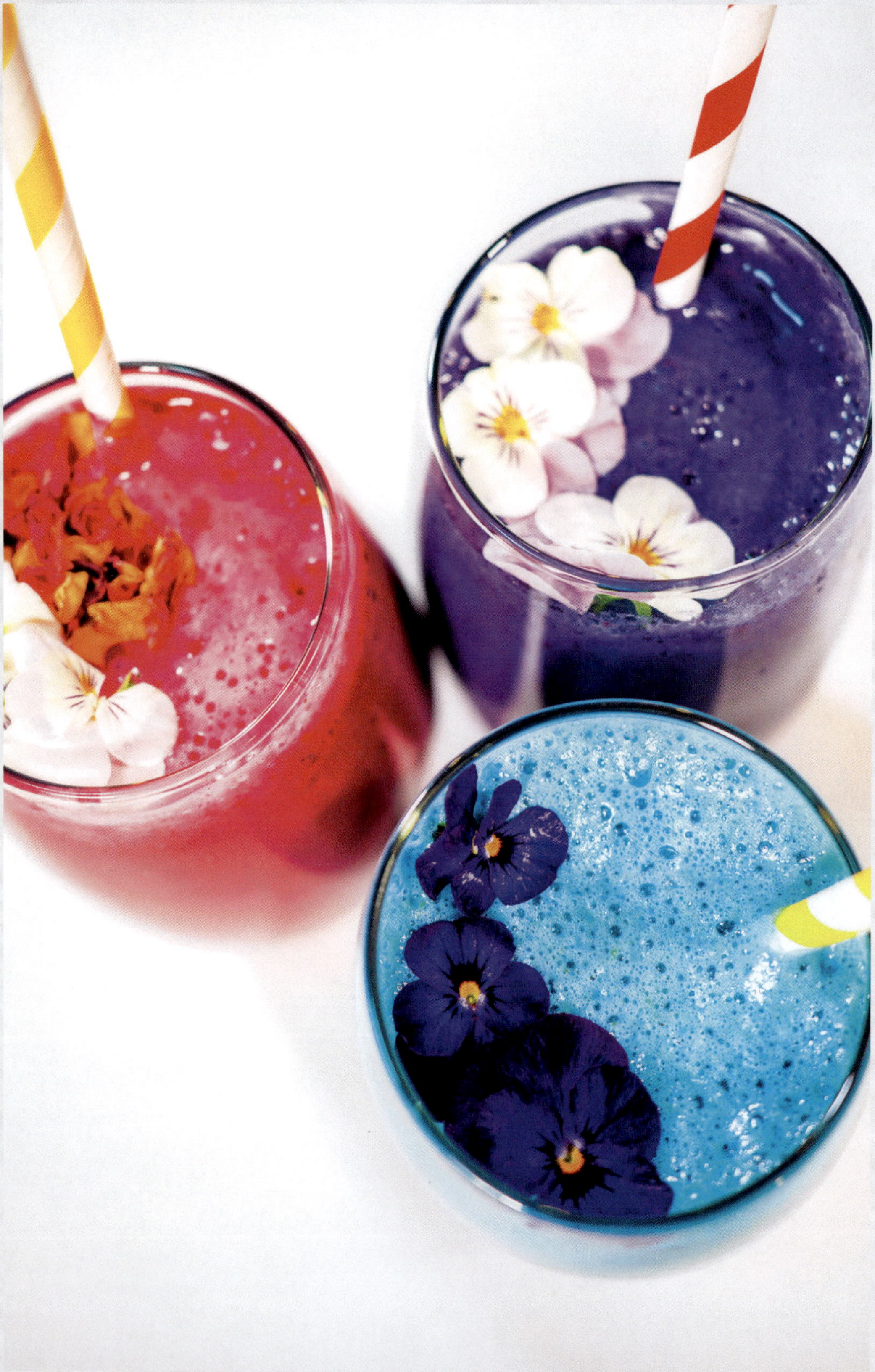

I AM: CHAKRA HEALING SMOOTHIES

Our Chakra Healing Smoothies have been created to raise the vibration, heal, and unblock each of the primary energy centres in the body. We all know food has a major effect on the physical, but did you know it also influences us on an emotional and mental level too. Each energy centre has its own unique vibration and the foods we eat, depending on the colour also carry the same unique vibration, helping us heal, unblock, and move any stagnant energy in the chakras. Each chakra also vibrates at its own frequency, and so do the words we use, reciting a mantra that resonates with this vibration also helps realign any imbalances and can have a profound uplifting effect on the energy field.

EQUIPMENT NEEDED:

A set of measuring cups, a high-speed blender, a sharp knife, a chopping board.

Start by setting an intention for your chakra healing to take place.

Prepare the ingredients mindfully and in a meditative state, channelling the breath to the energy centre, "energy flows where attention goes".

Place ingredients into a high-speed blender with 1-2 cups of liquid and blend until smooth while focused breathing.

Once blended pour the smoothie into a glass and repeat the Mantra I AM….. while receiving the healing benefits nutritionally and metaphysically.

TIP: The texture of smoothies are always better when made from frozen fruit, so set a day aside and prepare all your fresh produce into portions and freeze them down for the week ahead. This will not only save you time but will preserve and lock in all nutrients. You can also buy in frozen fruits which will save time further.

VIOLET CROWN SMOOTHIE

"I AM CONSCIOUSNESS, an extension of the Divine and at one with all that is."

The Crown Chakra is located on the top of the head and connects you to your higher self, consciousness, to God, the universe or the divine.

1 Cup Plums
1 Cup Purple Grapes
0.5 Cup Blackberries
1 Tsp Acai Berry Powder
1-2 Cup Plant Milk Or Water

INDIGO THIRD EYE SMOOTHIE

"I AM CONNECTED with spirit, and I trust my intuition."

The Third Eye Chakra is located in-between the brows and is the centre of intuition, foresight and is driven by openness and imagination.

0.5 Cup Blueberries
0.5 Cup Blackberries
1 Cup Plum
0.5 Tsp Butterfly Pea Powder
1-2 Cups Water or Plant Milk

BLUE THROAT SMOOTHIE

"I AM TRUTH and I express myself with a clear intention."

The Throat Chakra is located is in the centre of neck and represents truth, are ability to speak and communicate effectively.

2 Cup Pineapple
0.5 Cup Blueberries
0.5 Cup Banana
0.5 Tsp Blue Spirulina
1 Cup of Or Water Plant Milk

GREEN HEART SMOOTHIE

"I AM LOVE, I am open to give love and receive love."

The Heart Chakra is the colour green, which is located in the centre of the chest, representing love, self-love, and compassion and it governs our relationships.

0.5 Cup Apple
0.5 Cup Celery
0.5 Cup Kiwi
0.5 Cup Spinach
0.25 Tsp Green Spirulina
1-2 Cups Water

YELLOW SOLAR PLEXUS SMOOTHIE

"I AM WORTHY of pursuing my passion and purpose."

The Solar Plexus is bright yellow and is located just below the ribs. This chakra represents self-worth, confidence, will power, and strength.

0.5 Cup Banana
0.5 Cup Mango
0.25 Cup Pineapple
0.25 Cup Lemon
1-2 Cups Of Plant Milk

ORANGE SACRAL SMOOTHIE

"I AM CREATION and in tune with my entire reality."

The Sacral Chakra is a deep orange colour and is located just below the navel. It is connected to the reproductive organs and is deeply linked to creative and sexual energy. It is the second of the energy centres and it governs the water element inside of you, all that is fluid. Having the ability to adapt with emotions and feelings.

1 Cup Orange Segments
1 Cup Lemon Segments
0.5 Cm Fresh Turmeric
¼ Cup Carrots, Thin Sliced
2 Cm Fresh Ginger
3 Dates
2 Cups of Water

RED ROOT SMOOTHIE

"I AM GROUNDED, strong and supported."

The Root Chakra is deep red and located at the base of the spine, providing a foundation for the building blocks of life, it is the first of the energy centres and connected directly to the earth and is associated with all things necessary on this physical plane, like survival, safety, security, and stability.

0.5 Cup Strawberries
0.5 Cup Raspberries
A Squeeze of Fresh Lime
5 Mint Leaves
1 Tsp Beetroot Powder
1 Cup of Water or Plant Milk

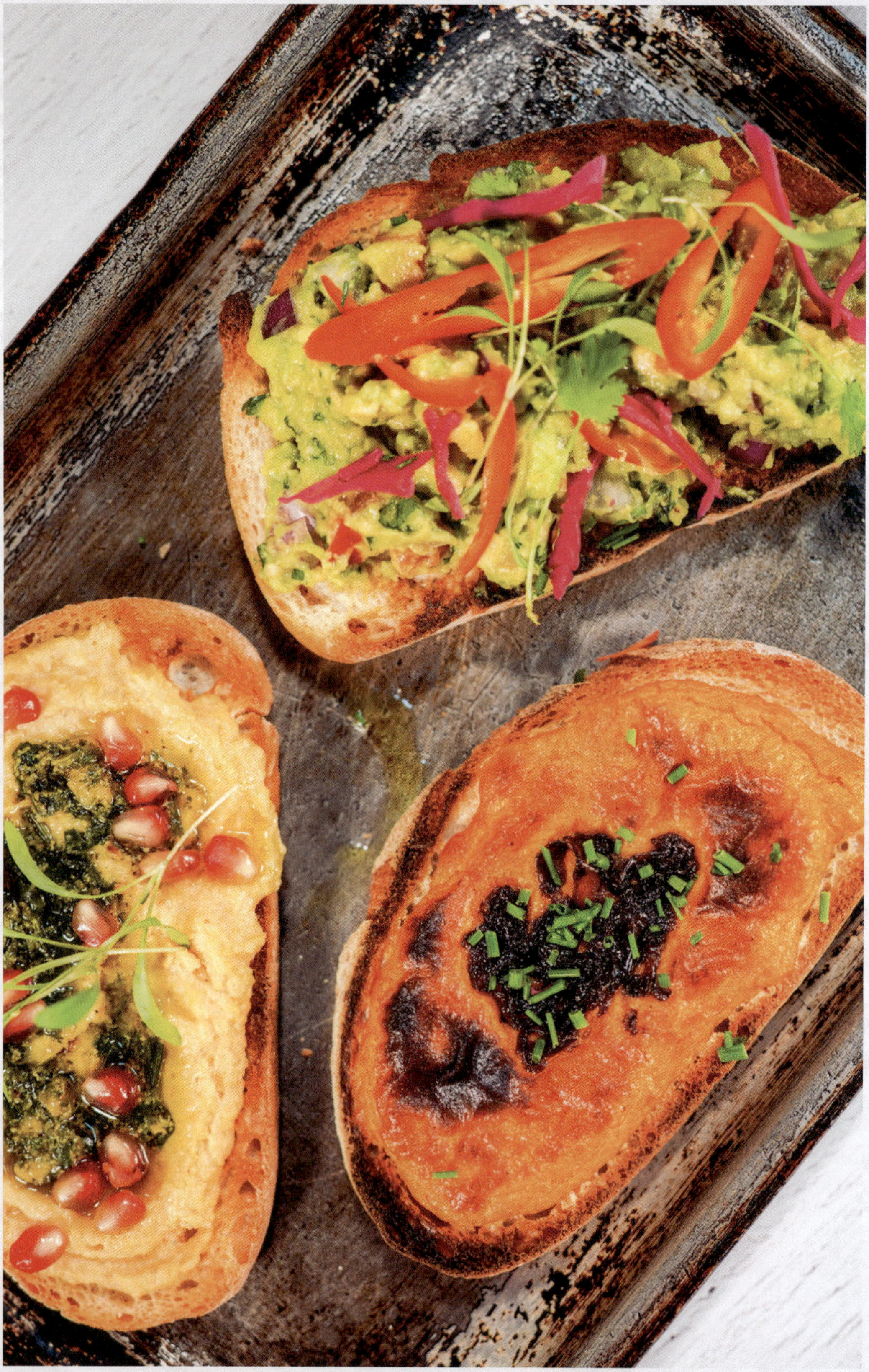

ON TOASTS

All our 'On Toast' options are served on toasted Sourdough Bread as it is much easier to digest and less likely to spike blood sugar levels as it relies on a mix of wild yeast and a lacto-fermentation process which increases the folate and antioxidant levels while reducing the anti-nutrients (phytates) making it easier to absorb the nutrients the bread contains.

PUMPKIN SEED PESTO AND POMEGRANATE HUMMUS

NUTS FREE • SOY FREE • GLUTEN FREE • REFINED SUGAR FREE

Hummus on toast, simple, satisfying and extremely refreshing, loaded with pumpkin seed pesto, pomegranates, and toasted seeds. Each burst of flavour releases huge amounts of nutrients, antioxidants, anti-inflammatory, and antibacterial properties. The colours say it all!!

1 Serving

EQUIPMENT NEEDED:
A baking tray, chopping board, knife.

INGREDIENTS:
2 Slices of Sourdough Bread or Quinoa and Chia Loaf for GF option (see page 42)
3-4 Tbs Creamy Smooth Traditional Hummus (see page 92)
2 Tbs Chunky Pumpkin Seed Pesto (see page 90)
2tbsp Pomegranate Seeds

To Garnish
Sesame Seeds
Pumpkin Seeds, Toasted
Coriander
Balsamic Glaze (see page 94)

Toast your choice of bread to your liking under a grill or in the toaster.

Add a big dollop of hummus to the centre of each piece and spread thickly in all corners.

Angle one piece of toast over the other on a plate.

Spoon over the pesto and sprinkle over the pomegranates, sesame seeds and toasted pumpkin seeds.

Serve straight away and enjoy.

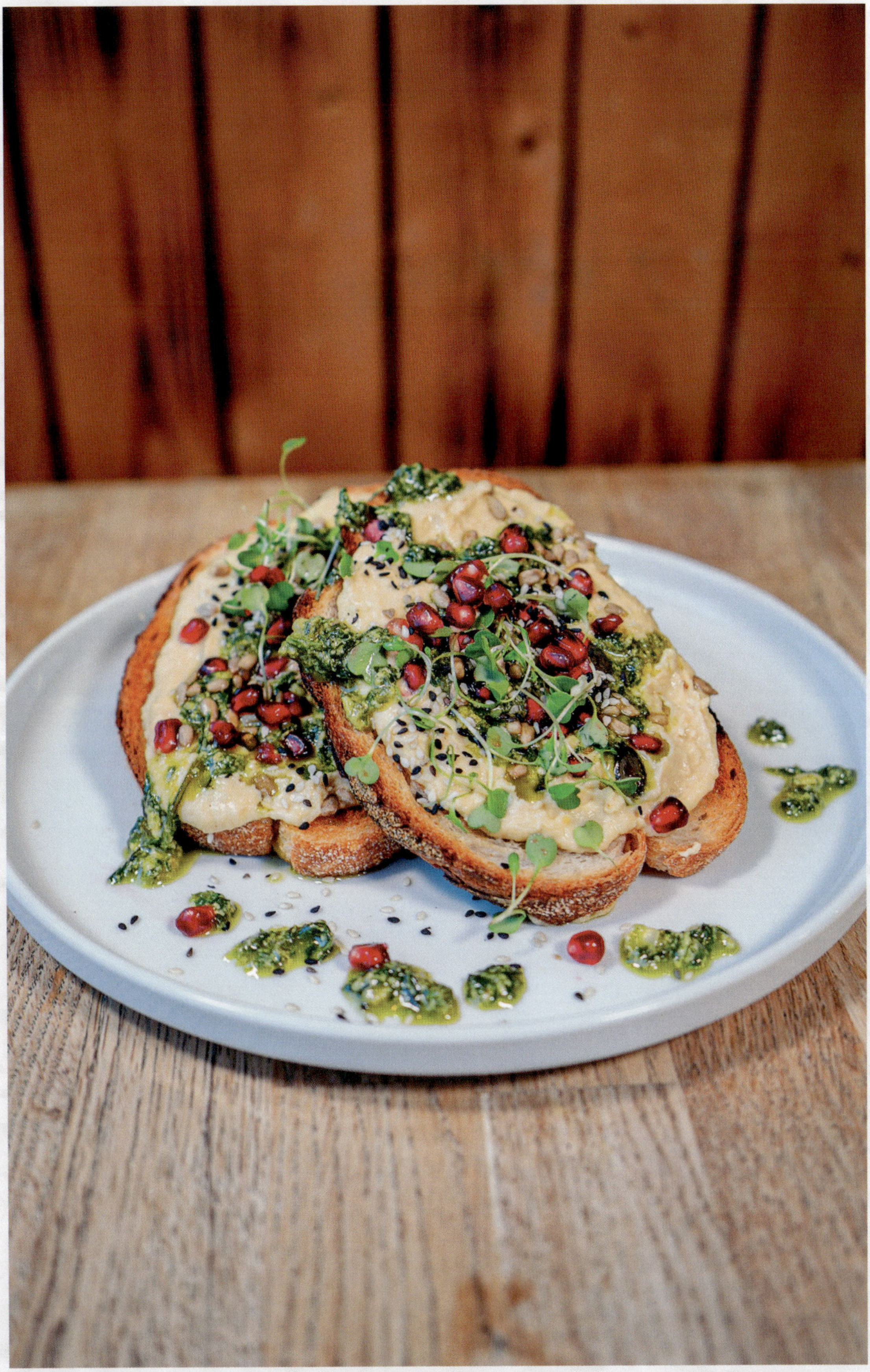

GRILLED CASHEW CHEESE, CHIVE AND CARAMELISED ONION CHUTNEY

Grilled Cheese, everyone's guilty of loving it…. but there's honestly no guilt necessary when indulging in our dreamy Smoked Cashew Cheese, it's definitely a popular choice in the restaurant and it's no surprise as the flavour combination is truly addictive. Complemented with our Caramelised Onion Chutney and charred under the grill to perfection. Cashew nuts are super diverse when it comes to plant-based cooking, they can literally be used for so many dairy alternatives, exchanging those saturated animal fats for heart healthy fats which help lower cholesterol instead of adding to it.

1 Serving

EQUIPMENT NEEDED:

A baking tray, chopping board, knife.

INGREDIENTS:

2 Slices of Sourdough Bread or Quinoa and Chia Loaf with Sunflower Seeds for GF option (see page 42)

3-4 Tbs Smoked Cashew Cheese (see page 101)

2 Tsp Caramelised Onion Chutney (see page 86)

To Garnish

Chives, Finely Chopped

Balsamic Glaze (see page 94)

Place your choice of bread under the grill and toast to your liking on one side only.

Flip the bread and spread the Smoked Cashew Cheese thickly across all corners, adding a spoon full of onion chutney to the centre of both pieces over the cheese.

Place it back under the grill on a high heat until the cheese starts to brown and gently caramelises for around 5-8 minutes.

Angle one piece of toast over the other on a plate and finish with chives and a good old drizzle of balsamic glaze.

Serve straight away and enjoy.

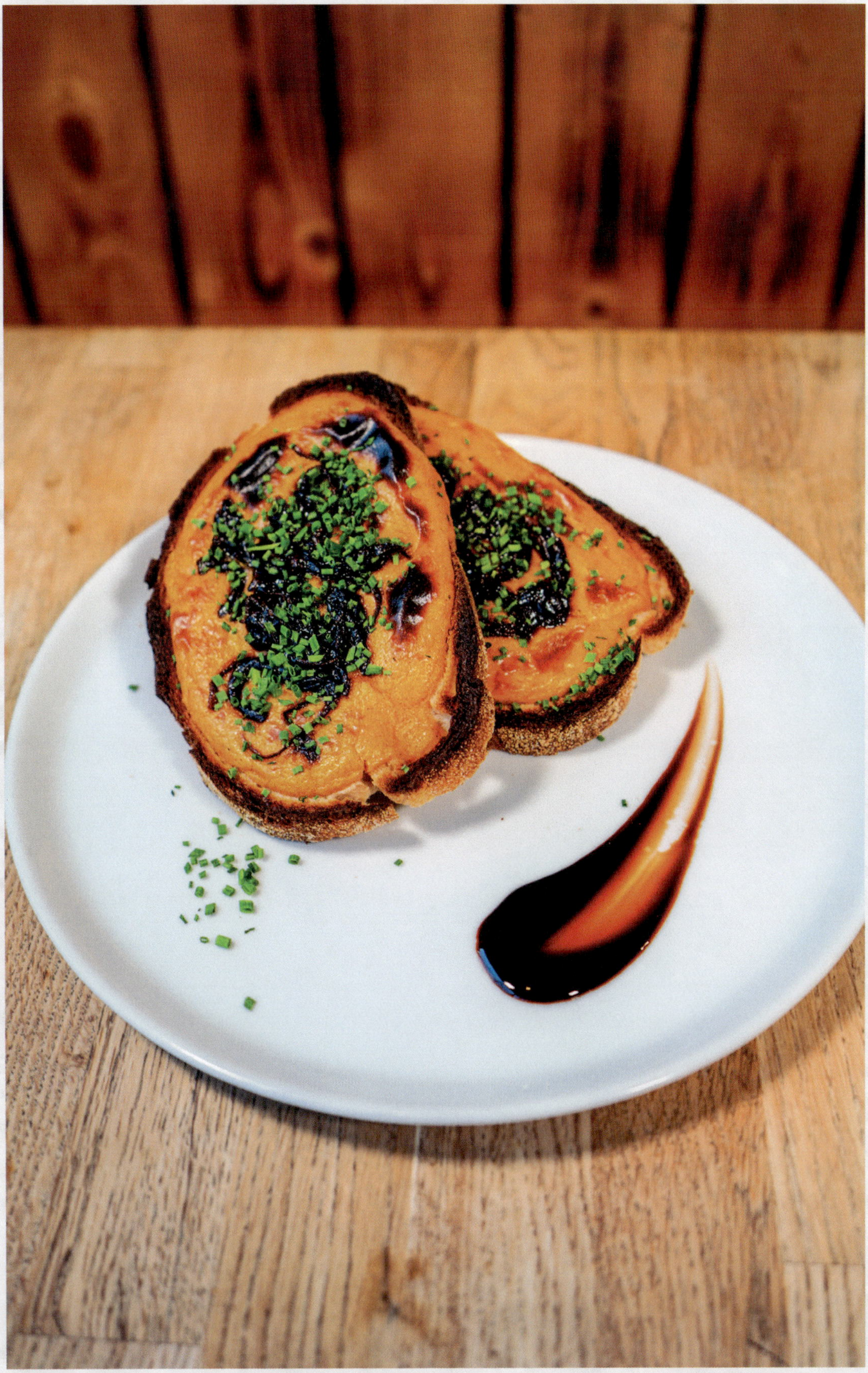

MASHED AVOCADO ON TOAST
WITH LIME, CHILLI AND CORIANDER

NUTS FREE *SOY FREE* *GLUTEN FREE* *REFINED SUGAR FREE*

Avocado on toast, it never gets old. Its rich and creamy flavour has undoubtably stole the hearts amongst health-conscious individuals for its super food properties over the years and although this fruit is over 77% fat, it contains no bad cholesterol and minimal saturated fats. The demonisation of fats over the decades has led people to fear of these highly nutritious fruits that not only offer excessive vitality, but they also dramatically help increase the nutrient value of other plant-based foods we eat too, as some nutrients are only effective if combined with the good fats like those found in avocados!!

1 Serving

EQUIPMENT NEEDED:

A baking tray, chopping board, knife.

INGREDIENTS:

2 Slices of Sourdough Bread or Quinoa and Chia Loaf with Sunflower Seeds for GF option (see page 42)

3-4 Tbs Guacamole (see page 99)

To Garnish

Coriander, Fresh

Red Chilli, Fine Slices

Sweet Pickled Cabbage, Drained (see page 136)

Toast your choice of bread to your liking under a grill or in the toaster.

Add a big dollop of mashed avocado to each piece spreading across thickly.

Angle one piece of toast over the other on a plate.

Top with fresh chilli's, fresh coriander, pickled red cabbage, and toasted pumpkin seeds.

Serve straight away and enjoy.

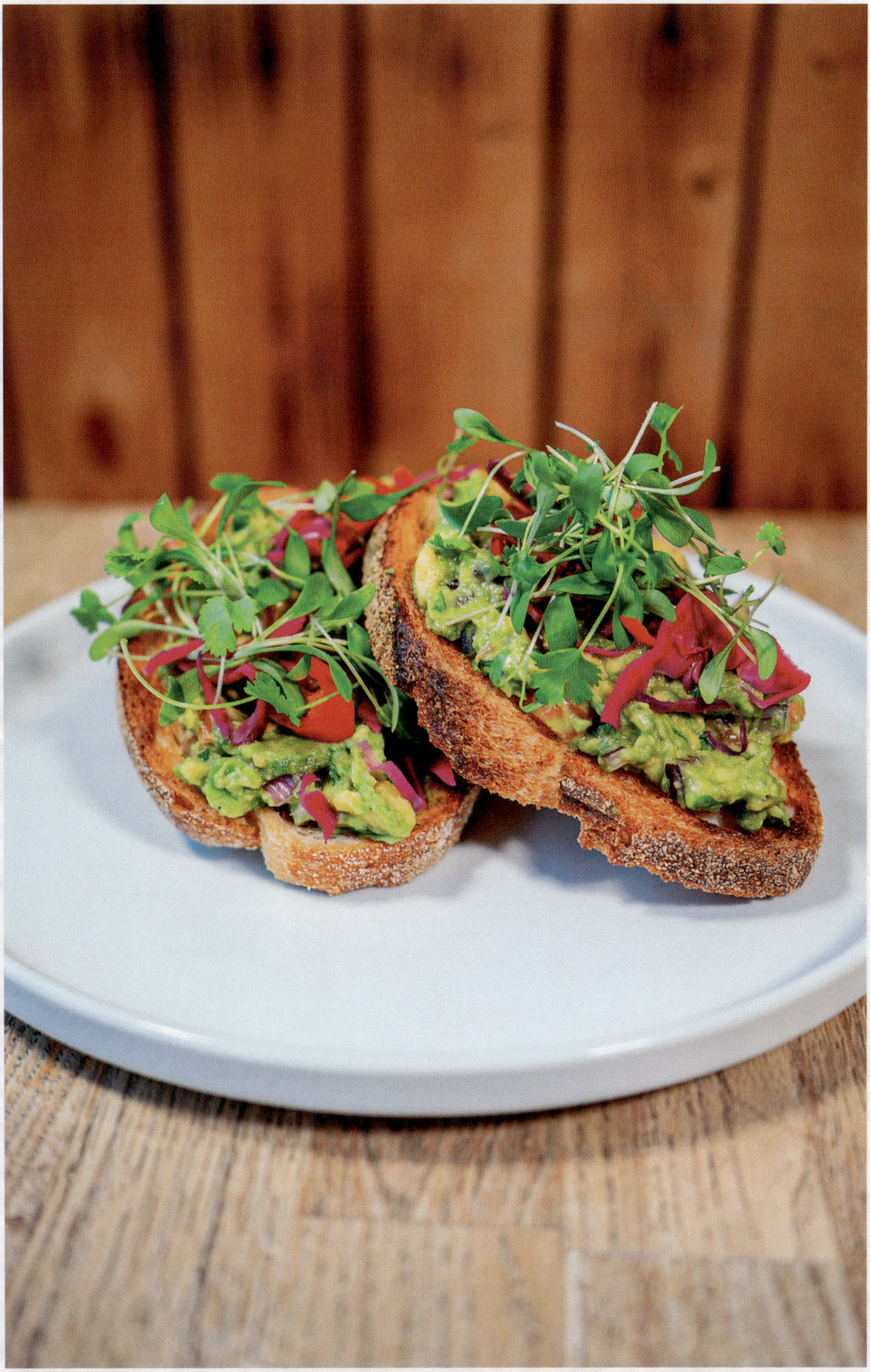

TOAST 3 WAYS

SOY FREE *GLUTEN FREE* *REFINED SUGAR FREE*

One for the indecisive ... 3-way toast, a firm favourite from the Indigo menu. A slice of mashed avo, chilli, lime and coriander, a slice of pesto and pomegranate hummus and a slice of grilled cashew cheese, caramelised onions and chives. There's definitely a party going on, on this plate. The question is, which one will be your favourite?

1 Serving

EQUIPMENT NEEDED:
A baking tray, chopping board, knife.

INGREDIENTS:
3 Slices Of Sourdough Bread
Or
Quinoa and Chia Loaf for Gf option with Sunflower Seeds (see page 42)
1.5 Tbs Smoked Cashew Cheese (see page 101)
1 Tsp Caramelised Onion Chutney (see page 86)
1.5 Tbs Creamy Smooth Traditional Hummus (see page 92)
1 Tsp Chunky Pumpkin Seed Pesto (see page 90)
1.5 Tbs Guacamole (see page 99)

To Garnish
Balsamic Glaze (see page 94)
Sweet Pickled Cabbage, Drained (see page 136)
Pumpkin Seeds Toasted
Pomegranates
Sesame Seeds
Red Chilli Slices
Coriander, Fresh

Place the 3 pieces of your choice of bread under the grill, toasting one side to your liking, flip the bread over and on one piece spread the cashew cheese thickly across all corners, adding a dollop of onion chutney to the centre of it.

Place all 3 pieces back under the grill and toast the other sides of the bread while the cheese on toast piece slowly cooks.

Once the other 2 slices are toasted, remove from the grill, and return the cashew cheese on toast until its well done and the cheese is starting to brown, about 5 more minutes.

Meanwhile add a big dollop of mashed avocado to one piece and garnish with fresh chilli's, fresh coriander, pickled red cabbage.

Add a dollop of hummus to other piece and spoon over the pesto, pomegranates, sesame, and pumpkin seeds.

Then angle one piece of toast over the other on a plate.

Remove the cashew cheese on toast from the grill once its browned and angle over the hummus on toast, sprinkle with chives.

Serve straight away and enjoy.

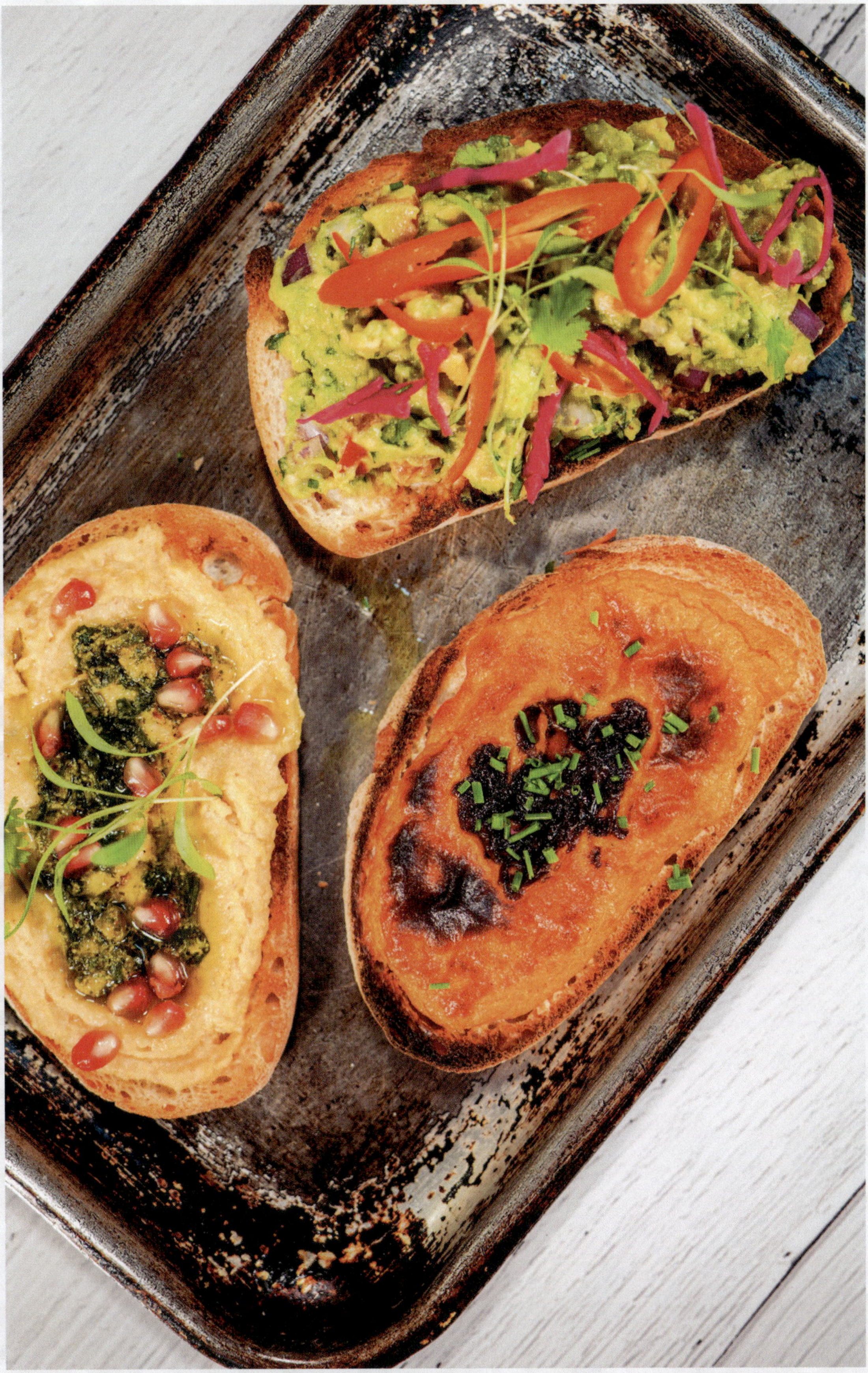

MUSHROOM BRUSCHETTA WITH PUMPKIN SEED PESTO

NUTS FREE · SOY FREE · GLUTEN FREE · REFINED SUGAR FREE

We put this one on the menu for those that were not so adventurous, I mean mushrooms on toast is pretty standard, right? But topped with our pumpkin seed pesto, balsamic glaze, toasted seeds, and sweet pickled cabbage turns something pretty standard into something pretty special, its fresh, vibrant and extremely nutrient dense. Pumpkin seeds are a great source of protein and unsaturated fats, including omega-3 and omega-6 fatty acids. They also contain a good range of nutrient's, including iron, calcium, B2, folate and beta-carotene, which the body converts into vitamin A.

1 Serving

EQUIPMENT NEEDED:

A set of measuring cups, chopping board, knife, skillet, or non-stick frying pan.

INGREDIENTS:

2 Slices of Sourdough Bread or Quinoa and Chia Loaf with Sunflower Seeds for GF option (see page 42)

3 Rosemary and Garlic Mushrooms, 1cm Slices (see page 70) or 3 large Raw Flat Mushrooms

¼ Small Red Onion, Sliced

1 Handful of Baby Spinach, Washed

2 Tbs Chunky Pumpkin Seed Pesto (see page 90)

1 tbsp Olive Oil to ingredients list

Sea Salt to Taste

Cracked Black Pepper

To Garnish

Balsamic Glaze (see page 94)
Pea Shoots
Sweet Pickled Cabbage (see page 136)
Pumpkin Seeds, Toasted

Heat the olive oil in a non-stick frying pan and sauté the garlic and rosemary mushrooms for 2 minutes (if using raw mushrooms, sauté for 4 minutes or until soft).

Add the onions and cook for a further 2 minutes until golden brown.

Briefly add the spinach and fold through, taking off the heat straight away so the spinach doesn't wilt too much.

Meanwhile toast your choice of bread to your liking under a grill or in the toaster.

Angle one piece of toast over the other on a plate and build the mushroom across both pieces.

Spoon over the pesto, drizzle with balsamic glaze, sprinkle with pumpkin seeds and a little pickled cabbage for colour.

Serve straight away and enjoy.

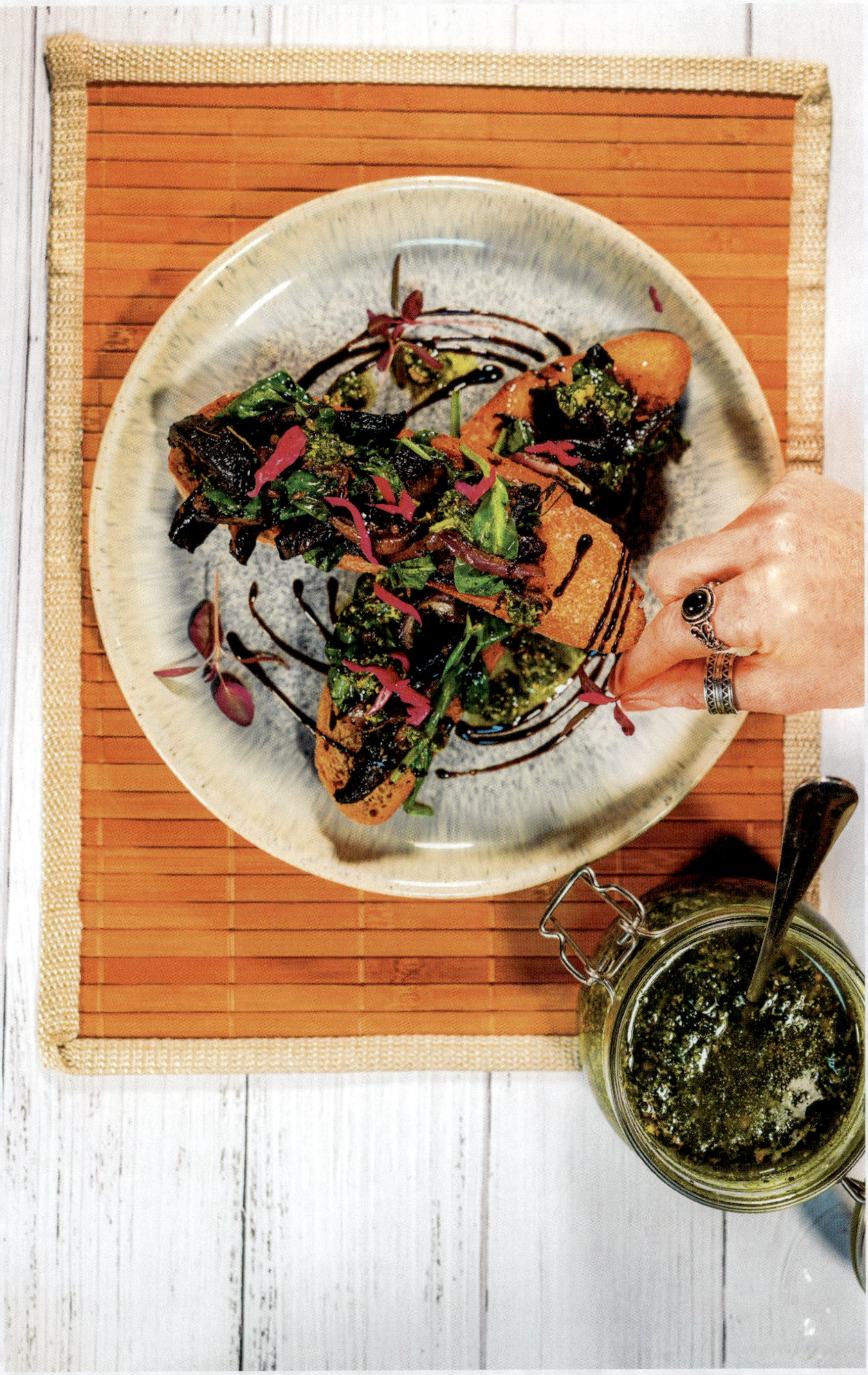

SAUSAGE ON

NUTS FREE | SOY FREE | GLUTEN FREE | REFINED SUGAR FREE

A good old sausage on... "Sausage on what"? You may be asking yourself if you're not from Liverpool, it's our lazy slang from the streets for a greasy Sausage on Toast. But our plant based, protein and fibre rich 'Sausage On' is not so basic, our hand rolled sausages are sandwiched between two thick slices of freshly baked sourdough, smothered in our slow cooked aromatic tomato chutney, and topped with melted cheese and spinach, it's like nothing you have ever tasted before and is far from the greasy gritty sausage you would of got from 'Pats café on the corner'.

1 Serving

EQUIPMENT NEEDED:

A baking tray, chopping board, knife.

INGREDIENTS:

2 Extra Thick Slices of Sourdough Bread or Quinoa and Chia Loaf with Sunflower seeds for GF option (see page 42)
3 X Herby Sausages (see page 70)
1-2 Tbs Tomato Chutney (see page 98)
1 Tbs Violife, Grated Mozzarella
1 Cup Baby Spinach, Washed

Follow the method to make the herby sausages needed for this dish and cook under grill as instructed on page 70.

Once the sausages are cooked, cut in half length ways, and keep warm.

Place your choice of bread under the grill and toast to your liking on one side only.

Flip the bread and add cheese to one piece, return to the grill and toast until cheese is melted and the other piece of bread is toasted.

Take the toast from the grill and start to build the sausage on with the cheese side as your base.

Add the spinach, sausages, spoon on the tomato chutney and finish with the top layer of toast.

Serve straight away and enjoy.

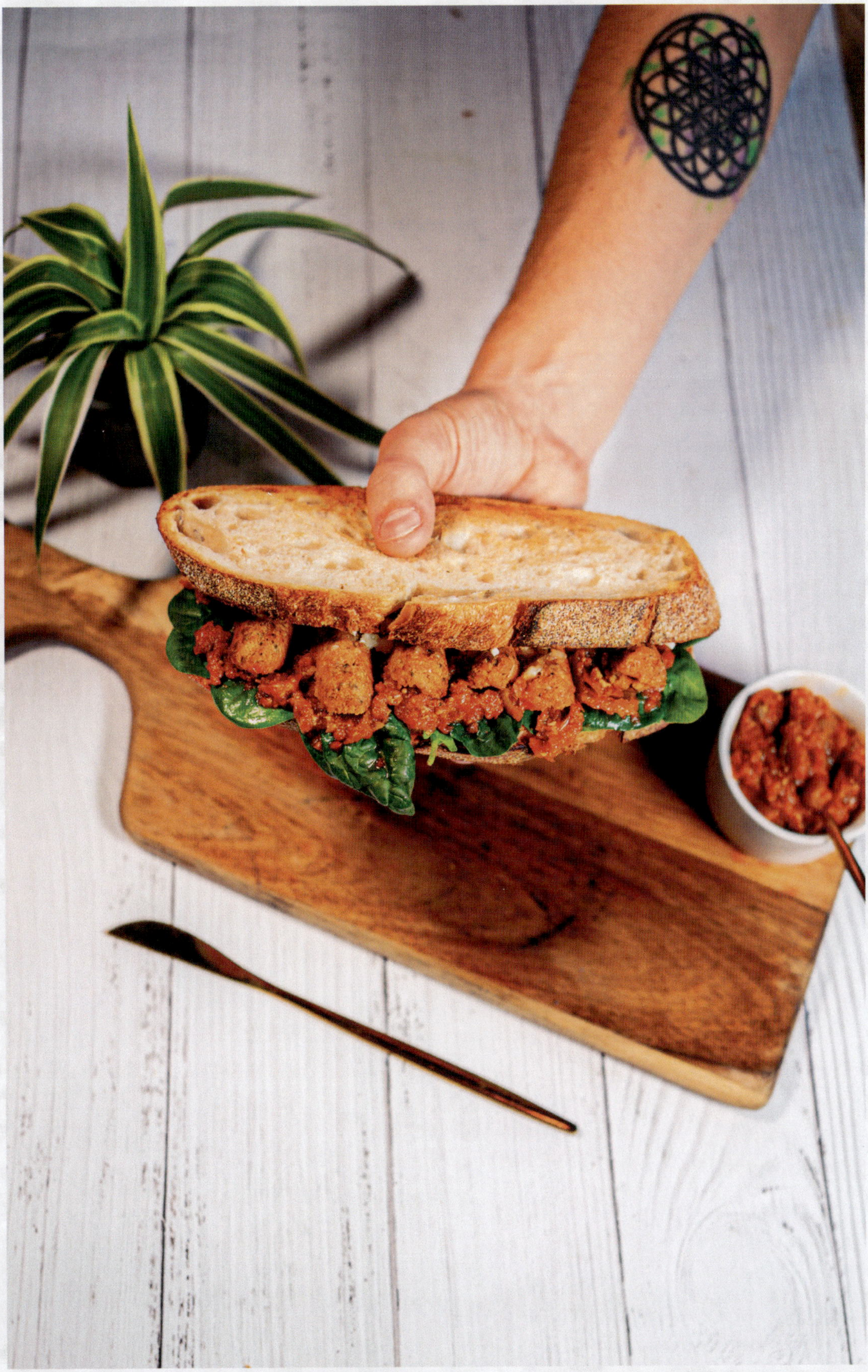

TERRACOTTA BEANS

NUTS FREE · SOY FREE · GLUTEN FREE · REFINED SUGAR FREE

If you grew up in Liverpool, 'Beans on Toast' was most definitely on the daily menu, well it was on mine anyway. We basically lived off it as kids and I could not resist to twist this dish up Indigo style. I chose to replicate the look of this dish by using the same kind of bean you find in a commercial tin of baked beans to create that familiarity from childhood, bringing back some memories and sparking those dopamine receptors. But although they may look the same, our sweet and smoky, protein and fibre rich beans are on a totally different spectrum of taste. Loaded with hummus, mexican chipotle, sesame seeds, coriander, and balsamic glaze - they're certainly not the average beans on toast we grew up loving, but the familiarity is there, releasing tiny hits of happy hormones that really take us back in time while offering bigger hits of energy, zinc, fibre, folate, and B vitamins.

1 Serving

EQUIPMENT NEEDED:

A set of measuring cups, a small saucepan.

INGREDIENTS:

2 Slices of Sourdough Bread Or Quinoa And Chia Loaf with Sunflower Seeds for GF option (see page 42)

1 Cup Smokey Breakfast Beans (see page 74)

1-2 Tbs Creamy Smooth Traditional Hummus (see page 92)

1 Tbs Spicy Chipotle Sauce (see page 95)

Balsamic Glaze (see page 94)

Coriander

Sesame Seeds

Place the beans in a small saucepan and gently bring to the boil on medium heat until piping hot.

Meanwhile toast your choice of bread to your liking, under a grill or in the toaster.

Angle one piece of toast over the other on a plate and pour over the beans.

Add a big dollop of hummus to the centre of the dish and spoon on the chipotle sauce.

Drizzle with balsamic glaze, sprinkle of sesame seeds and finish with coriander.

Serve straight away and enjoy.

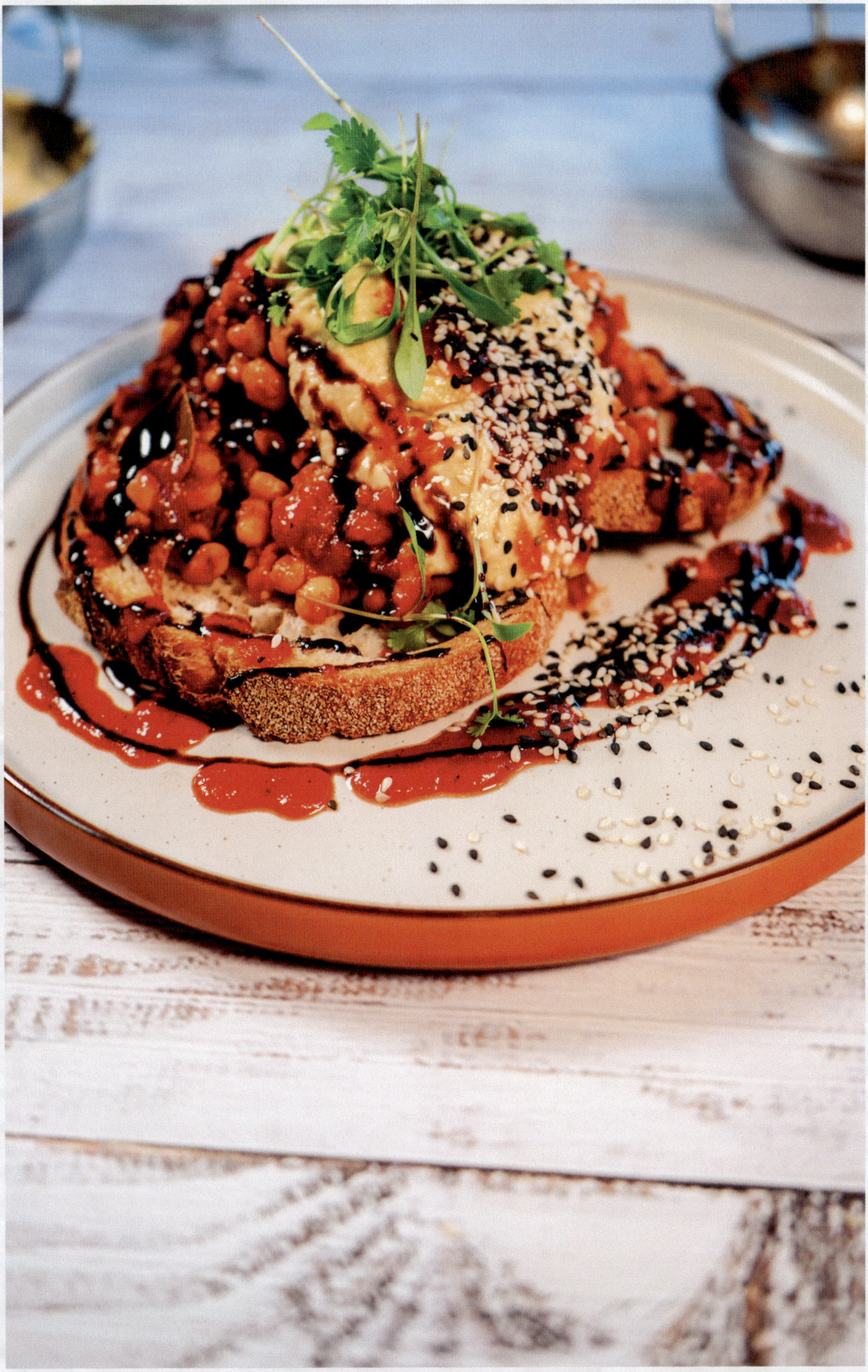

TLT - TOFU, LETTUCE, TOMATO ON TOAST

NUTS FREE | *GLUTEN FREE* | *REFINED SUGAR FREE*

Upgrading the classical BLT into a TLT with crispy slices of Chipotle Smoked Tofu, glazed under the grill and served with fresh tomato, red onion, plant-based mayo, and crunchy baby gem lettuce. Tofu's high protein count, variety of all essential amino acids and the wide range of vitamin and minerals is a great alternative making sure this sandwich is a sensational and nutritional delight!!

1 Serving

EQUIPMENT NEEDED:

A set of measuring cups, a small baking tray, chopping board, knife, colander.

INGREDIENTS:

2 Slices of Extra Thick Sourdough Bread Or Quinoa And Chia Loaf with Sunflower Seeds for GF option (see page 42)
3-4 Slices Extra Firm Tofu, 1cm Thick
3-4 Tbs Spicy Chipotle Sauce (see page 95)
2 Slices Beef Tomato
5 Slices Red Onion, Thin Sliced
3 Pieces Baby Gem Lettuce
2 Tbs Vegan Mayonnaise
2 Tbs Violife, Grated Mozzarella
Sea Salt To Taste
Cracked Black Pepper

Drain and slice the tofu, lay on some kitchen roll to soak up any excess water, pressing down with more kitchen roll if needed.

Meanwhile wash and prepare vegetables.

Place the tofu on a lined baking tray with a drizzle of oil and grill for 5 minutes on a high heat.

Flip the tofu and spread a 1tbsp thick layer of chipotle sauce over each slice, season, and place back under the grill on high heat for 8-10 minutes, until the sauce becomes glazed and slightly charred.

Place your choice of bread on a flat baking tray and toast under the grill until toasted to your liking, flip the bread, and add cheese to one piece, return to the grill and toast until the cheese is melted and the other piece of bread is toasted.

Start to build the TLT with the cheese side as the base, then layer it with baby gem, tomatoes, and onions.

Add the perfectly glazed chipotle tofu and drizzle with mayo, finishing with the top layer of toast.

Serve immediately and enjoy.

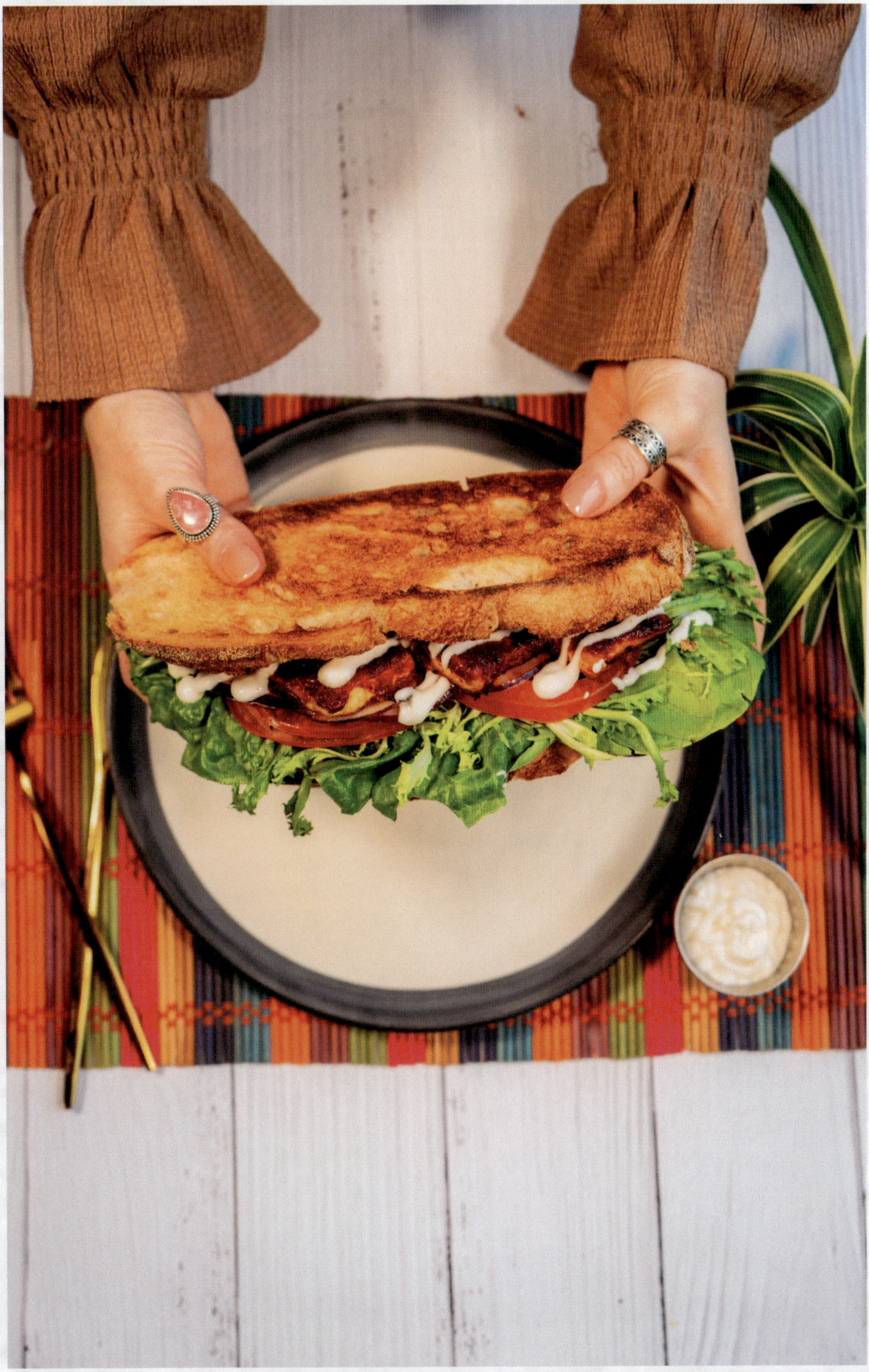

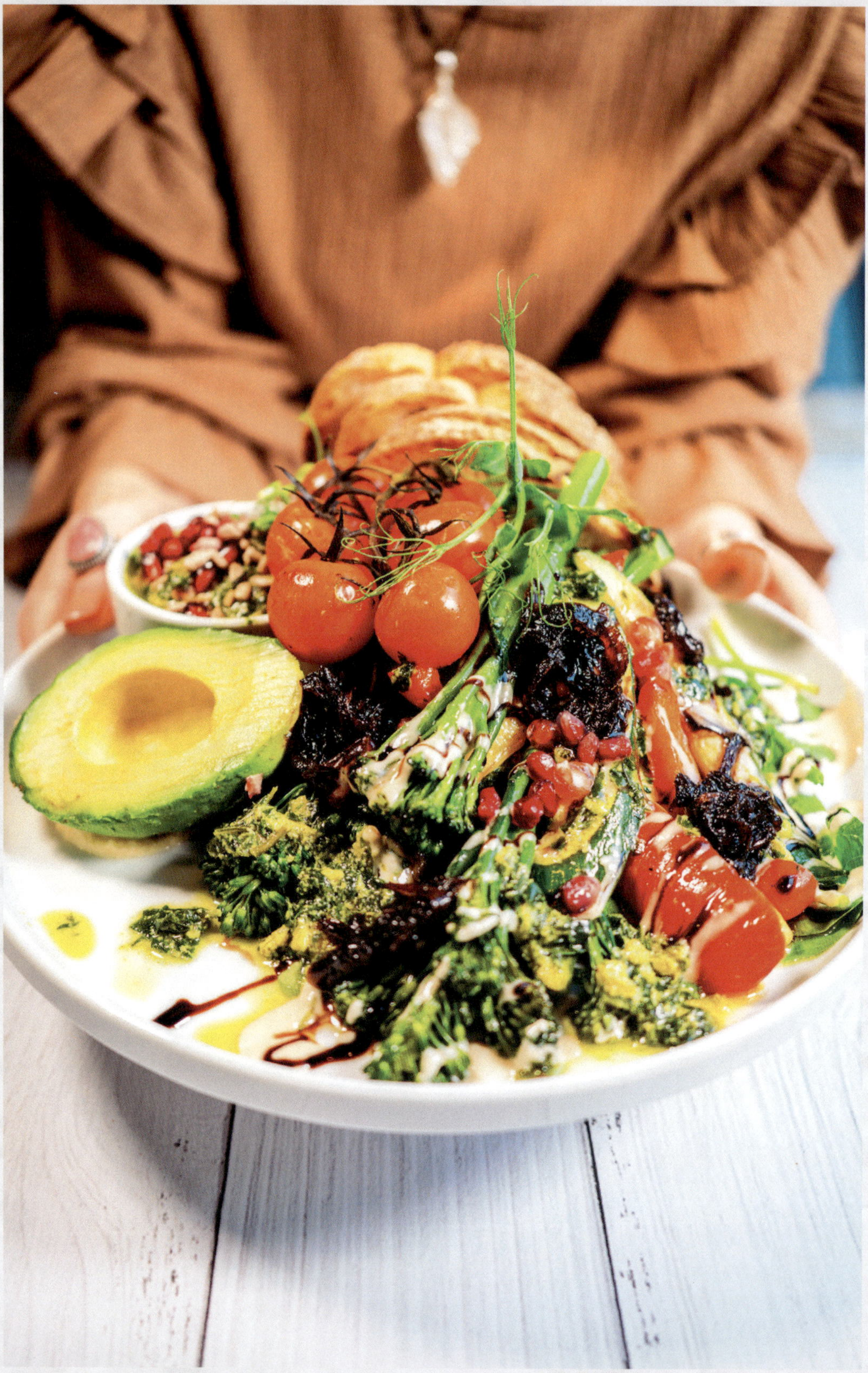

BIG BREAKFASTS

Our big breakfasts are mouth wateringly good, there is quite a lot of work that goes into each dish but when it all comes together you will be glad you tried them. As so much time and effort is required when making all the different components to build each breakfast, we have purposely made the batch recipes to produce larger quantities, saving you plenty of time next time. Once the batches are pre-made, they will last in the fridge for 4-5 days and can be frozen down for up to 3 months, Also, some of the bulk recipes are found in other recipes throughout the book, so again it will save you a lot more time later if you decide to indulge in more of our plant-based creations.

THE FULL INDIGO GRILL

NUTS FREE · REFINED SUGAR FREE

Our Full Indigo brings the worldwide well-known greasy fry up back to life with its plant-based nutrient dense spin on the traditional English breakfast. Our slow sweet roasted baby vine tomatoes, garlic and herb roasted mushroom, grilled potato hash, herby sausage, and smoky beans, wilted super green spinach and golden turmeric tofu brings back the good old days without a guilt-ridden food coma. This breakfast dish is not only bursting with flavour it is also packing with dietary fibre, protein and many nutrients that will satiate and nourish the entire body till way after noon!

1 Serving

EQUIPMENT NEEDED:
See individual recipes.

INGREDIENTS:
2 Herby Sausages (see page 70)
2 Grilled Hash Browns (see page 72)
½ Cup Golden Turmeric Scrambled Tofu (see page 80)
1 Bunch Balsamic Glazed Baby Vine Tomatoes (see page 78)
1 Rosemary and Garlic Mushrooms (see page 76)
½ Cup Smokey Breakfast Beans (see page 74)
1 cup Raw Spinach, washed
2 Slices of Sourdough Bread or Quinoa and Chia loaf with Sunflower Seeds (see page 42)
Chives, finely chopped
Olive oil or Plant Butter
Pea shoots

Follow the individual recipes below for each item and then plate as followed. If you have pre-made all your ingredients, heat up until piping hot.

Toast your choice of bread in the toaster or under the grill.

Once all the ingredients are heated, pot up the beans in a ramekin and place it at the back, lean the mushroom against the ramekin and place the 2 sausages in front of the mushroom keeping it upright.

Add on the hash browns and spoon on the scrambled tofu.

Add the wilted spinach keeping it stacked high in the middle of the plate.

Top with baby vine tomatoes.

Drizzle your toast with olive oil or butter.

Sprinkle with chives and garnish with pea shoots.

Serve straight away and enjoy.

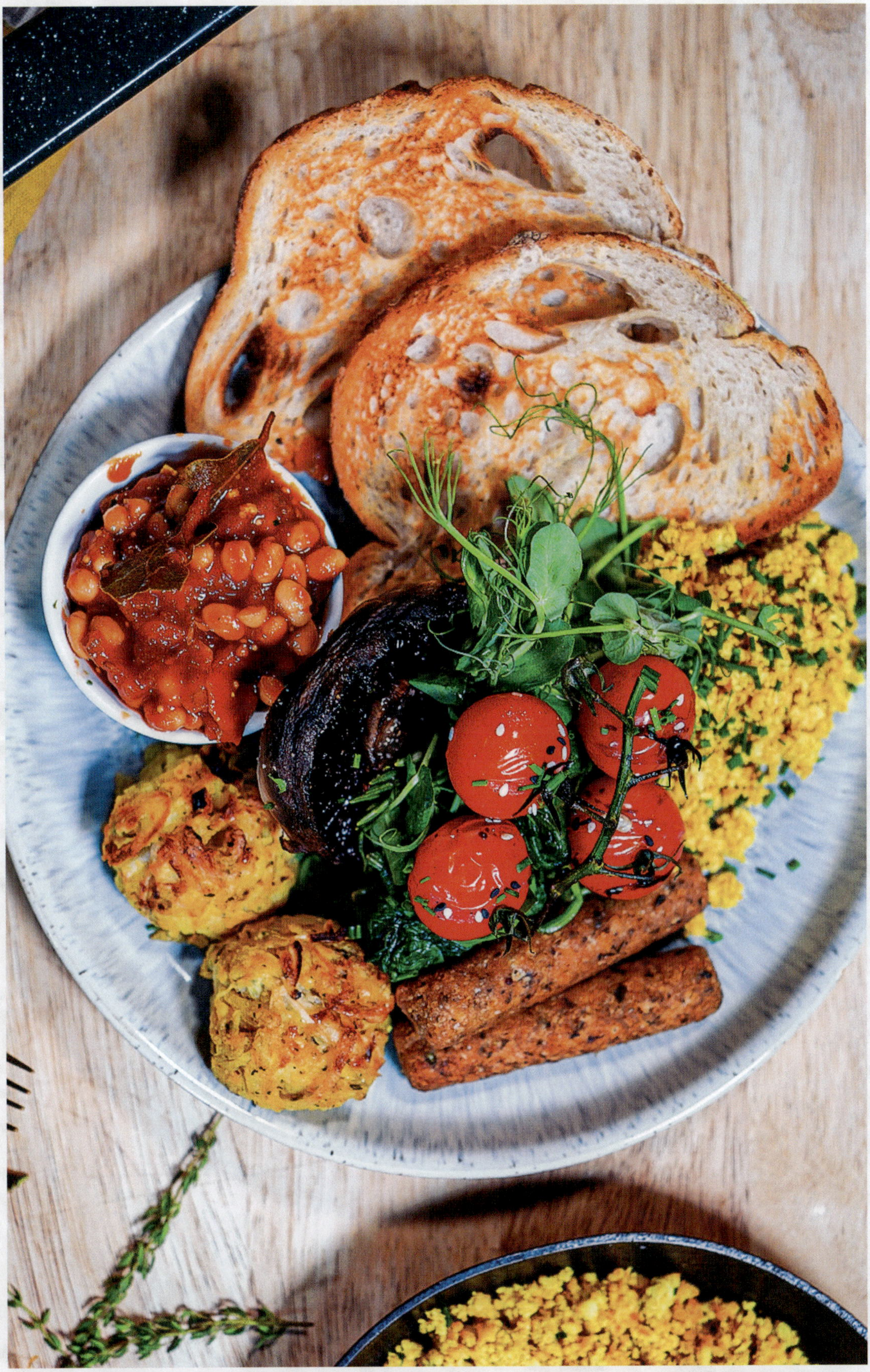

HERBY SAUSAGES

Our sausages are handmade, and hand rolled, yes, every single sausage. A combination of a soya and wheat sausage mix which is high in fibre and protein. A slightly different texture than that gritty consistency of scraps you would find squashed into sausage skin or should I say the sub mucosa of animal intestines. We also add lots of herbs and spices, not only for flavour but for their medicinal benefits too. Oregano is full of essential vitamins and minerals and is a great antibacterial agent that fights against infections. Garlic, paprika and cumin are also full of antioxidants which help prevent cell damage, oxidative stress, reduce the risk of cancer, improve immunity, and alleviate gas.

PLEASE NOTE – This mix can vary in texture batch to batch so the water amounts may need adjusting slightly. If the mix is cracking and won't roll it means it's too dry, wetting the hands slightly while handling each ball will work some extra moisture into the mix. If the mix is super tacky and sticking to your hands, it's too wet and will need more dry mix adding to absorb up the excess moisture. This recipe is created using Sos mix from Suma Wholefoods which you can buy online or from health food stores like Mattas in Liverpool City Centre, if you are using a different sausage mix, please follow the instructions from the manufacturers, as we have perfected this recipe using Sos Mix only.

6 Servings - 2 each

EQUIPMENT NEEDED:
A set of measuring cups, measuring jug, scales, 5cm ice-cream scoop with leaver (optional), large tray, mixing bowl.

INGREDIENTS:
400g Sos Mix
3 Tbs Oregano, Dried
2 Tsp Smoked Paprika
1 Tsp Chilli Powder
3 Tsp Garlic Powder
600ml Cold Water
½ Tbs Sea Salt
1 Tsp Cracked Black Pepper
Olive oil

Store in the fridge for 4-5 days or freeze for up to 3 months.

Weigh out all the dry ingredients and mix in a large mixing bowl.

Add the COLD water and mix well.

Cover the mix and place in the fridge for an hour whilst it sets, the mix should be moist but firm and easy to roll.

Once the mix is set, use a 5cm ice cream scoop to ball onto a tray, use boiling hot water to clean the scoop after each ball, this will make sure each of them are neat, tidy, and uniform in size.

Alternatively measure them by eye and hand or using scales weighing 40g per ball.

To make them into sausage shapes, start by massaging the balls in your hands to soften and roll between both palms to create a sausage shape.

Place on a clean surface and use your 3 middle fingers to smooth out the shape, as it lengthens, gently squeeze the ends with your thumb and index finger to flatten the ends.

Repeat this until your sausages are even with a smooth surface area.

Cover and store in the fridge, when you are ready to cook, drizzle with oil and place under the grill on a medium to high heat for 15-18 minutes, flipping halfway.

Try making our famous 'Sausage On' (see page 60) or making meatballs, burgers or hotdogs from the same mix with additional herbs and spices to heat things up.

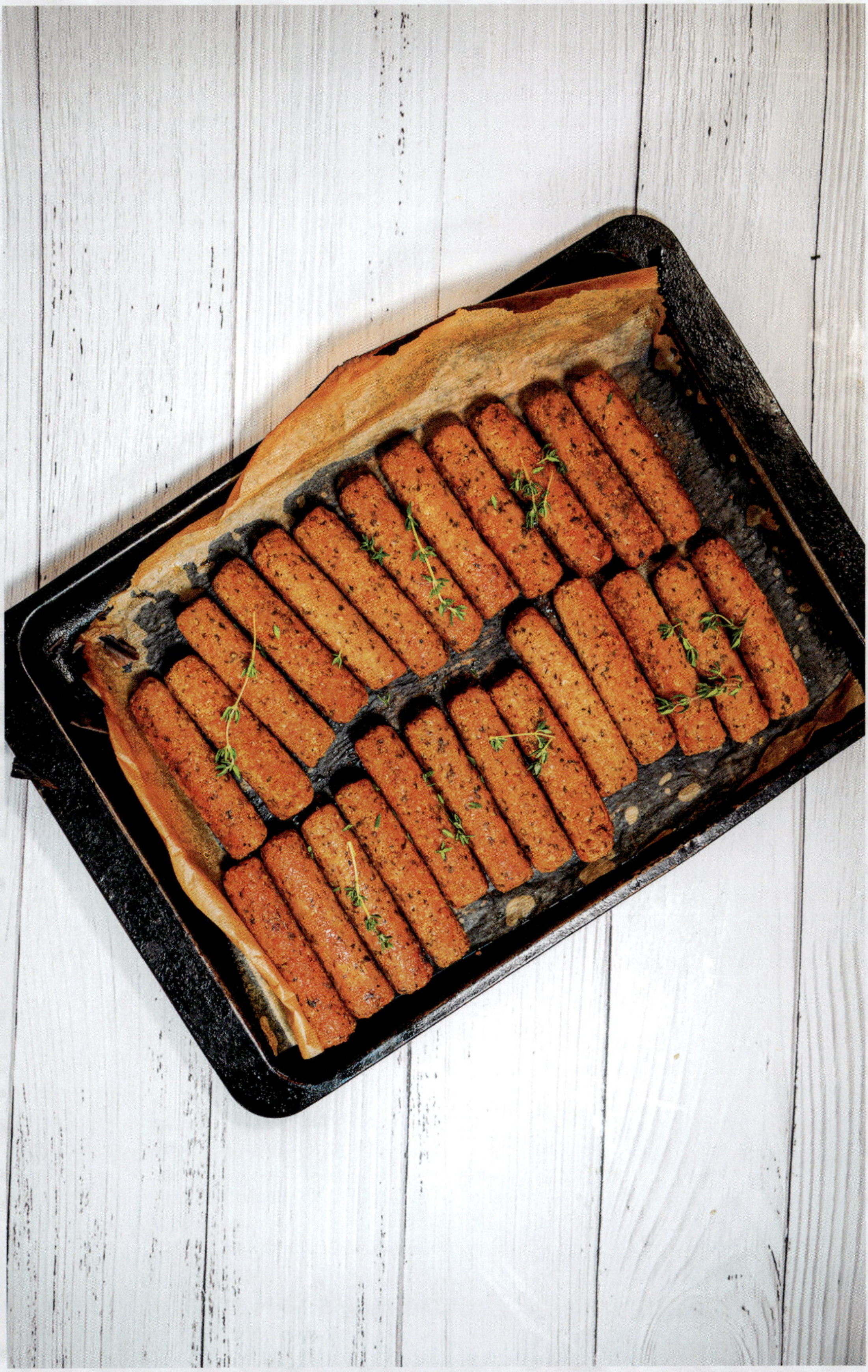

GRILLED HASH BROWNS

NUTS FREE | SOY FREE | GLUTEN FREE | REFINED SUGAR FREE

These crispy little flavour bombs of grated potato are every brunch lover's dream. The key component to this recipe is a B12 fortified ingredient called nutritional yeast which gets its name from all the proteins, trace minerals antioxidants and vitamins it contains. It adds a subtle cheesiness making our hash browns even more satisfyingly good, and as they're high in B12, a vitamin many vegans are deficient in, gives you even more of a reason to make them. We need B12 for healthy red blood cell formation and the development of the central nervous system, adding B12 fortified nutritional yeast to your recipes will not only enhance the flavour but will also improve energy levels too as B12 deficiency has been linked to anaemia.

6 Servings - 2 per person

EQUIPMENT NEEDED:

A set of measuring cups, scales, 5cm ice-cream scoop with leaver (optional), extra-large deep sided tray or extra-large mixing bowl, box grater, large pan, mandolin, or sharp knife, colander.

INGREDIENTS:

1/2 Small White Onion, Finely Sliced

10 Sprigs Thyme, Fresh, Picked

7.5 Sprigs Rosemary, Fresh, Chopped

5tbs Nutritional Yeast with B12

2 Tsp Garlic Powder

1kg Medium Red Rooster Potatoes, Peeled, Halved

Sea Salt to Taste

Cracked Black Pepper

Store in the fridge for 4-5 days or freeze for 1 month.

Wash, peel and prepare potatoes so they are the same size, always use red, waxy potato's as they hold their shape when boiling better than other potatoes.

Place the potatoes in a large pan and add enough cold water to cover them by 2 inches, with a pinch of salt.

Place on a high heat and bring the potatoes up to the boil, reduce heat to a simmer and cook for 20-25 minutes, checking the potatoes with a sharp knife, the knife should pierce the potatoes but still be firm and not able to fall off the knife easily.

Drain the potatoes and leave for a couple of minutes in a colander allowing them to air dry before returning them to the pan, tightly cover the pan with cling film and allow them to steam the rest of the way.

Once cool enough, place the potatoes in a tub in the freezer for an hour or in the fridge for at least 4 hours, they need to be cold and hard before grating otherwise they will end up very starchy.

Meanwhile, measure out the rest of the ingredients.

Slice the onions very fine using a sharp knife or mandolin and place in the tray, add a pinch of salt to the onions to soften them up.

Once the potatoes are completely cold, grate on the large side of a box grater and spread out the grated potatoes over the onions.

Evenly sprinkle the rest of the ingredients over the potatoes and carefully mix the ingredients together straight away to avoid any clumping of the dried ingredients. Avoid using heavy hands and don't squash the mix together - loosely run fingers through the mix, twisting and turning your hands gently until it's all combined.

Preheat the oven on 180c / 350f / gas mark 4 while you mould the hash browns.

Using an ice cream scoop, start balling and tightly pack the potato mix into the scoop, using the palm of your hand to push in the mix and flatten, scooping out onto a lined baking tray, use boiling hot water to clean the scoop after each ball, this will make sure each of them are neat, tidy, and uniform in size. (Alternatively measure out into equal balls using your hands to mould tightly together).

If you're cooking straight away, drizzle with olive oil and place in the oven for 25-30 minutes until golden brown and crispy, flipping halfway.

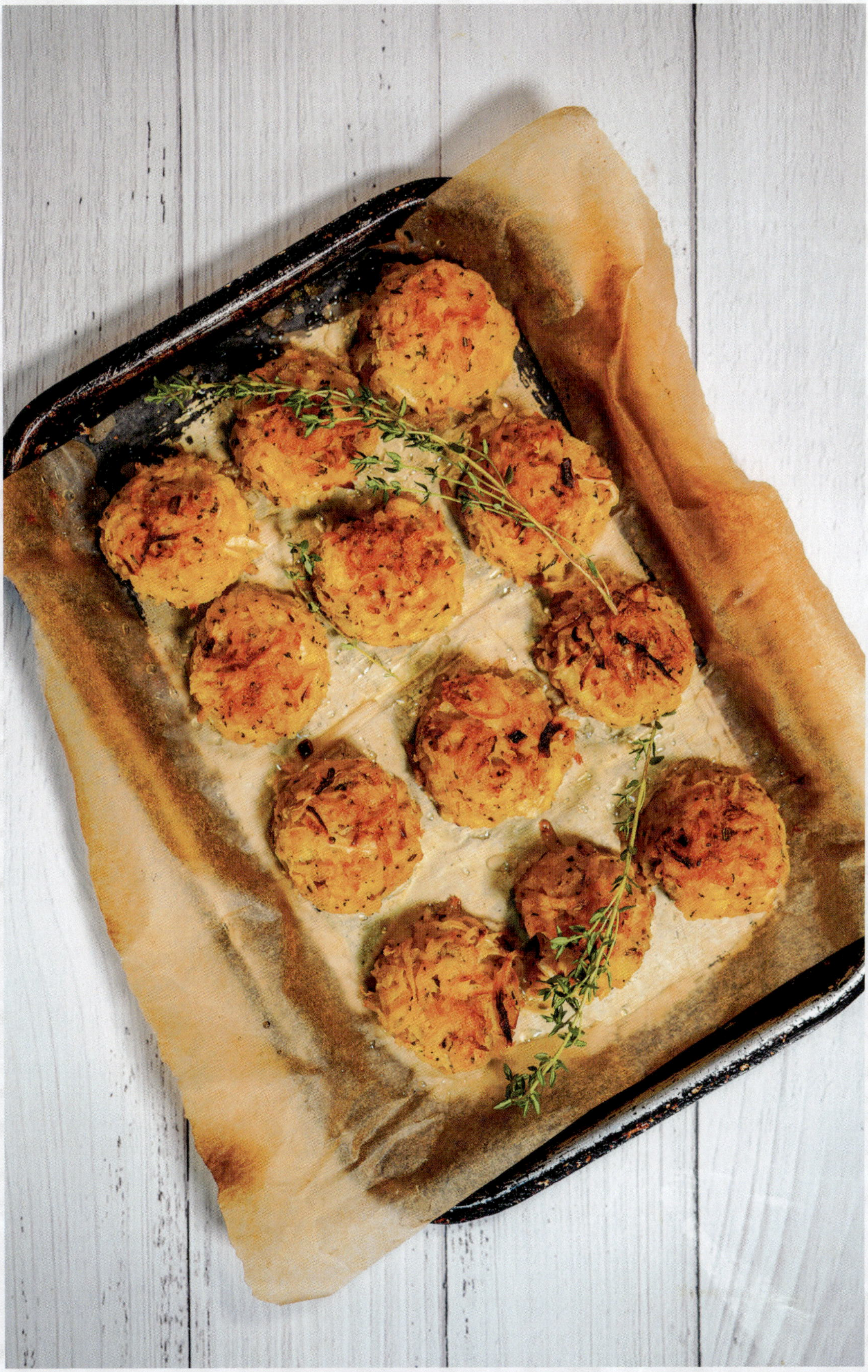

SMOKEY BREAKFAST BEANS

NUTS FREE · SOY FREE · GLUTEN FREE · REFINED SUGAR FREE

Beans beans they're good for your heart, the more you eat, the more you fart!! Yes, this childhood rhyme is no fable, all beans are high in fibre which help unblock the digestive tract. Depending on what other foods are lingering about in there, will result in whether you get gaseous bowel movements or not. When diets consist of highly processed or animal-based ingredients, their fibre intake is extremely low, which means the digestive tract may be backed up. The body needs fibre to pull and push out congested food that is stuck in the intestines. Think of fibre as a potion you pour down your drain when it is blocked up with all kinds of debris, rotting and decaying, as the potion starts to work, things start moving and breaking down causing a chemical reaction ie, gas, when the drain is finally released the smell is very unpleasant due to the back up of rotting foods. The bowels move in the same way, this is exactly what's happening in the body when there is insufficient fibre intake. So, if you pong after you have eaten beans or anything high in fibre, I suggest you eat more as the magic potion is working on your own physical draining system!!

8-10 Servings

EQUIPMENT NEEDED:
A set of measuring cups, chopping board, a large saucepan, a colander, measuring jug. An airtight container to store.

INGREDIENTS:
1 Tbs Olive Oil
1 Medium Onion, Small Diced
3 Garlic Cloves, Minced
1 Tsp Cumin Seeds
1 Tsp Mustard Seeds
1 Tbs Smoked Paprika
3 Bay Leaves
2 Tbs Tomato Puree
400g Tin Chopped Tomatoes
5 Sprigs of Thyme, chopped
800ml Water
800g Haricot Beans, canned
2 Tbs Maple Syrup
1 Tbs Balsamic Vinegar
¼ Lemon, Juice
Sea Salt to Taste
Cracked Black Pepper

Store in the fridge for 4-5 days or freeze into smaller portions for up to 3 months.

Add mustard seeds and cumin seeds to a large dry saucepan and heat for 10-20 seconds until they start to crackle and pop, remove from the pan, and set a side.

In the same saucepan sauté the onions in olive oil for about 8 minutes on a medium to high heat, until they are golden, this is when all the natural sugars start to caramelise.

Add the garlic and cook for a further 30-45 seconds

Spoon in the smoked paprika, add in the bay leaves and gently cook out for a further 30 seconds.

Apart from the beans and thyme, add the rest of the ingredients, including the toasted seeds from earlier.

Bring the tomato sauce to the boil and then lower to a simmer. Reduce until the sauce becomes nice and thick (for about 30 minutes). Meanwhile drain the haricot beans and rinse well.

Once the sauce has reduced by a third, add the drained beans to the sauce along with the thyme and bring the pan back up to gently simmer and cook for 5 minutes, adding a drop of water if the beans become too thick. Season to taste.

Serve immediately or allow them to cool fully before storing.

Served with our Full Indigo Grill (see page 68) or Terracotta Beans on Toast (see paage 62).

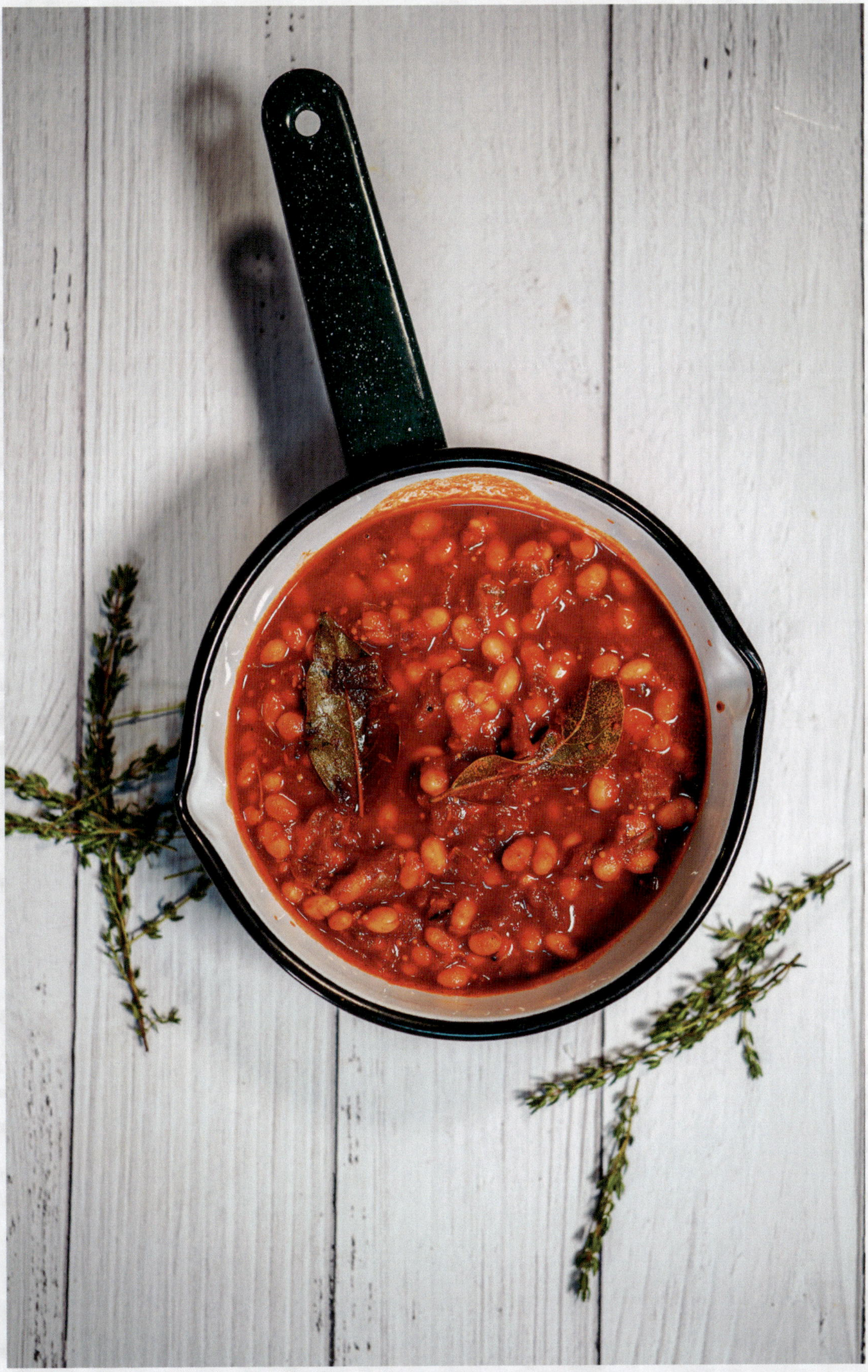

ROSEMARY AND GARLIC MUSHROOMS

Nuts Free / Soy Free / Gluten Free / Refined Sugar Free

The perfect flavour combination to be soaked right up. Did you know that mushrooms act like a sponge when it comes to soaking up flavours and will literally absorb anything? They even have the ability to absorb UVB energy from the sun that converts into vitamin D3, the only plant-based food that can do this, meaning mushrooms grown in direct sunlight are an amazing source of Vitamin D which is an important component for bone growth, reproduction, and immune health. So, when the darker days close in and you're not getting enough sunlight on your skin, make sure you're eating plenty of mushrooms. Especially the wild kind!

6 Servings

EQUIPMENT NEEDED:
A medium baking tray.

INGREDIENTS:
6 Large Flat Mushrooms, peeled
6 Sprigs Rosemary
1 Tbs Garlic Granules
6 tbsp Olive Oil
30ml Water
Sea Salt to Taste
Cracked Black Pepper

Store in the fridge for 4-5 days in an airtight container.

Pre heat the oven on 180c / 350f / gas mark 4.

Meanwhile peel the outer layer of skin from the mushrooms, and rinse mushrooms of any muck. You can keep the skins to add to a stock later in the week or discard.

Lay the mushrooms flat in a lined baking tray with the nose facing upwards, dust with garlic powder and season with salt and pepper.

Drizzle with olive oil and add a sprig of rosemary to each mushroom.

Add a dash of water to the base of the baking tray, this will gently steam the mushrooms in the oven as well as roasting them avoiding them drying out and going all wrinkly.

Place in the oven for 15-18 minutes.

Serve straight away or allow proper cooling before storing.

These mushrooms are also used on our Mushroom Bruschetta (see page 58), so if you have any left over you know what you can have for breakfast tomorrow!

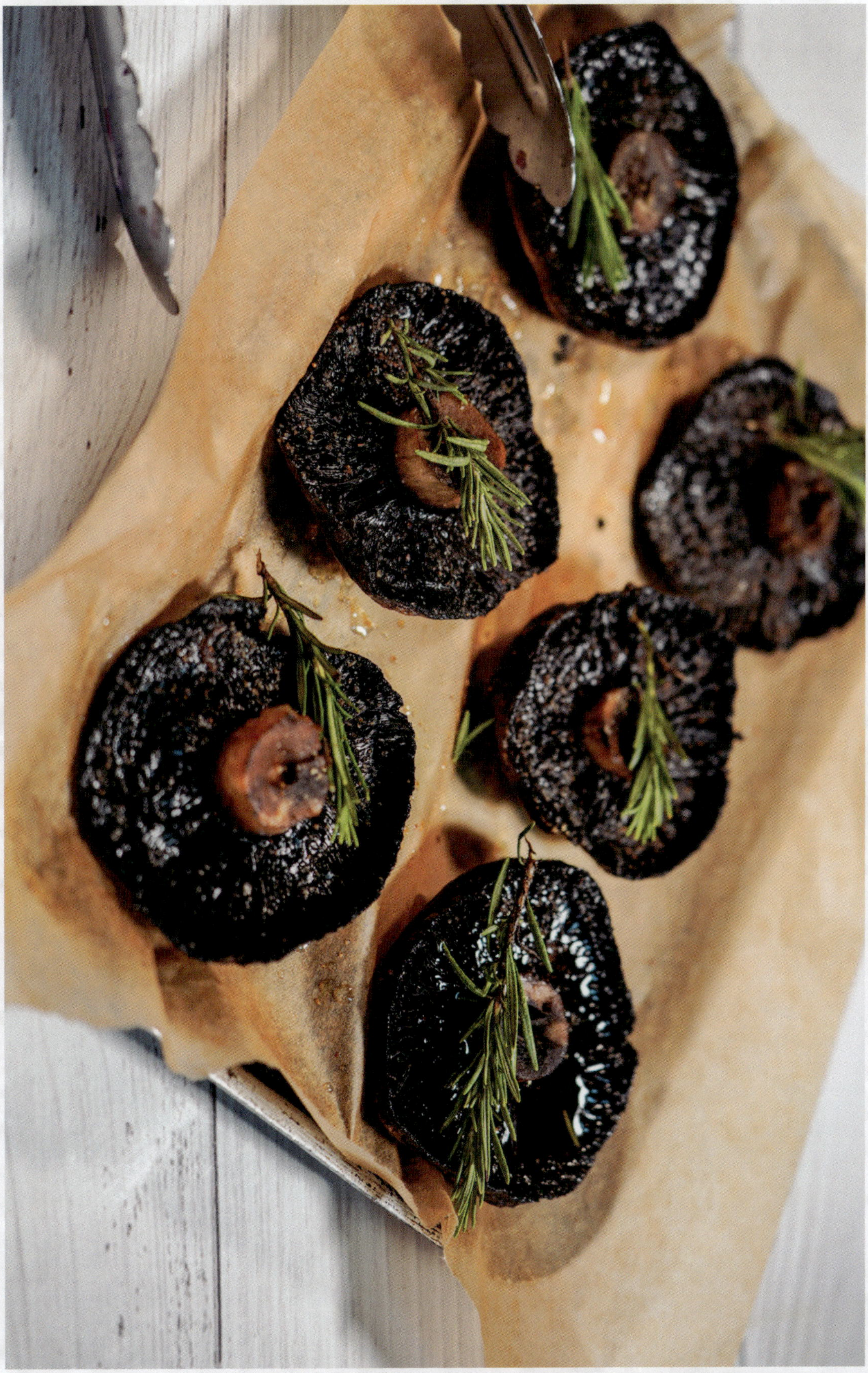

BALSAMIC GLAZED BABY VINE TOMATOES

Ripened on the vine tomatoes, there's nothing better than the ripest of the ripest fruit. These sweet and juicy mini flavour bombs literally explode with antioxidants, vitamins and minerals, such as vitamin C, potassium, vitamin K, and folate. Once they pop, you just can't stop!

6 Servings

EQUIPMENT NEEDED:
A medium baking tray.

INGREDIENTS:
500g Baby Vine Tomatoes
15ml Balsamic Glaze (see page 94)
Olive Oil, Drizzle
Pinch Of Sea Salt
Cracked Black Pepper

Store in the fridge for 4-5 days in an airtight container.

Preheat the grill on medium to high heat.

Wash and prepare tomatoes by using scissors to cut into bunches of 4-6 tomatoes and place on a lined baking tray.

Drizzle with olive oil and balsamic glaze and then season with salt and pepper lastly so the seasoning grips to the tomatoes.

Place under the grill for 5-8 minutes or until the skin starts to burst open and the juices begin to bubble and foam.

Serve and enjoy.

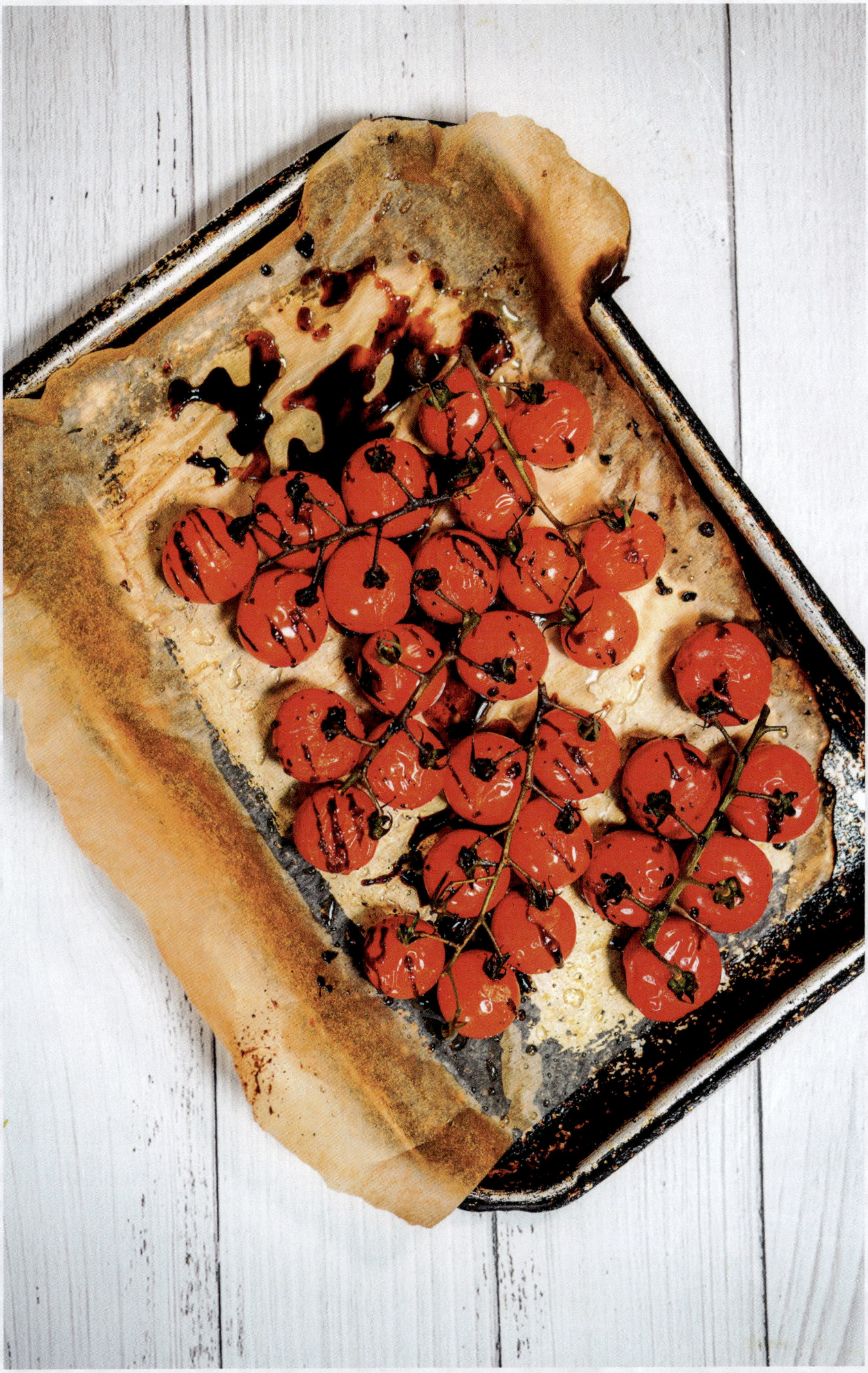

GOLDEN TURMERIC SCRAMBLED TOFU

Tofu also known as a 'culinary chameleon' takes on the flavours of whatever you marinade it in as its sponge like texture absorbs everything its mixed with. Our Golden Tofu Scramble is lightly spiced with turmeric and garlic which are both anti-inflammatory ingredients that aid in gut and brain health. Adding a pinch of black pepper activates the live compound curcumin in the turmeric which is necessary to benefit from any of the medicinal effects.

6 Servings

EQUIPMENT NEEDED:

A skillet or non-stick frying pan, a mixing bowl, a colander, chopping board, chives.

INGREDIENTS:

600g Pack Firm Tofu, drained 500g net
¼ Tsp Turmeric Powder
¼ Tsp Garlic Powder
Chive, finely chopped
2 Tbs Olive Oil
1 Tbs Plant Butter
Sea Salt to Taste
Cracked Black Pepper

Store in an airtight container for 3-4 days in the fridge.

Drain the tofu well and place onto some kitchen paper to remove any excess moisture.

In a mixing bowl, add the tofu, turmeric and garlic powder and then begin to crumble the blocks of tofu into a scramble-like texture with your hands, mixing all the ingredients together gently in the bowl until it's all yellow in colour.

Heat the olive oil in a large non-stick frying pan on a medium to high heat and add the scrambled tofu, cook for 7-8 minutes stirring occasionally until all the moisture has evaporated and the tofu starts to dry out.

Season well and finish with chives and a dollop of plant butter.

Serve immediately or allow proper cooling before storing.

BUTTERED SPINACH

Popeye was onto to something wasn't he? These bright green leaves are loaded with strength building vitamins and minerals and are one of the most nutrient rich plant foods available. Simply sautéing spinach with some butter and a pinch of sea salt can be so tasty and great side for any dish, be careful not to overcook it in the pan as it diminishes in front of your eyes.

1 Serving

EQUIPMENT NEEDED:

A skillet or non-stick frying pan, a colander.

INGREDIENTS:

2 Cups Spinach, washed
1 Tsp Plant Butter
Sea Salt to Taste
Cracked Black Pepper

Place the pan on a medium to high heat, add the butter being careful not to burn.

Once melted add the spinach for 10 seconds and remove off heat immediately, season to taste and stir until lightly wilted.

Serve straight away.

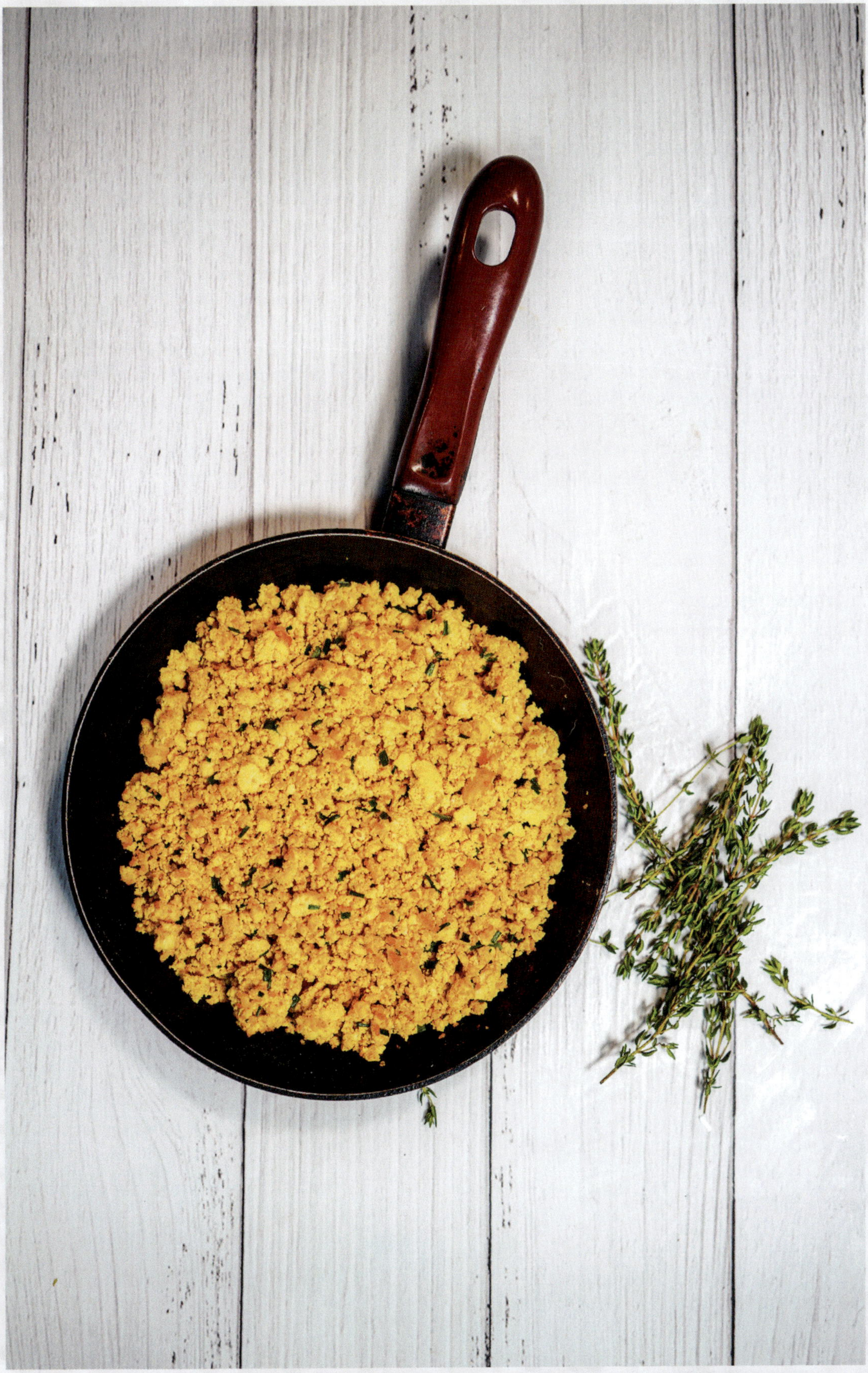

THE GREEN GRILL

NUTS FREE | SOY FREE | GLUTEN FREE | REFINED SUGAR FREE

When I put this dish on the menu, I had no idea what it was going to be. It kind of had its foundations, but it was never quite finalised due to the launch date coming around so fast. From what I envisioned, it was going to be a plate full of green goodness (hence the name) with avocado and hummus, fresh flavours, vibrant colours and of course the healthier looking option on the menu. Even though everything is healthy, this dish would be screaming out health. Our first week launching Indigo Greens was chaotic and we sold everything on the menu apart from The Green Grill, it was total madness, no one knew what to expect, it just boomed. But the Green Grill never got a look in until around day 5 - right in the peak hour when the restaurant was full and the tickets were rolling in - the order came in. The panic was real, I had no idea what to do, my mind went blank for a second, but If you know me then you know how I work, I kind of cross bridges when I come to them. In a moment of madness, from an on-the-spot adrenaline rush of whatever I had in front of me, the Green Grill was randomly created. The charred crunchy greens got smothered in pumpkin seed pesto, tahini whip and caramelised onion, topped with toasted seeds, sweet roasted tomatoes and finished with juicy pomegranates that burst in the mouth. The Green Grill was birthed in minutes and has grown into one of our best-selling dishes - being described as a 'party on a plate'. Its packed full of antioxidants, vitamins, minerals, and heart healthy fats that keep your brain healthy and gut intact by helping maintain a balance of good and bad bacteria. No wonder people keep coming back for more!

1 Serving

EQUIPMENT NEEDED:

A set of measuring cups, a skillet or non-stick frying pan, a mixing bowl, a ramakin (optional) a colander, chopping board, knife.

INGREDIENTS:

2 slices of Sourdough Bread or Quinoa and Chia loaf with Sunflower Seeds for GF option (see page 42)
2 Tbs Olive Oil
4 Pieces Tender-Stem Broccoli, Thinly Trimmed
¼ Courgette, Sliced 1cm, ½ Moon Angled
¼ Large Red Pepper, 1cm Slices
1 Cup Baby Spinach, Raw
2 Tbs Chunky Pumpkin Seed Pesto (see page 90)
2 Tbs Whipped Tahini
Balsamic Glaze (see page 94)
2 Tbs Caramelised Onion Chutney (see page 86)
2-3 Tbs Creamy Smooth Traditional Hummus (see page 92)
Pumpkin Seeds, Toasted
½ Avocado, Halved, pitted
1 Bunch Balsamic Glazed Baby Vine Tomatoes (see page 78)
Pomegranate, seeds
Sesame Seeds, Toasted
Sea Salt to Taste
Cracked Black Pepper

Wash and prepare all the vegetables.

Carefully heat the oil up in a large non-stick frying pan or wok on a high heat.

Add tender stem and cook for 3-5 minutes until it starts to brown and add a splash of hot water to steam the tender-stem through.

Add the courgettes and peppers and cook for a further 2 minutes or until vegetables are nicely charred and still al dente, season to taste.

Meanwhile arrange a plate with a bed of spinach, a large ramekin of hummus topped with pesto pomegranates and then half of an avocado leaning up against on the side.

Dish out the charred greens on top of the spinach and drizzle each of them with 2 tbsp tahini, pesto, and caramelised onions each.

Drizzle balsamic and sprinkle with sesame, pomegranates and top with some baby vine tomatoes and pea shoots for hight.

Finish with some toasted sourdough or our quinoa and chia loaf, cut it on an angle and fan it across the greens.

Serve straight away and enjoy.

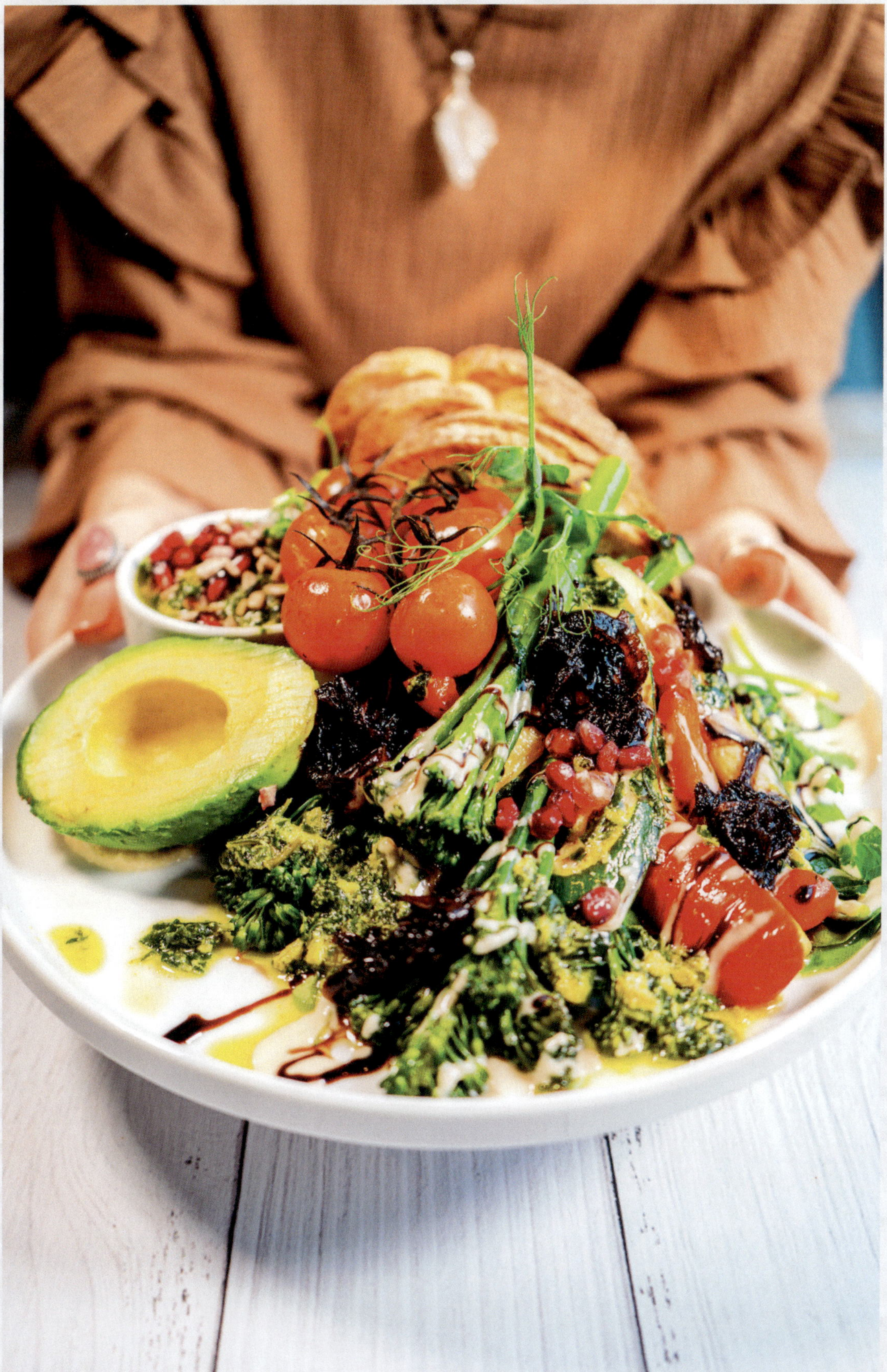

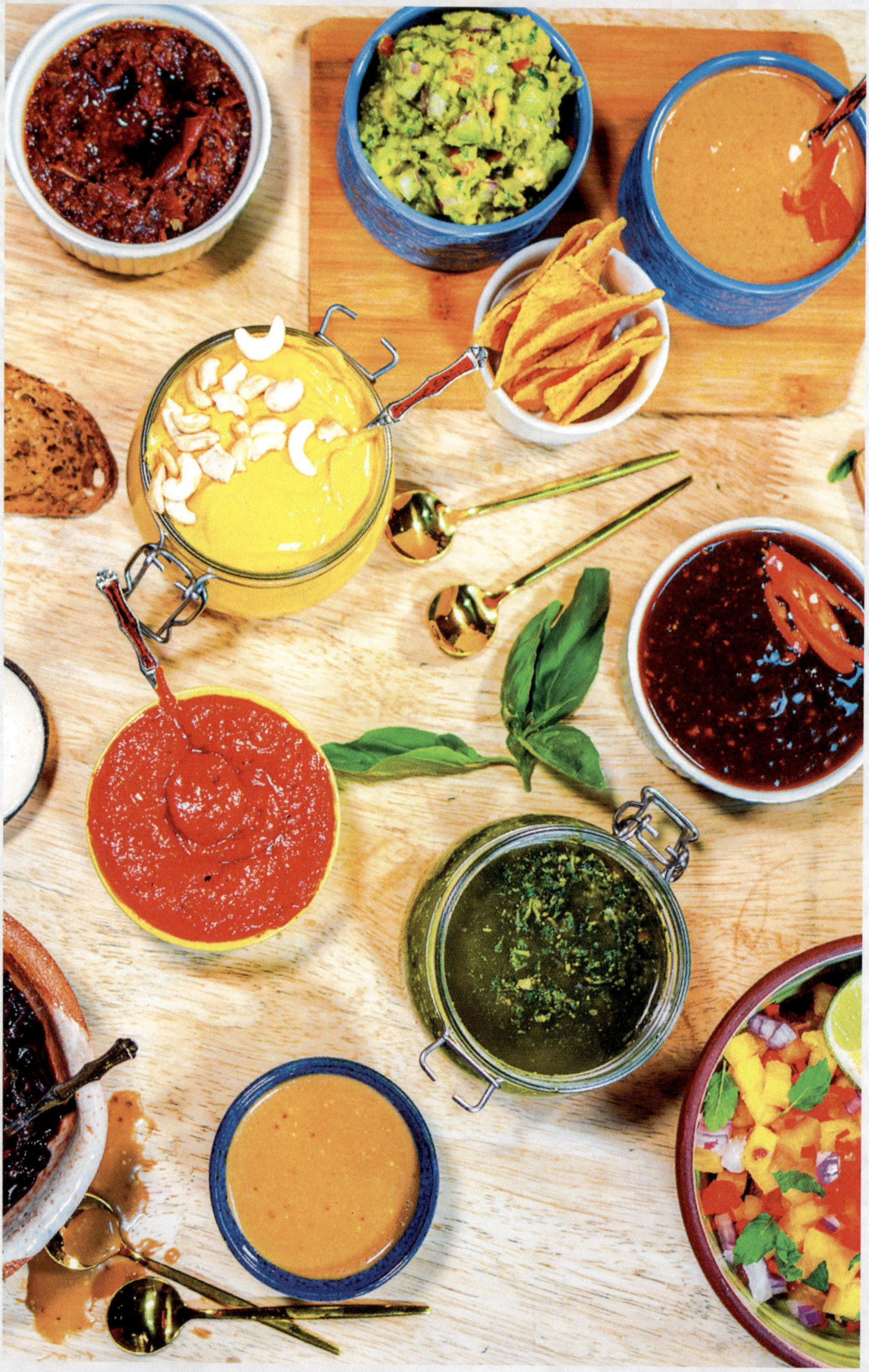

SAUCES AND DIPS

All our different 'Sauces and Dips' at Indigo Greens are what make up the phenomenal flavours of each of our dishes. We consciously bring dishes together by infusing them with layers, upon layers of different flavor notes that literally blow people's minds. With that, we have purposely scaled the recipes in this section to create a larger batch, so that you and your family can enjoy layers upon layers of sauces later on through the week. All our sauces are freezable too, so we recommend freezing half of them down for future convenience. That is if you dont demolish them all first!

CARAMELISED ONION CHUTNEY

NUTS FREE | SOY FREE | GLUTEN FREE | REFINED SUGAR FREE

Caramelised red onions, reduced in balsamic vinegar and sweetened to perfection, a balance of flavours that enhances everything it's added too.

Quantity 400g

EQUIPMENT NEEDED:

A measuring jug, a mandolin or sharp knife, chopping board, heavy based saucepan, airtight jar for storing

INGREDIENTS:

4 Medium Red Onions, Fine Sliced
2 Tbs Olive Oil
100ml Balsamic Vinegar
125ml Water
120ml Maple Syrup
3 Sprigs Fresh Thyme,
Sea Salt to Taste
Cracked Black Pepper

Store in an airtight jar for up to 1 month in the fridge.

Wash and prepare onions and measure out the rest of the ingredients.

Add oil into a medium saucepan and sauté the onions and a large pinch of salt on a medium heat for 10 minutes until they are caramelised, the salt helps break down the onions by releasing all the water.

Add the liquid ingredients, thyme, lemon and bring to the boil.

Once boiling, lower the heat and simmer until the liquid has reduced for around 20 minutes, stirring frequently, be careful not to burn towards the end as the liquid reduces right down.

Once the onions are tacky and liquid has gone, take of the heat and allow to cool before storing.

Served on our Green Grill (see page 76) or our famous Grilled Cashew Cheese on Toast (see page 46).

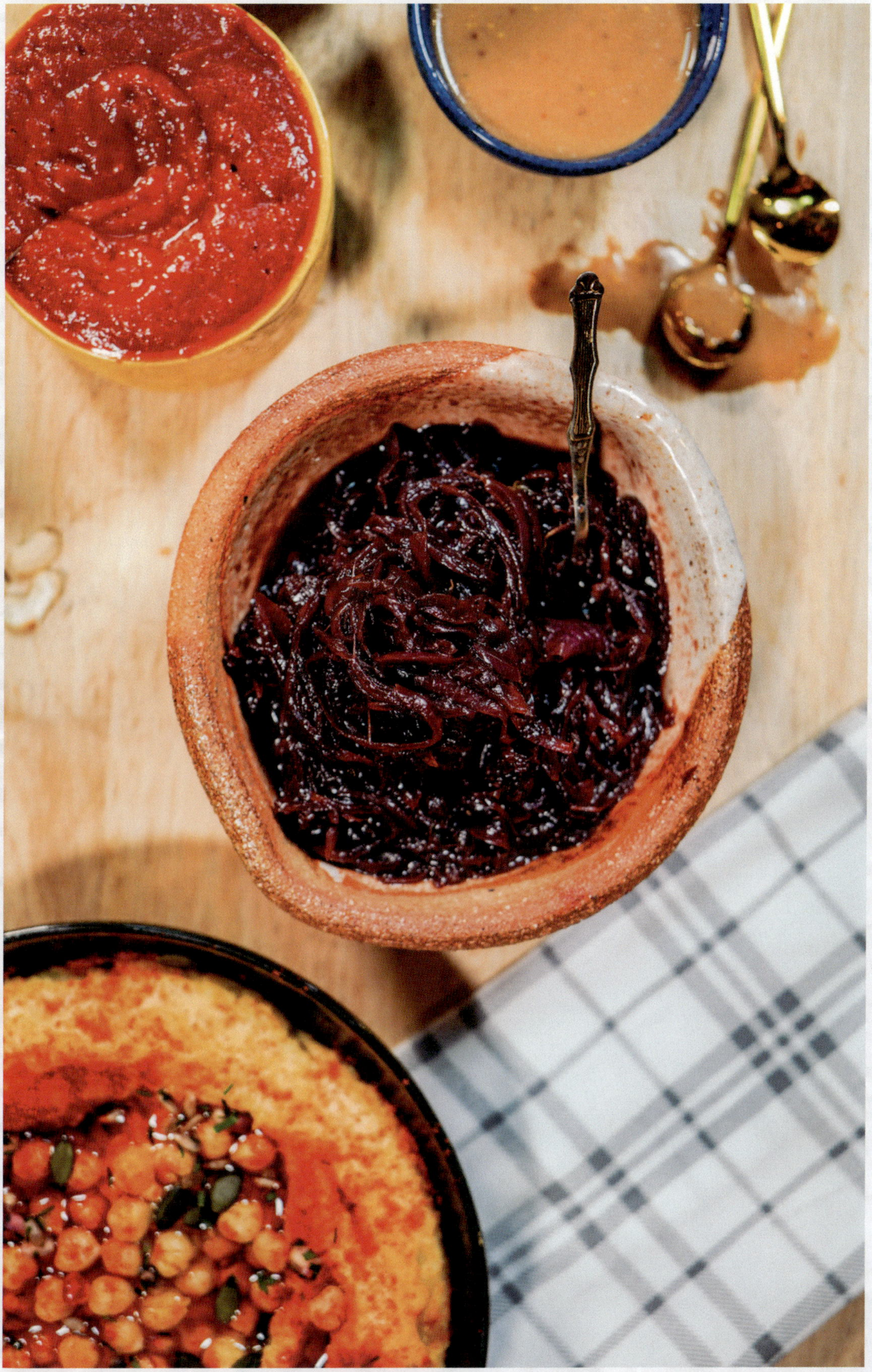

TAHINI WHIP

NUTS FREE | SOY FREE | GLUTEN FREE | REFINED SUGAR FREE

Tahini, it's a distinctive taste that some people may find it a little bit bitter, but I say the more bitter something is, the better for us it is. However, whipping tahini with some water, a squeeze of fresh lemon, garlic and drizzle of maple will help cut through what may be unpleasant for some, turning it into a delicious light and fluffy dressing. Tahini is made from ground toasted sesame seeds which are full of calcium, manganese, copper, and zinc keeping the bones, joints, and blood vessels intact. Copper is also known for its use in pain relief and swelling due to its anti-inflammatory and antioxidant enzyme system.

Quantity 450ml

EQUIPMENT NEEDED:

A set of measuring cups, small mixing bowl, whisk, lemon juicer, garlic crusher.

INGREDIENTS:

1 Cup Tahini Paste
1 Cup Water
2 Garlic Cloves, Minced
1 Small Lemon, Juiced
1 Tsp Maple Syrup or To Taste (optional)
Sea Salt to Taste
Pinch Of Cracked Black Pepper

In a mixing bowl whisk together all the ingredients until light and fluffy - The mix will be hard to whisk at first as the water and oil emulsify, but it will soon loosen becoming light, fluffy and will drip perfectly from the whisk.

Served on our Green Grill (see page 76).

Store in an airtight jar for 4-5 days in the fridge.

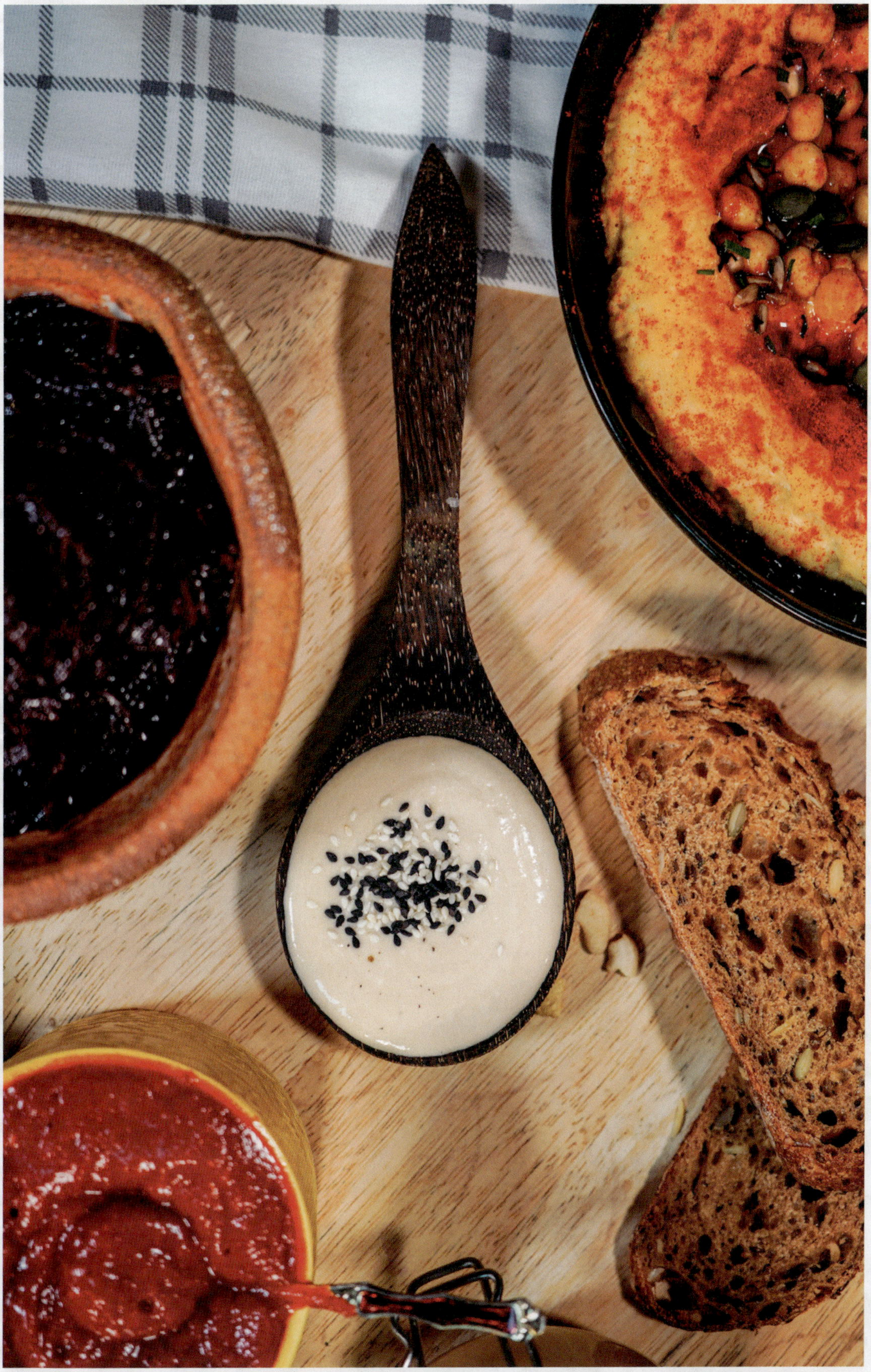

CHUNKY PUMPKIN SEED PESTO

Our fresh, vibrant, and nutrient dense pesto isn't your usual pesto recipe as we make ours with pumpkin seeds instead of pine nuts, the taste isn't far off but in comparison to the nutrient profile, pumpkin seeds have double the amount of protein, 400% more fibre, 50% less calories and are a lot more cost effective.

8-10 Servings
Quantity 500g

EQUIPMENT NEEDED:

A set of measuring cups, food processor or blender, lemon juicer, an airtight jar for storing, colander.

INGREDIENTS:

1 cup of Pumpkin Seeds
2 cups Fresh Basil, washed
1 cup Fresh Coriander, washed
2 Cups Olive Oil, Cold
3 Tbs Nutritional Yeast Flakes With B12
1 Lemon, Juice

Store in an airtight jar for up to 10 days in the fridge or freeze for 3 months

Pre-soak all the pumpkin seeds for 8 hours overnight – optional but advised (see page 14 for benefits on soaking).

Put the olive oil in the fridge to get cold, this will keep the pesto green.

Once soaked rinse well and set a side on some kitchen roll to absorb any excess moisture.

Place pumpkin seeds on a baking tray and bake in the oven on 200c / 400f / gas mark 6 for around 15 -20 minuets until golden.

Meanwhile measure out all the ingredients.

Once the seeds are ready, add everything - except the nutritional yeast - to the jug of a blender or to the bowl of a food processor and blend for 30 seconds, until all the leaves are blitzed and the seeds are broken down slightly but still quite chunky. You dont want it to become a paste, so be careful not to over blend the seeds.

Add the nutritional yeast and season, pulse once or twice until the flakes are dissolved. (We add the nutritional yeast last as it can make the pesto a not-so-vibrant 'yellowy' color if it's blended for too long through the mix, that's why you only once or twice at the end.)

Served on our Loaded Sweet Potato Wedges (see page 130) Mushroom Bruschetta (see page 58) and Green Grill (see page 82) Earth Bowl (see page 112).

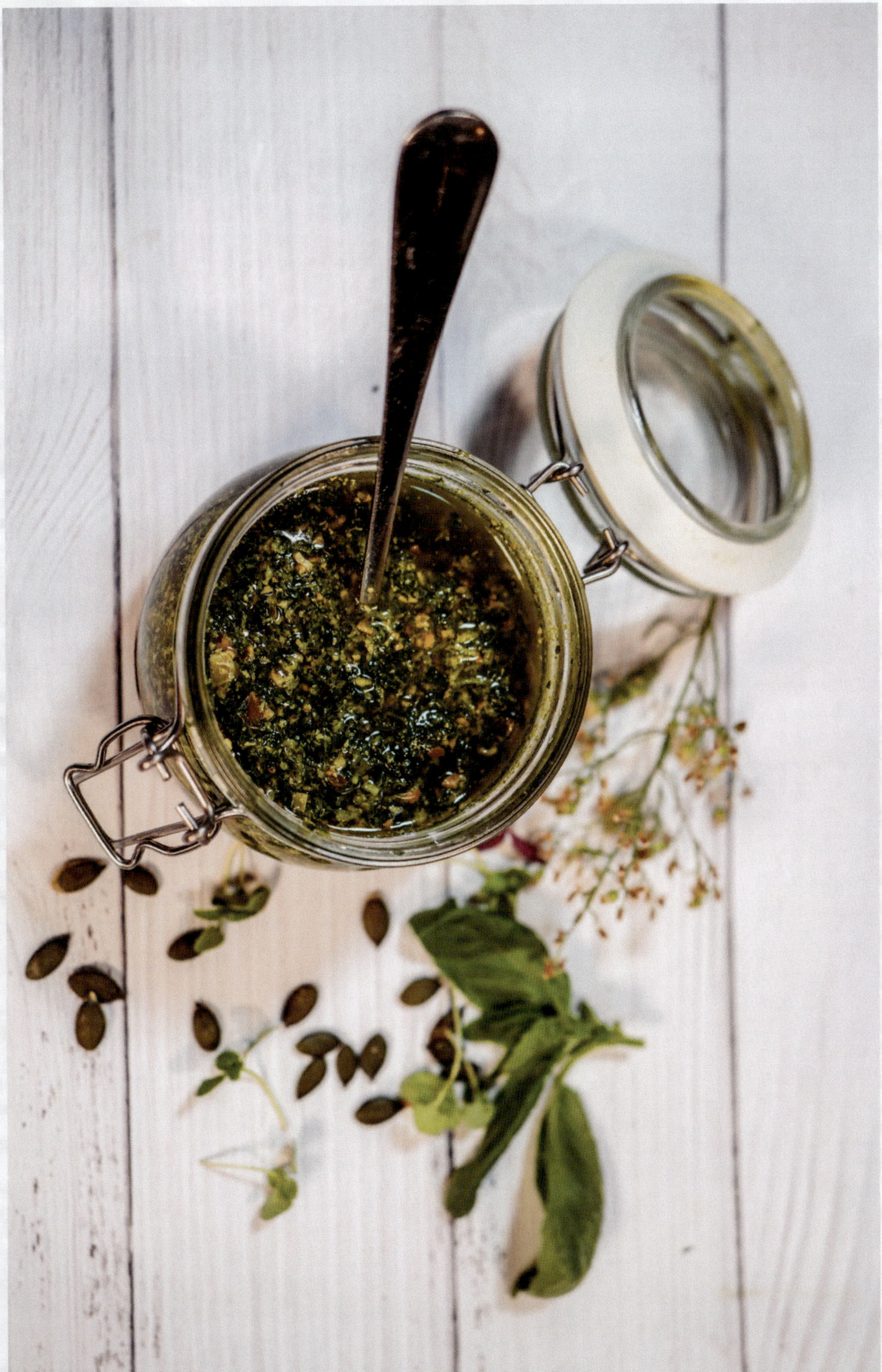

CREAMY SMOOTH TRADITIONAL HUMMUS

NUTS FREE · SOY FREE · GLUTEN FREE · REFINED SUGAR FREE

Hummus is such a simple, but delicious dip that's made from chickpeas, tahini, lemon, garlic, and spices that comes from the middle east. Chickpeas by weight have the same protein profile as chicken making it an excellent meat replacement, as well as a rich souse of fibre, vitamins and minerals that host a range of health benefits. Our recipe has the basic foundations for a traditional hummus, so once you have mastered that you can start adapting it to more exciting flavours. Try adding some roasted red peppers, olives, or sun blush tomatoes to the blender to enhance the flavours even more!

Quantity 300g

EQUIPMENT NEEDED:

A set of measuring cups, food processor, lemon juicer, small saucepan, a colander, garlic crusher, air tight jar for storing.

INGREDIENTS:

- 2 Cans Chickpeas, Drained
- 1 Tsp Gluten Baking Powder
- 1.5 Medium Lemon, Juiced
- 2 Medium Garlic Cloves, Minced
- 5 Tsp Tahini Paste
- ¾ Tsp Cumin Powder
- ¾ Tsp Smoked Paprika
- 5 Tbs Olive Oil
- 30ml Water
- Sea salt to taste
- Pinch of cracked black pepper

Store in an airtight container for 4-5 days in the fridge.

Open, drain and rinse the chickpeas in cold water until chickpeas are clean from brine, using a colander.

Place in a saucepan and cover with cold water 2cm above the chickpeas, add the baking powder and bring to the boil to soften for 12 minutes, until the skin starts to peel on the chickpeas, and they can mush in between your fingers easily.

Drain chickpeas and allow natural cooling. Do not run under cold water, this will reduce the flavour of the peas.

Meanwhile, blend the lemon juice, water and garlic for 30-60 seconds in the blender. This will help reduce the potency of raw garlic.

Add the rest of the ingredients and blend for 3-4 minutes adding a dash of water if needed to blend through, season to taste.

Dish up and garnish with some smoked paprika, olive oil and whole chickpeas.

Try loading it with our Chunky Pumpkin Seed Pesto (see page 90) Caramelised Onion Chutney (see page 86) and Pomegranates.

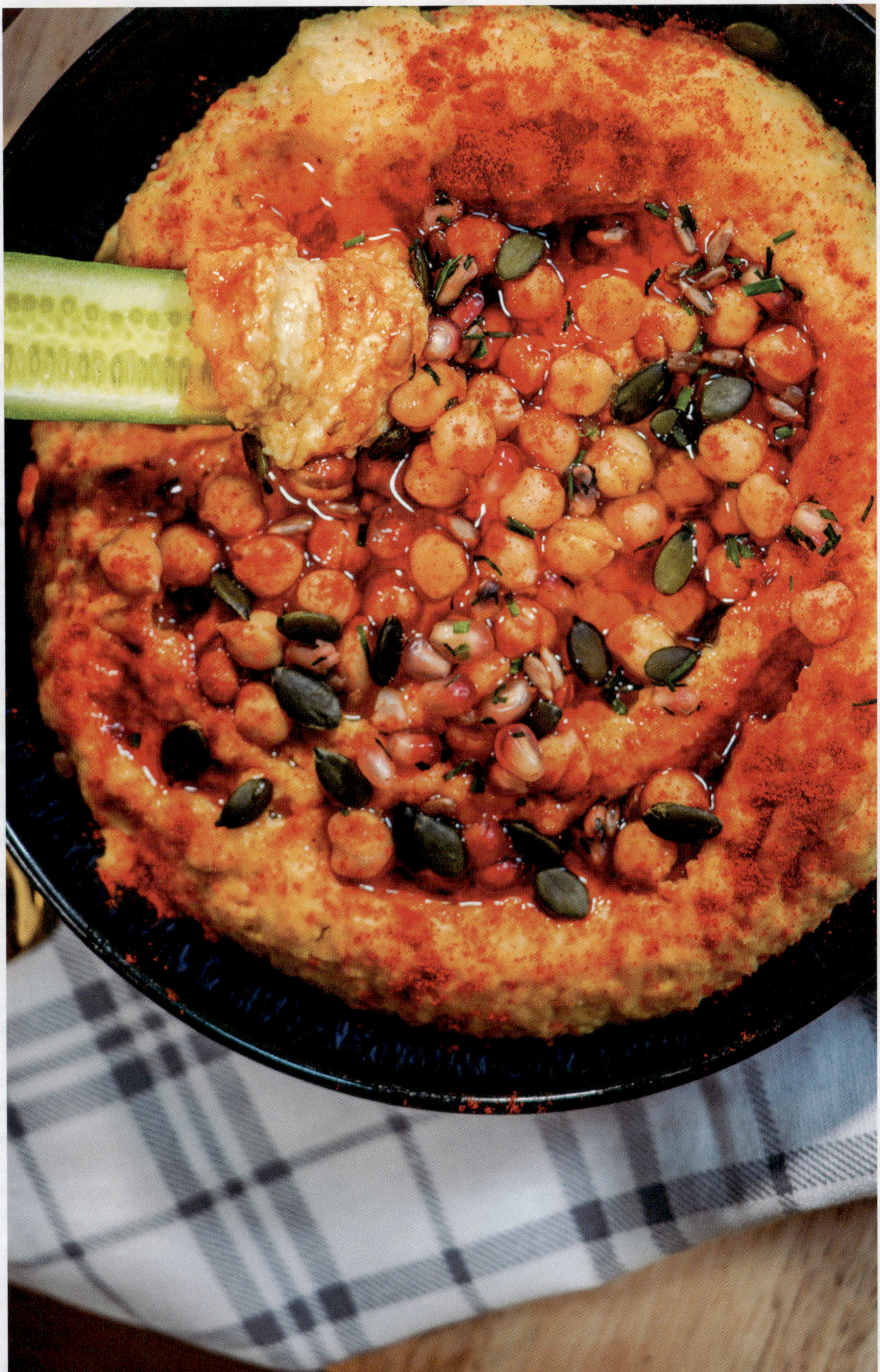

BALSAMIC GLAZE

Nuts Free · Soy Free · Gluten Free · Refined Sugar Free

This sweet and sticky reduction of balsamic vinegar, maple, lemon, and thyme is delicious drizzled over almost everything and is also a very effective glossy elixir to spruce up the décor of one's plate.

Quantity 500ml

EQUIPMENT NEEDED:

Measuring jug, heavy based saucepan, airtight jar for storing, chipping board, knife, whisk.

INGREDIENTS:

250ml Balsamic Vinegar
250ml Water
240ml Maple Syrup, whole
1 Sprig Rosemary
½ Lemon, sliced

Store in an airtight jar at room temperature up to 1 month.

Put all ingredients in a small, heavy based saucepan on a medium to high heat and bring to the boil, be careful it doesn't overflow as it will bubble right up due to the heating of sweet maple.

Reduce heat and simmer for 20-25 minutes until its reduced by a third, you can check its done by spooning a line of it on to a cold plate and then run your finger through the middle of the line, if the gap in the line remains firm, its done.

Allow to cool, before storing, as it cools it will thicken. If it becomes too thick once cooled, add a dash of boiling hot water and whisk to loosen, keep the thyme and lemon in to infuse.

Served on our Green Grill (see page 82), Mushroom Bruschetta (see page 58) and as a garnish to decorate our plates.

MAPLE AND MUSTARD DRESSING

Nuts Free · Soy Free · Gluten Free · Refined Sugar Free

A light emulsion of balsamic vinegar, maple syrup, mustard and pomace oil blended into a sweet salad dressing full of essential fatty acids from the olive oil that help absorb the immune boosting fat soluble vitamins A, D, E and K.

Quantity 650ml

EQUIPMENT NEEDED:

A measuring jug, a whisk, or a blender/stick blender, mixing bowl, garlic crusher, an airtight jar to store.

INGREDIENTS:

2 Tbs Dijon Mustard
1 Large Clove Garlic
50ml Maple Syrup
100ml Balsamic Vinegar
500ml Olive Oil
2 Tbs Wholegrain Mustard
50ml Hot Water, to loosen
Sea Salt to taste
Pinch Of Cracked Black Pepper

Store in an airtight jar for up to 1 month in the fridge.

Measure the vinegar, maple, mustard, and garlic into the blender or alternatively a bowl if you don't have one, you will need to mince the garlic if you're making by hand.

Turn on the machine on a medium setting or begin to whisk the ingredients by hand quite quickly.

As the dressing is being whisked, from a height, drizzle in the oil as slowly as possible, the slower the better, this will avoid the emulsion from splitting.

The dressing should start to emulsify after half of the oil has been added, becoming thick and creamy.

Once all the oil has been added, spoon in the whole grain mustard and pulse once or twice to keep the texture of the grains and season to taste. If the dressing is too thick, add some hot water slowly at the end to loosen.

Used as the dressing on our Rainbow Earth Bowl (see page 112) and can be used as a glaze to make maple and mustard sausages with our Herby Sausages recipe (see page 70).

IG BURGER SAUCE

Although it's called 'Burger Sauce', it doesn't necessarily mean it's just for burgers, this creamy, sweet, and spicy sauce will make any salad, sandwich, wrap or burger taste unbelievably better. It's even great just for dipping!

Quantity 500g

EQUIPMENT NEEDED:

A set of measuring cups, a whisk, a mixing bowl, an airtight jar to store.

INGREDIENTS:

2 Cups Vegan Mayonnaise, Soy Free
2 Tbs Tomato Puree
4 Tbs American Mustard
3 Tbs Maple Syrup
1.5 Tbs Onion Powder
1 Tbs Cayenne Pepper
1 Tbs Garlic Powder
2 Tsp Smoked Paprika
4 Tbs Pickled Vinegar Out of a Jar Of Gherkins
Sea Salt to taste
Pinch Of Cracked Black Pepper

Add all the ingredients to mixing bowl and whisk until evenly combined.

Season to taste.

Serve and enjoy with our Ultimate Beyond Burger (see page 120) or as the perfect dip with Salt and Pepper Wedges (see page 126).

Store in an airtight jar in the fridge for up to 1 month.

SPICY CHIPOTLE SAUCE

This sweet and smoky combination of flavours has the perfect hit of heat, a blend of roasted red peppers and chipotle peppers in adobo sauce is what gives this a kick, literally adding some zing to any dish it served with. Red peppers are high in beta-carotene which is a pigment found in plants that give them their red, yellow, and orange appearance, beta-carotene converts into retinol the active form of vitamin A which the retina of the eye needs to do its job in converting light into neural signal and transmitting them to the brain for visual recognition. They say carrots help you see in the dark, well so do peppers!

Quantity 500g

EQUIPMENT NEEDED:

A set of measuring cups, a high-speed blender, food processor or stick blender, a colander airtight jar to store.

INGREDIENTS:

3 Tsp Garlic Powder
2 Tbs Tomato Puree
1 Tsp Smoked Paprika
1.5 Cup Roasted Red Peppers, Tinned
1/3 Cup Liquid from Roasted Red Peppers
¼ Cup Chipotle Peppers in Adobo Sauce
½ Cup Maple Syrup
Sea Salt to taste
Pinch Of Cracked Black Pepper

Measure out all the ingredients straight into the jug or bowl of a food processor and blitz until silky smooth.

Season to taste.

Served on our Loaded Sweet Potato Wedges (see page 130) and TLT (see page 64).

Store in an airtight jar for up to a week in the fridge or freeze for up to 3 months.

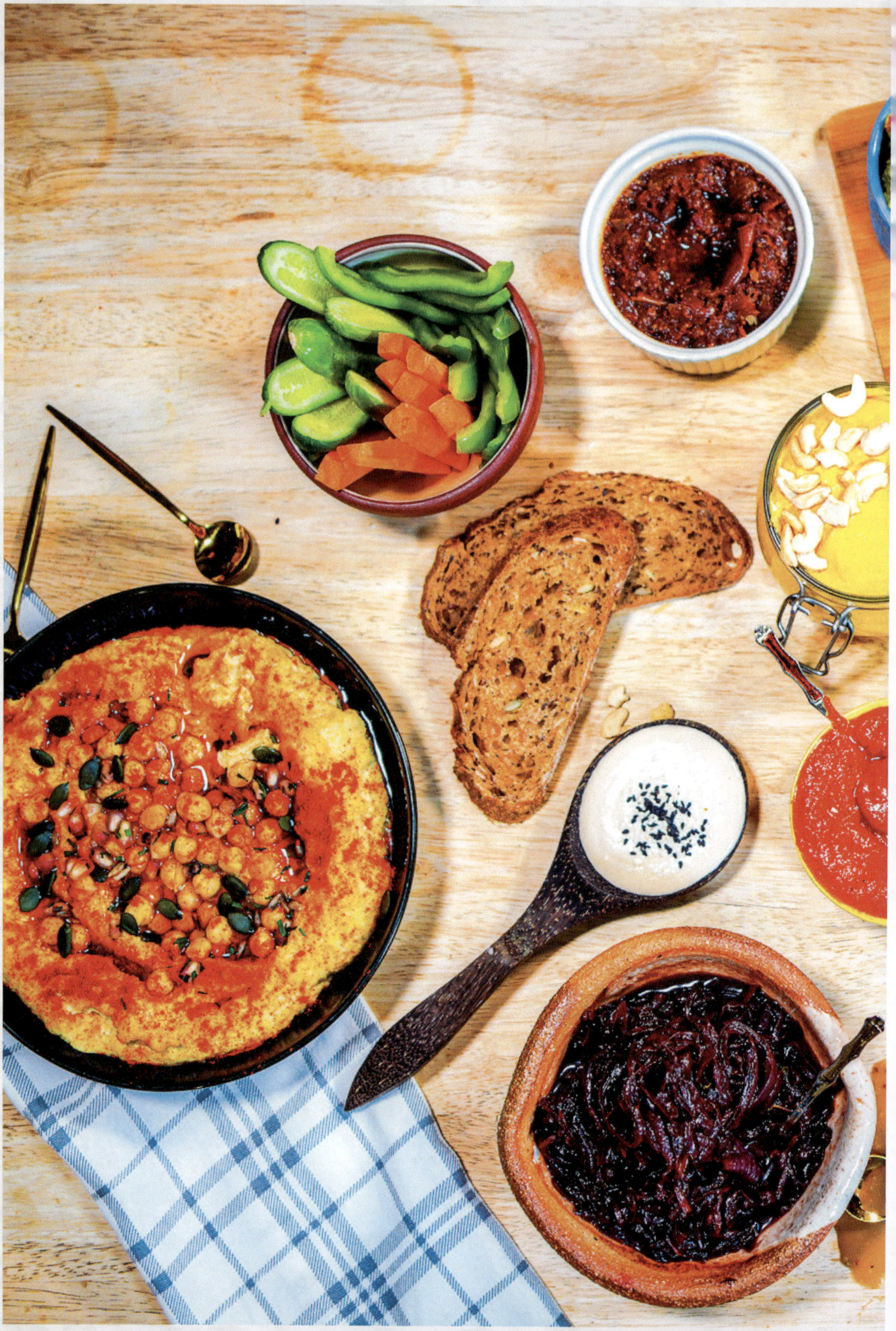

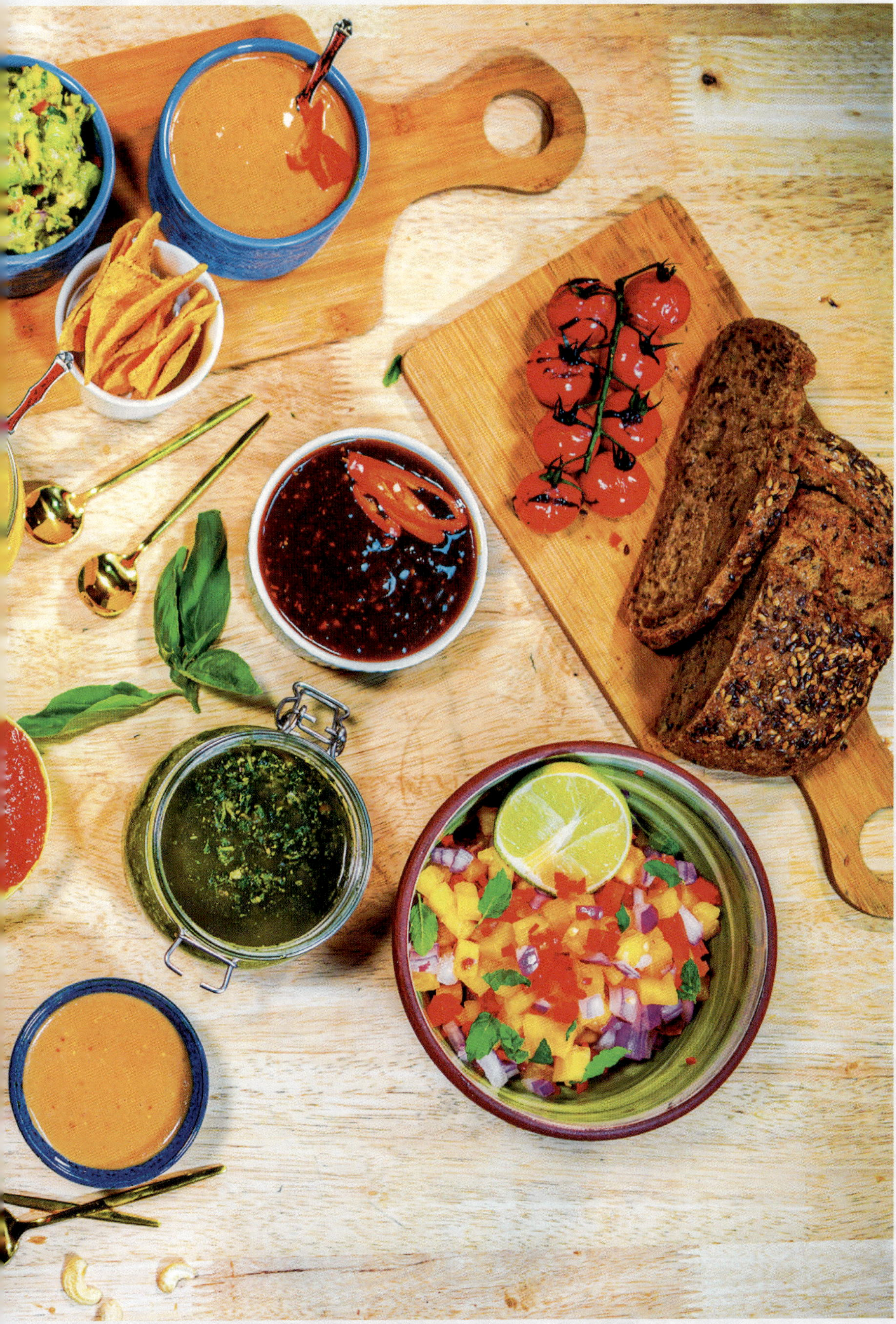

TOMATO CHUTNEY

NUTS FREE | SOY FREE | GLUTEN FREE | REFINED SUGAR FREE

Slow cooked tomatoes, lightly infused with fresh herbs and aromatic spices leaving a slight hint of the East on the pallet, it takes us around 48 hours to reduce and cook down but don't worry, we have to make it for the masses, a small batch can be done in an hour at home. Which means you can smoother it on almost anything and reap the rewards from all the benefits of lycopene it contains. Lycopene is an antioxidant found in tomatoes from the carotenoid family which can protect your body from damage caused by pesticides, herbicides, certain types of fungi and monosodium glutamate- also known as MSG.

Quantity 500g

EQUIPMENT NEEDED:

A set of measuring cups, a garlic crusher, chopping board, sharp knife, a medium sized heavy based saucepan, airtight jars to store.

INGREDIENTS:

7 Medium Tomatoes, Small Diced
1 Medium White Onion, Small Diced
2 Medium Garlic Cloves, crushed
2 Tbs Olive Oil
1 Tsp Mustard Seeds
1 Tsp Cumin, Seeds
5 Fresh Sprigs Thyme, chopped
3 Bay Leaves
¼ Cup Maple Syrup
½ Tsp Balsamic Vinegar
A squeeze of Lemon
Sea Salt to Taste
Pinch Of Cracked Black Pepper

Wash and prepare all the vegetables.

Heat up the pan on a low to medium heat, add the cumin seeds and mustard seeds for about 10-20 seconds, once they begin to crackle and smoke, this signals that the flavours have started to release, remove from the pan, and set aside.

In the same pan, sauté the onions with some olive oil for 8 minutes until soft, golden brown and caramelised, then add the garlic and cook for a further minute.

Add the rest of the ingredients, saving the thyme until the end, simmer for 1 hour, stirring frequently until a jam-like consistency is created.

Season to taste. Allow the chutney to cool fully before storing.

Serve with our famous Sausage On (see page 60) and The Ultimate Beyond Burger (see page 120)

Store in an airtight jar for up to 10 days in the fridge.

GUACAMOLE

A traditional Mexican dish best kept simple with just a few fresh ingredients. Firstly ripe, but firm avocados are the foundation of this desirable dip, soft and mushy avos are a big no-no! Also no-one likes a watery guac, so removing the juicy seeds from the tomatoes before dicing will keep it super thick and creamy. The flavours in this dip are what does it for me, they really zing things up. Onion, chilli, lime, coriander, and garlic, all my favourite ingredients mashed up in a bowl full of luxurious heart healthy, brain boosting fats that I just can't get enough of. Adding this dip to any meal, not only enhances the flavours, but also enhances your potassium levels, a nutrient we just don't get enough of!

4 Servings

EQUIPMENT NEEDED:
A chopping board, a sharp knife, a mixing bowl, a garlic crusher, an airtight jar to store.

INGREDIENTS:
4-6 Ripe Avocados, Scooped and Stone Removed
1 Medium Tomato, De-Seeded and Fine Diced
¼ Small Red Onion, Fine Diced
1 Small Garlic Clove, minced
½ Lime, Juiced
Pinch Of Coriander, Chopped
Pinch Of Chilli Flakes to Taste
Sea Salt to Taste
Pinch Of Cracked Black Pepper

Wash and prepare vegetables.

Place all ingredients into a bowl and mash up using a fork until your desired texture - I like to leave it quite chunky so it still has some bite throughout.

Season well.

Consume within 24 hours as the avocado oxidises turning brown and loses its fresh flavour.

Served on Toast (see page 54) or with our Mexican Chilli Bean (see page 116) or with Nachos.

Store in an airtight container like a mason jar for up to 24 hours.

STICKY KUNG PAO SAUCE

A sweet and spicy, tangy taste of Asia! This sauce is extremely addictive and perfect for stir-fry's and grilled or tempura vegetables. It's packed with pepper, chilli, ginger, and garlic - all extremely strong and powerful ingredients with antibiotic properties that keep away common colds and viruses.

This recipe can be enjoyed two different ways, the way it's traditionally served at Indigo as a thick intense sticky sauce by cooking and thickening it up, which enhances the flavours. Or you can just simply mix the ingredients together and have a super light Asian dressing that can be served over noodles and salads.

Quantity 500g

EQUIPMENT NEEDED:

A measuring jug, a medium heavy based saucepan, airtight jars to store, sharp knife, garlic crusher, box grater, chopping board, whisk, mixing bowl.

INGREDIENTS:

3-Inch Fresh Ginger, grated
5 Large Garlic Cloves, Minced
250ml Tamari or Gluten Free Soy
250ml Water
180ml Rice Vinegar
2 Tbs Siracha Chilli
1 Tbs Black Pepper
Pinch Ground Cardamom
100ml Maple Syrup
1/4 Nori Sheet, Sliced
Pinch Fresh Coriander, Chopped
4 Tbs Arrow Root / 4 Tbs cold water

Measure out and prepare the ingredients into the pan.

Bring up to the boil on a high heat, once boiling reduce heat and simmer for 2-3 minutes.

Meanwhile, mix the arrowroot and water together to make a paste and slowly add it to the centre of the simmering sauce, whisk constantly while pouring to avoid lumps.

Take off the heat and allow to cool before storing Ingredients.

Served on our Kung Pao Wings, Spicy Vegetable Stir-fry or Asian Glazed Greens.

Store in an airtight jar for up to 1 month in the fridge.

SMOKED CASHEW CHEESE

Our Cashew Cheese recipe is definitely one of the most sought after recipes at Indigo Greens - people literally go crazy for this "cheese". It's creamy, dreamy texture, is super rich, with a nutty twist and a mouth-watering flavour that's high in protein, iron, zinc, B12, magnesium and essential fatty acids. Making this recipe an excellent alternative on a plant-based diet. If you can get this recipe right, there's no turning back!!

Quantity 500g

EQUIPMENT NEEDED:

Vitamix or high-speed blender, bowl for soaking, mason jar for storing, measuring jug, measuring cups, spoon, lemon juicer

INGREDIENTS:

390ml Water
3 cups, Soaked Cashew Nuts
4 tsp Smoked Paprika
2tsp Turmeric, ground
2 Cloves of Garlic, large
1 Lemon, small, juiced
7tbsp Nutritional Yeast with B12
Sea Salt, generous pinch
Cracked Black Pepper

Tip: You will need a high-speed blender or food processor to get the silky-smooth finish on this recipe. We use a Vitamix, other blenders and food processors may not have the same effect.

Pre-soak the cashew nuts for 90 minutes before starting this recipe and rinse well once soaked.

Once soaked, measure all the ingredients into the jug of the blender and blend for 4-5 minutes on a medium speed, turning off the machine halfway and scraping down the sides.

The cashew cheese should be a silky and smooth consistency, falling off a spoon nicely, leaving a ribbon effect on the top of the mixture. If the mix is too thick and grainy, add a dash of water and re-blend until creamy.

Season well and store in an airtight jar for 4-5 days in the fridge or freeze for up to 3 months.

PINEAPPLE AND MINT SALSA

NUTS FREE | SOY FREE | GLUTEN FREE | REFINED SUGAR FREE

This delicious fruit salsa recipe is fuelled with life-force healing properties, a sensational sweet and spicy taste of the tropics, that can be served with salads, stir-fry's, grilled vegetables or as an appetiser with some home-made nachos.

Quantity 500g

EQUIPMENT NEEDED:

A chopping board, a sharp knife, a mixing bowl, lemon juicer, an airtight jar to store.

INGREDIENTS:

1 Small Pineapple Fresh, Fine Diced
1 Small Red Onion, Fine Diced
1 Large Tomato, Deseeded, Fine Diced
Fresh Mint, Finely Chopped
1 Medium Red Chilli, Finely Chopped
½ Lime, juice, squeezed

Wash and prepare all ingredients into a bowl, mix together and serve.

Served with our Vegetable Stir-fry, Rainbow Earth Bowl, Mexican Chilli Bean, as a side dish or topper on our Ultimate Beyond Burger.

Store in an airtight container for 3-4 days.

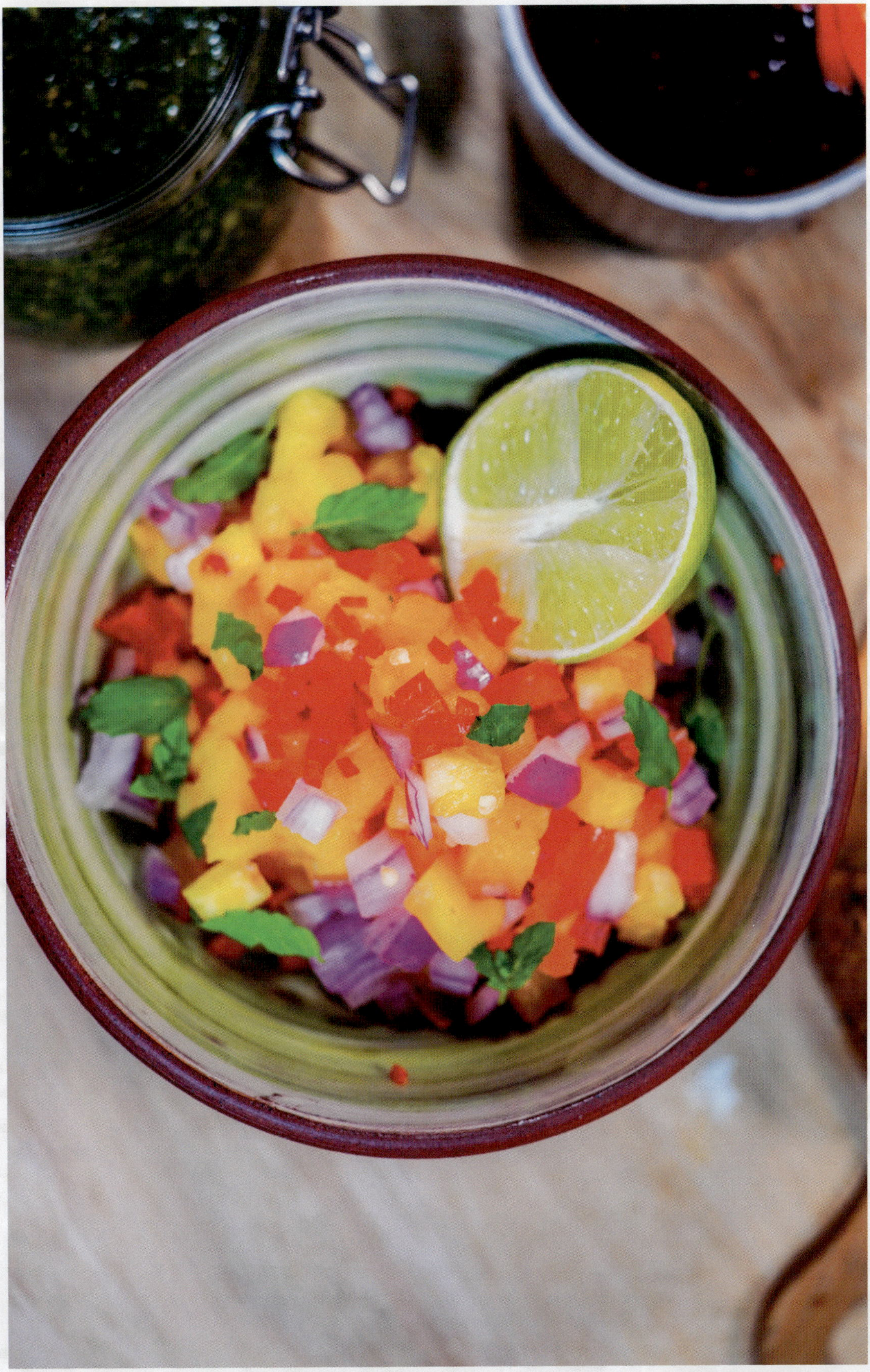

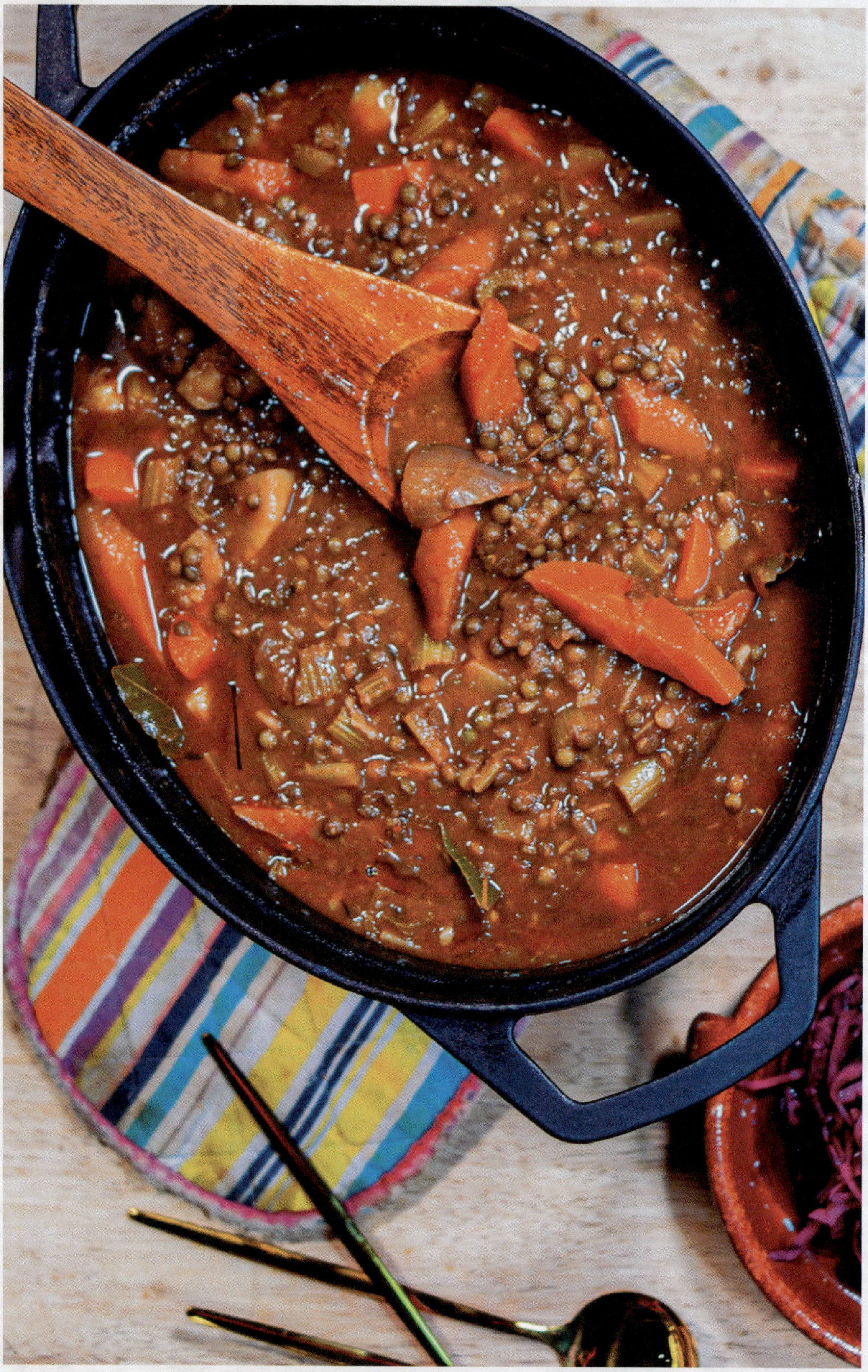

INDIGO FAVOURITES

Our grounding and comforting 'Mains' at the eatery are always wholesome, filling and full of delicious ingredients, flavours and textures from around the world. Some of our one pots require an extra large pan as we have made sure you have enough to share or to meal prep and freeze down for convenience. If you haven't got a large pan or would just prefer to cook a smaller batch, simply half the recipes.

BLIND BUT AWAKE SCOUSE

NUTS FREE · SOY FREE · GLUTEN FREE · REFINED SUGAR FREE

Our famous Scouse has made a name for itself in the heart of Liverpool, a tradition us Liverpudlians have grown up in the city with since childhood. It's a type of stew that was previously thrown together from the leftovers of vegetables and red meat. But our Scouse, is made with love, and lots of lentils instead. Lentils are made up of over 25% protein, making them an excellent alternative to meat, they are also high in fibre making them easier to digest and they have plenty of iron too.

Scouse for me was a tradition every Saturday at my Nans house and although this recipe wasn't her recipe, her house was where I sourced our secret ingredient which makes ours luxuriously rich. When I recreated the plant-based version of Scouse, I had to find a way to make a gravy base with the slight saltiness a traditional Scouse would have, some colour too as my first-time attempts were bland and pale. As I was rattling my brain for ways to achieve this richness, I was taken back to my nan's kitchen, watching her crumble this dark brown block into to her roux for our Sunday roast gravy. I remembered how it turned her blonde flour mix into a rich, dark brown, salty gravy that I would literally be found every Sunday drinking out of a cup, that's how good it was!! The foundation of my nans gravy, was what I needed to make our Scouse - the best Blind Scouse about! For years customers and friends have asked us how we get it so good, but nanna's secret crumb has been all hush-hush ... until now!

7-8 Servings

EQUIPMENT NEEDED:

A chopping board, a sharp knife, an extra-large casserole pan, measuring jug, a peeler, a bowl for soaking, a garlic crusher, an airtight container for storing.

INGREDIENTS:

- 1.5 Large White Onion, Medium Diced
- 2 Tbs Olive Oil
- 8 Large Potatoes, Peeled, Cut into 6
- 4 Large Carrots, Peeled, Halved Lengthways, Angle Sliced 2 Cm
- 5 Sticks of Celery, Chopped 2cm
- 4-5 Medium Cloves Garlic, Minced
- 3-4 Tbs Compton's Gravy Salt (Nannas Secret Crumb)
- 2 Cups Puy Lentils, Pre-Soaked
- 5 Sprigs Fresh Thyme, chopped
- 3 Dried Bay Leaves
- 3 Tbs Tomato Purée
- 2.5 Litres Water, More If Needed
- Pinch Of Cracked Black Pepper

Store in the fridge in an airtight container for 4-5 days or freeze for up to 3 months.

Pre-soak lentils for 2 hours – optional but advised (see page 20 for benefits on soaking).

Meanwhile wash and prepare the rest of the vegetables.

Once the lentils are soaked, wash and rinse.

Then in a large thick based casserole pan sauté the onions in olive oil on a medium heat for about 5-8 minutes until they start to soften and brown.

Add the celery and carrots for a further 8 minutes until they also start to brown.

Add in the garlic and cook for 1 minute.

Add the potatoes, bay leaves, tomato purée and pour in just 2.2 litres of cold water.

Crumble in the gravy salt making sure it's all dissolved.

Bring the pan up to the boil on a higher heat. Once boiling, add the lentils.

Reduce to a simmer and cook for 20-25 minutes, stirring occasionally and adding the rest of the water if needed. (If you didn't soak your lentils, they will need another 20 minutes or so.)

Add the chopped thyme for the last 5 minutes, season with pepper to taste, we don't usually add any sea salt, as it has the gravy salt, but if you wish to add more, now's the time.

Once the sauce has thickened and the lentils are softened, serve straight away in a bowl with some crusty Sourdough Bread and Sweet Pickled Cabbage (see page 136).

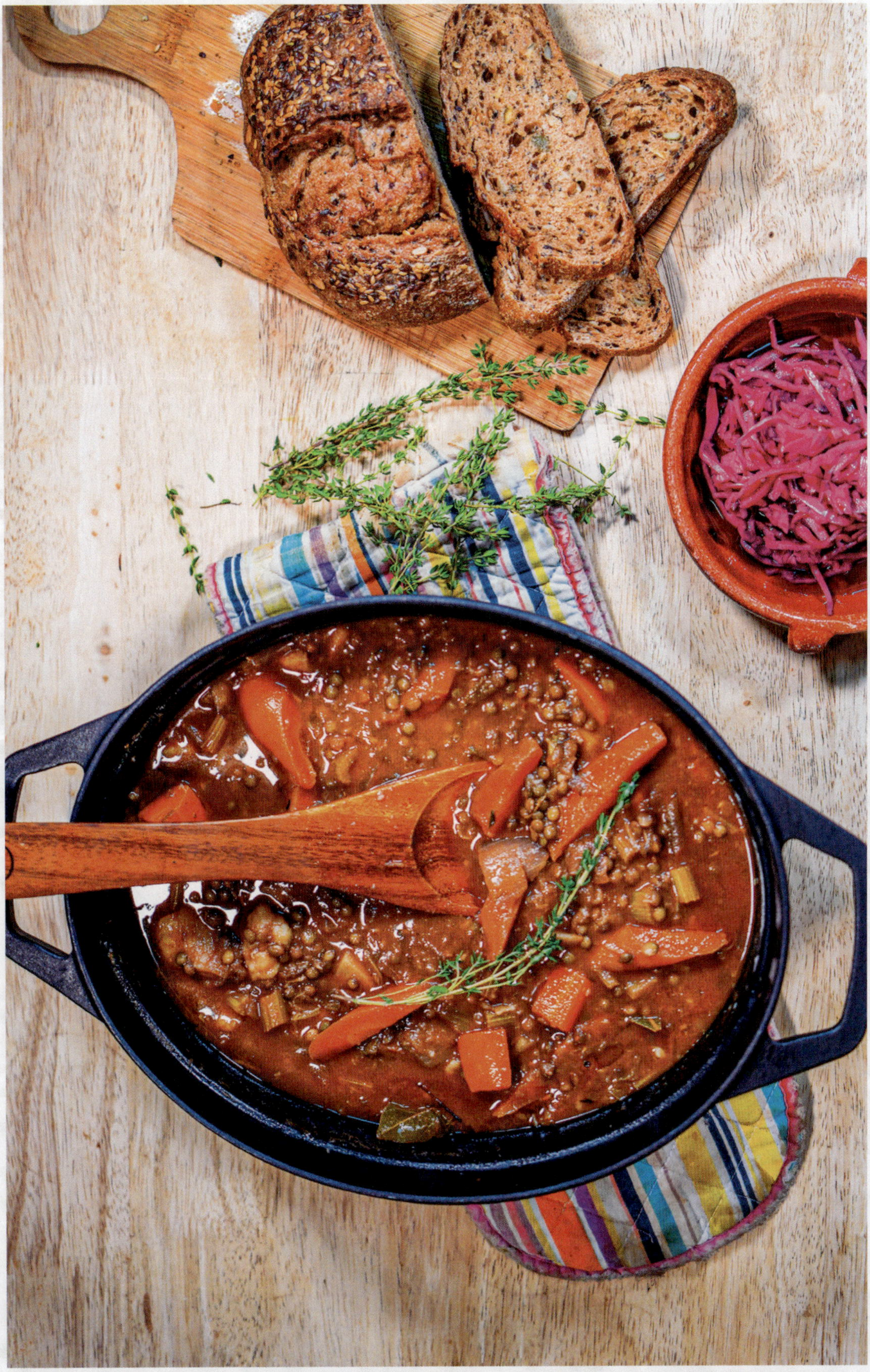

PERUVIAN QUINOA AND VEGETABLE STEW

SOY FREE — GLUTEN FREE — REFINED SUGAR FREE

This colourful stew can be enjoyed throughout the year as it's not too heavy nor too light. It's gently spiced, fresh and colourful ingredients will cheer the entire nervous system right up. Quinoa is typically a seed not a grain, so it's much easier to digest. In saying that, quinoa can mimic the same molecule of gluten when eaten by someone who suffers with coeliac disease or has a really bad gluten intolerances which can cause serious inflammation, even though quinoa is naturally gluten free. In this case try making it with amaranth, it's a much finer seed and is again even easier on the digestive tract, it contains more fibre, more protein and even more lysine which are the building blocks we need to break down protein. In general, amaranth is much better to use, but not as widely available as quinoa.

8-10 Servings

EQUIPMENT NEEDED:

A chopping board, a garlic crusher, a sharp knife, measuring jug, bowl for soaking an extra-large, heavy based casserole pan, a bowl for soaking, an airtight container for storing.

INGREDIENTS:

1 Large White Onion, Diced
3 Tbs Olive Oil
4 Garlic Cloves Minced
4 Celery Stalks, 1cm Chopped
3 Large Carrots, 2cm Diced
4 Large Courgette, 3cm Diced
3 Large Red Pepper, 3cmDiced
1.5 Cups Red Quinoa
1 Tsp Cumin Seeds
1 Tsp Cayenne Ground Pepper
4 Tsp Smoked Paprika
2 Tsp Oregano, Dried
5 Tbs Tomato Puree
650ml Water
2 Stock Cubes
800g Chopped Tomatoes, Tinned
½ Cup Sweetcorn, Frozen
20g Fresh Coriander, Chopped
Sea salt to taste
Pinch of cracked black pepper

Garnish
Fresh coriander, chopped
Lime, slices
Red chilli, slices

Pre-soak the quinoa or amaranth for 8-12 hours or overnight – optional but advised (see page 20 for benefits on soaking).

Wash and prepare vegetables.

On a medium to high heat, sauté the onions in some olive oil until golden brown for about 5-8 minutes.

Add the celery and carrots and cook for a further 5 minutes, until they also start to brown.

Add the garlic and all the spices, cook for a further minute, then add the rest of the fresh vegetables, cold water and dried herbs, crumble in the stock cubes and bring up to the boil, once boiling reduce heat to a simmer and cook for 20 minutes.

Meanwhile, wash and rinse the soaked quinoa until the water runs clear and then add it to the stew for the last 15 minutes of cooking.

Add the frozen sweetcorn for the last 5 minutes.

Serve immediately in a bowl and garnish with some fresh chilli, coriander, lime and crusty sourdough or gluten free bread (see page 42).

Store in the fridge in an airtight container for 4-5 days or freeze for up to 3 months.

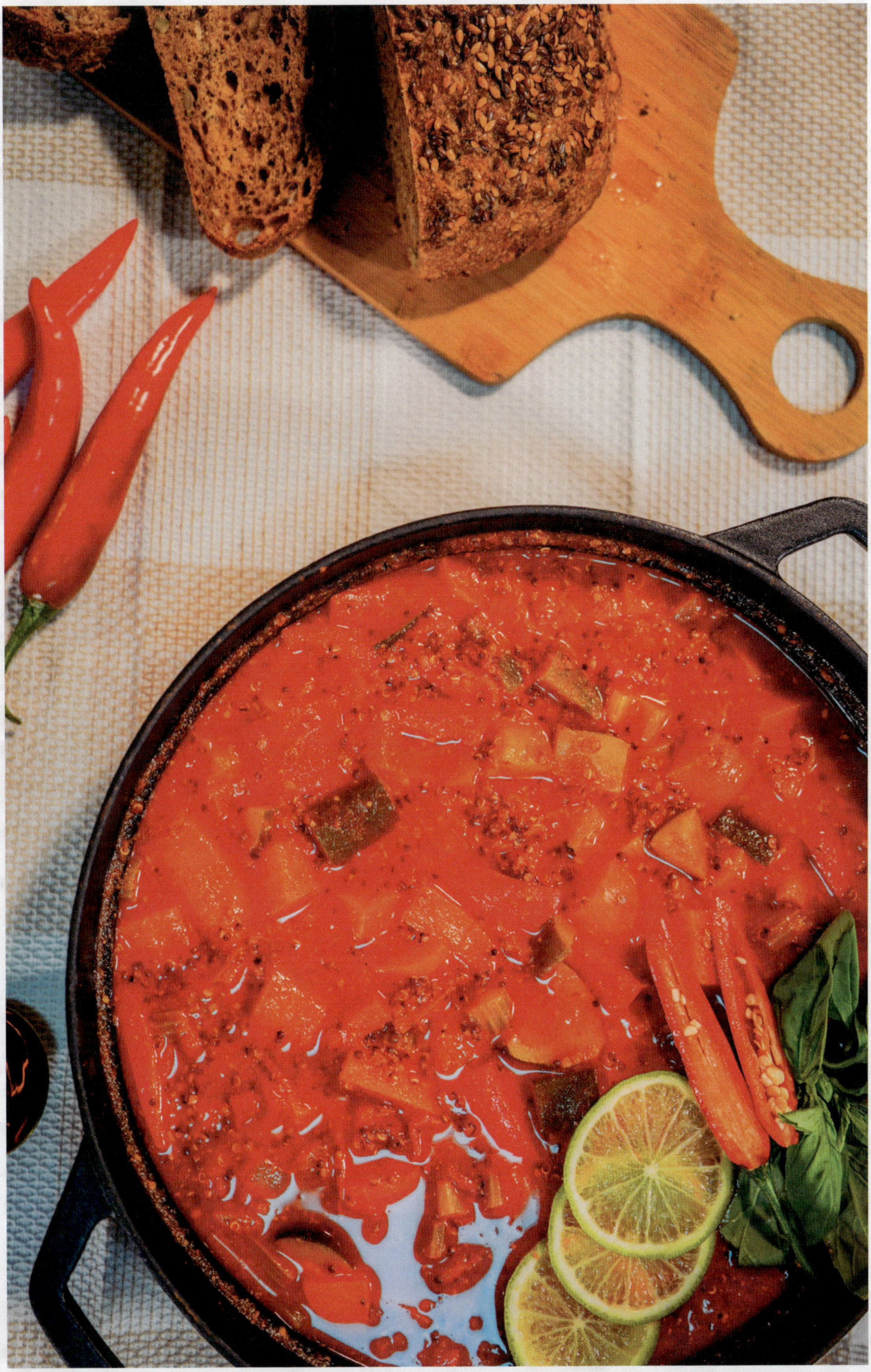

CHUNKY PEA NO HAM STEW

NUTS FREE · SOY FREE · GLUTEN FREE · REFINED SUGAR FREE

A traditional British stew that gets its main flavour from the smokiness of gammon ham, an ultra processed piece of pork that is strongly linked to cancer due to its high carcinogenic level and nitrate-based preservatives. Whereas our Pea No Ham recipe gets its smokiness from natural, oat-smoked paprika that reduces the risk of cancer, while boosting the immune and cardiovascular system. Traditional Pea Soup was one of my favourites growing up, so to recreate this one for the winter months brought back lots of comforting memories of family life.

---

8 Servings

EQUIPMENT NEEDED:

A chopping board, a peeler, a garlic crusher, a sharp knife, measuring jug, bowl for soaking an extra-large, heavy based casserole pan, a bowl for soaking, an airtight container for storing.

INGREDIENTS:

3tbsp Olive Oil
1.5 Large White Onion, Diced
5 Medium Celery Stalks, Chopped 2cm
4 Medium Carrots, 1cm, ½ Moon Angled
4 Large Garlic Cloves, Minced
6 Large Potatoes, Peeled and Cut Into 6
3 tbsp Tomato Puree
100g Curly Kale, Chopped
2 Cups Yellow Split Peas, Soaked 1.5 Cups
Red Lentils, Soaked
10 Sprigs Thyme, chopped
4 Bay Leaves
3 Litres Water
2 Vegetable Stock Cubes
2 tbsp Smoked Paprika
Sea Salt to Taste
Pinch Of Cracked Black Pepper

Store in the fridge in an airtight container for 4-5 days or freeze for up to 3 months.

Soak yellow split peas for a minimum of 12 hours or overnight, rinse well. (see page 20 for benefits on soaking).

Once the yellow lentils have been soaked fully, in a separate bowl soak red lentils for a maximum of 1-2 hours and rinse well - optional but advised.

While you're waiting for your red lentils to soak, measure the rest of the ingredients, wash and prepare the vegetables.

Sauté the onions for 5-8 minutes until soft and nicely caramelised, add the celery and carrots, cook for a further 5 minutes or so until browned.

Add the garlic and smoked paprika, lower heat slightly and cook for 60 seconds.

Add the cold water, tomato puree, yellow split peas and sprinkle in the stock cubes along with the bay leaves.

Bring the pan up to the boil on a high heat, once boiling reduce heat to a simmer and cook for 35-45 minutes.

Add the potatoes 15-20 minutes after the yellow split peas are added, and then add the red lentils 10-15 minutes after the potatoes are added and cook until all the lentils are broken down, the base is thick, and the potatoes are soft.

The stew will be really thick towards the end as the red lentils break right down, so keep stirring and scraping the base of the pan with a wooden spoon to avoid it catching, adding a dash of water as and when, if needed.

Add the thyme, kale and turn off the stove, the heat from the soup will cook the kale out and keep it nice and green while the thyme infuses.

Serve straight away with some Pickled Cabbage (see page 136) warm crusty sourdough, or gluten free bread (see page 42)

Allow proper cooling before storing.

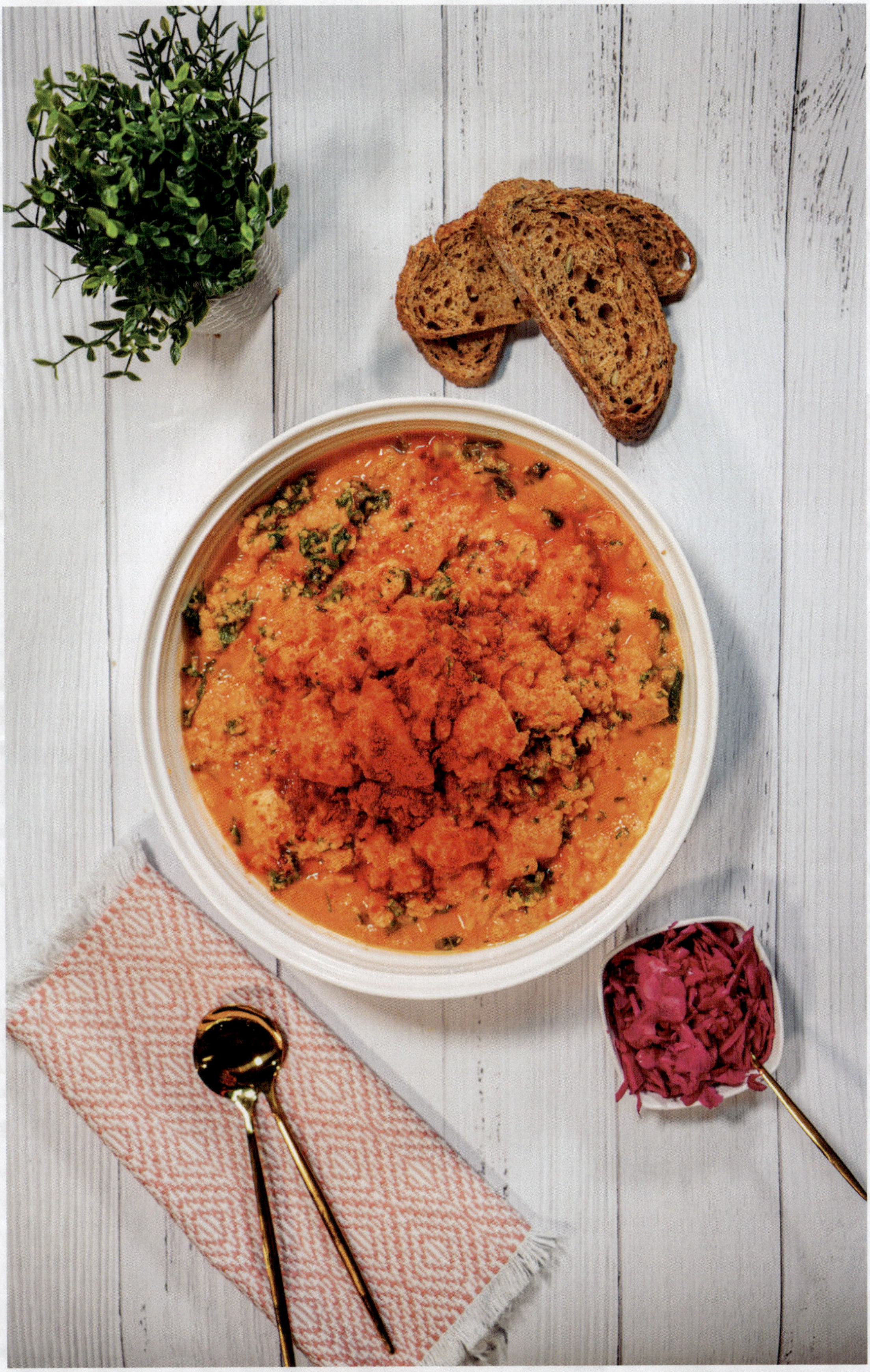

RAINBOW EARTH BOWL

NUTS FREE | SOY FREE | GLUTEN FREE | REFINED SUGAR FREE

Taste the rainbow with this one bowl wonder, its light, crisp, fresh, and fruity flavours are a perfect lunch during the warmer months of the year. This bowl is filled with a very good source of fibre, heart healthy fats, protein, and lots of raw food goodness, keeping all those vital vitamins and minerals in their most natural form. The closer the food is to its natural state the more optimal the food is.

1 Serving

EQUIPMENT NEEDED:
A chopping board, a sharp knife, a small pan, colander.

INGREDIENTS:

½ Cup Spinach
½ Cup Mixed Grains or Chickpeas, Cooked
½ Cup Tortilla Chips
1.5 tbsp Spicy Kale Slaw (see page 138)
1.5 tbsp Pickled Cabbage (see page 136)
1.5 tbsp Pineapple Salsa (see page 102)
2 Spring Onions, Fine Sliced
½ Cup Beansprouts
2 Baby Cucumbers, Halved
½ Avocado, Halved, Stone Removed
1 Tbsp Creamy Hummus (see page 92)
1 Tsp Pumpkin Seed Pesto (see page 90)
2 Tbsp Maple and Mustard Dressing (see page 94)
Pumpkin Seeds, Toasted
Pomegranates, Seeds
Sesame Seeds, Toasted
¼ Red Chilli, Sliced
Fresh Coriander

Wash and prepare all the vegetables.

Arrange the spinach, grains, kale slaw, pickled cabbage, cucumbers, peppers spring onions, beansprouts, tortilla chips and pineapple salsa into small sections around the bowl contrasting the colours.

Place the avocado in the centre and scoop the hummus into the hole, spoon the pesto onto the hummus and the add a pinch of pomegranates.

Circle over the maple and mustard dressing, sprinkle with sesame and pumpkin seeds.

Garnish with fresh coriander, toasted seeds, sesame, and chili.

Serve and enjoy straight away.

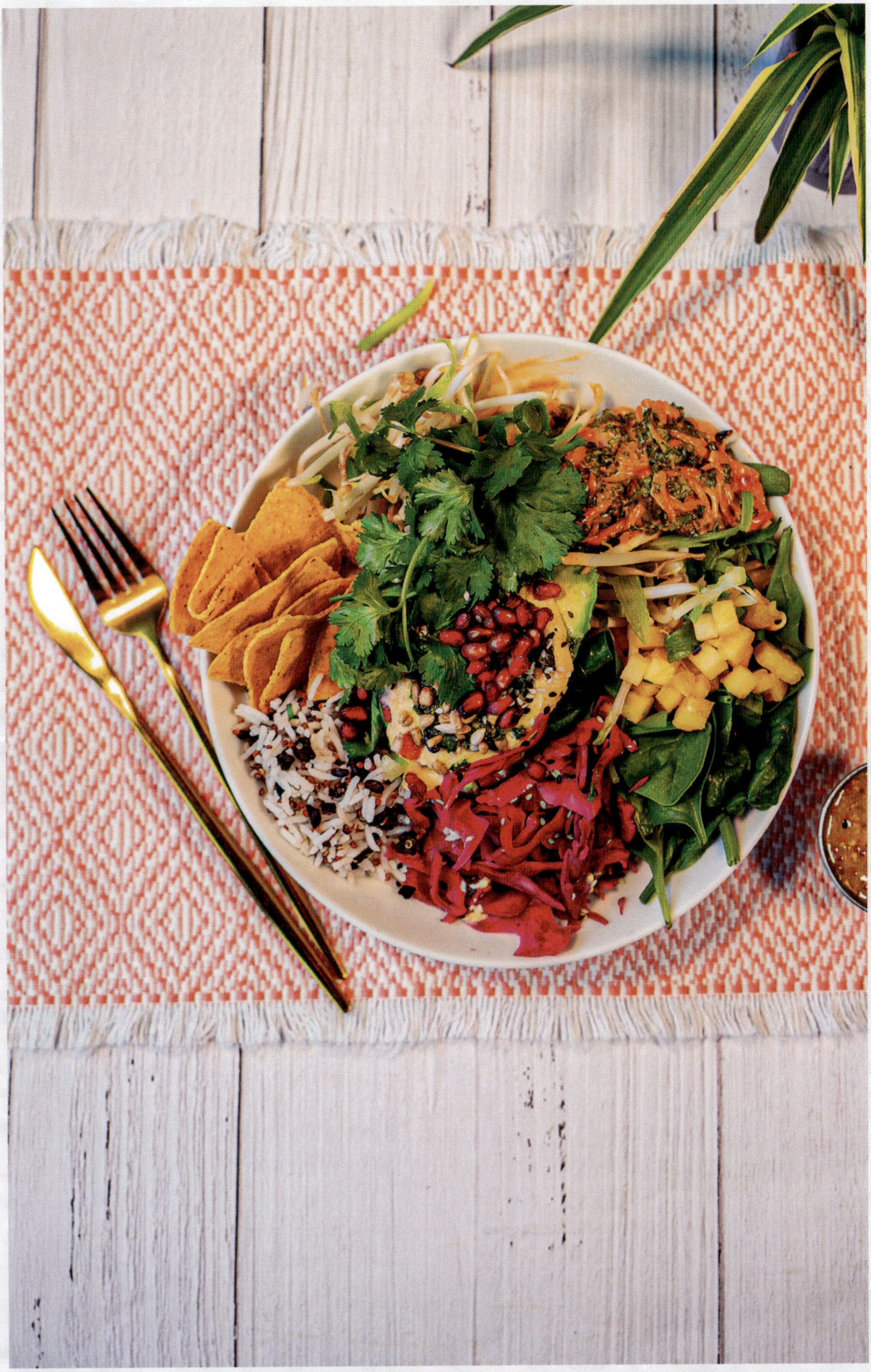

SPICY VEGETABLE STIR-FRY

NUTS FREE · GLUTEN FREE · REFINED SUGAR FREE

The great thing about stir-fry's is they literally take minutes to knock up and can be extremely diverse from season to season, you can bulk them out with noodles, rice, quinoa or just simply have a load of wok fried vegetables. I personally believe it is important to have a variety of cuts and textures from both cooked and raw vegetables for crunch, also adding lots of fresh herbs, nuts, seeds, and some kind of fruit as these ingredients add so much more fun and flavour to the plate. There're so many different sauces to use in a stir-fry but to keep things simple we use our famous Kung Pao sauce as the flavours are intense!

4 Servings

EQUIPMENT NEEDED:

A chopping board, a sharp knife, a large wok, non-stick frying pan or skillet, medium saucepan, colander, mixing bowl, a medium pan, a colander.

INGREDIENTS:

2-3 tbsp Pure Sesame Oil or Olive Oil
½ Red Onion, 1cm Sliced
12 Pieces Tender Stem, Trimmed Down
1 Courgette, 1cm Sliced, Half Moon, Angled
1 Large Red Pepper, 1cm Sliced
2 Tsp Chinese Salt and Pepper Mix (see page 128)
4 Cups Brown Rice, Quinoa, Or Noodles, Cooked
½ Cup Kung Pao Sauce (see page 100)
¼ Cup Water
1 Cup Sweet Pickled Cabbage, Drained (see page 136)
2 Pak Choi, Fine Sliced
4 Spring Onion, Fine Sliced, Angled
2 Cups Bean Sprouts
Squeeze of lime
Pineapple Salsa (See Page 102)

To Garnish

Sunflower Seeds, Toasted
Sesame Seeds, Toasted
Coriander, Fresh
Red Chilli, Thinly sliced

Store in an airtight container in the fridge for 3 days.

Wash and prepare all the vegetables, cook grains or noodles following the instruction on the packet.

In a mixing bowl mix together the spring onions, beansprouts, pickled red cabbage and bok choi with a squeeze of lime, set aside for later.

Carefully heat the oil up in the pan on a high heat

Add tender stem and cook for 4-5 minutes until it starts to char, then add a splash of water to the hot pan and let the steam cook them through for 30 seconds, remove from the pan and set a side till later.

Add the courgettes and peppers to the same pan and cook for 2 minutes, there should still be traces of oil in the pan, so no need to add more.

Once the vegetables are nicely charred, add the tender-stem back to the pan and season with Chinese Salt and Pepper Mix.

Toss in the grains or noodles of your choice and add a splash of water to avoid them sticking to the pan as they heat through.

Stir in the Kung Pao Sauce, once it starts to bubble and steam, remove from the heat straight away so the sticky sauce doesn't burn the pan. Transfer to a plate or bowl.

Begin to build the stir-fry up with the raw salad mix prepared earlier, top with some coriander, toasted pumpkin seeds, sesame seeds, and chilli.

Finish off by spooning the Pineapple Salsa around the plate.

Serve straight away and enjoy or allow proper cooling before storing.

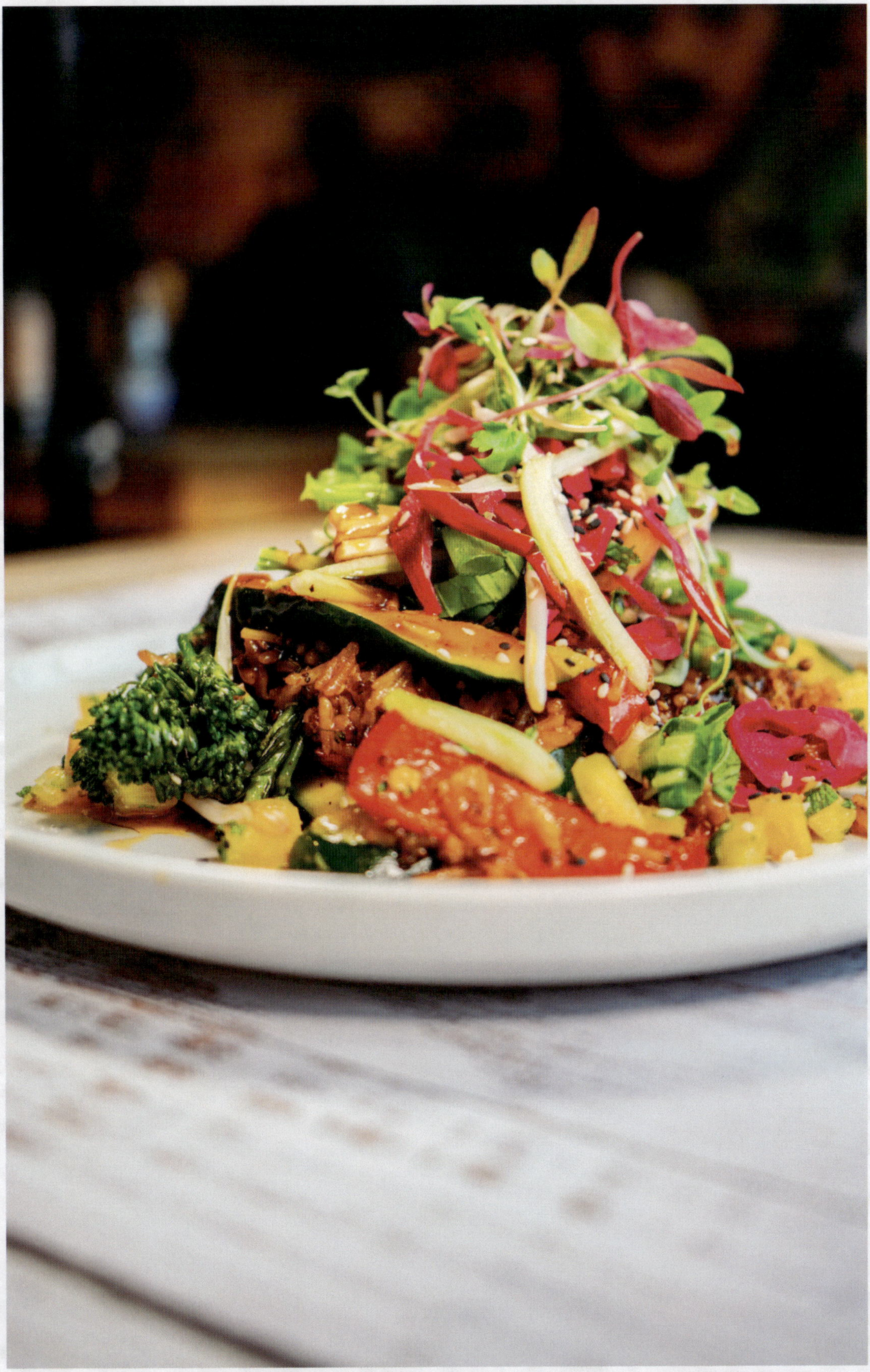

JENS MEXICAN 3 BEAN CHILLI WITH LIME AND CORIANDER

NUTS FREE | SOY FREE | GLUTEN FREE | REFINED SUGAR FREE

This tongue tantalising Chilli dish actually comes from our meal prep menu 'The Vegan Meal Prep Company'. Jen - our talented meal prep chef - has this one hands down and it certainly is one of my personal favourites. It takes me right back to when my brother and I were children, once a year on the 5th November, we would gather around community built street fires with friends and family, wrapped up with our hats, gloves and scarfs on, eating chilli jacket potatoes on a freezing cold bonfire night, staring into the blazing flames. This one warms you right up from the inside.

6-8 Servings

EQUIPMENT NEEDED:

A chopping board, a sharp knife, a large casserole dish, box grater or zester, a colander, measuring jug, garlic crusher, measuring jug.

INGREDIENTS:

2 Small Onions, Fine Diced
3 Tbs Olive Oil
3 Celery Stalks, Small Diced
1 Tsp Cumin, Ground
1 Tsp Smoked Paprika
2 Tsp Chilli Flakes, crushed
5 Large Garlic Cloves, Minced
1 Large Red Pepper, Diced, 2cm
1 Large Yellow Pepper Medium Diced, 2cm
1 Large Green Pepper Medium Diced, 2cm
800g Chopped Tomatoes, Canned
2 Tbs Tomato Puree
800ml Water
1.5 Tbs Compton's Gravy Salt (Nans secret crumb)
400g Black Beans, Canned, Drain and Rinse
400g Red Kidney Beans, Canned, Drain and Rinse
400g Cannellini Beans, Canned, Drain and Rinse
1.5 Tsp Cacao Powder, raw
1 Small Lime Zested, To Taste
Coriander To Taste
Sea Salt, To Taste
A pinch of Cracked Black Pepper

Wash and prepare all the vegetables.

On a medium-high heat sauté the onions in olive oil in a medium heavy based pan for about 8 minutes until golden brown.

Add the celery and continue to sauté until they also start to brown.

Add the garlic and all the spices, cook for a further minute and stir in the tomato puree.

Add the peppers, tomatoes, water, gravy salt and cacao, bring up to the boil, once boiling reduce heat to a simmer and cook for 20 minutes until the sauce is reduced into a thick tomato sauce.

Meanwhile if you're having the Chilli with the Pea and Mint Fritters or any other side dish, this would be a perfect time to make them.

Add the the beans for the last 5 minuets.

Sprinkle in some chopped coriander, lime zest and season.

Serve in a bowl with our Pea and Mint Fritters (see page 118) alongside some mixed grains or loaded in a sweet potato with our Pineapple and Mint Salsa (see page 102) or Guacamole (see page 99).

Store in the fridge for 4-5 days in an airtight container or freeze for up to 3 months.

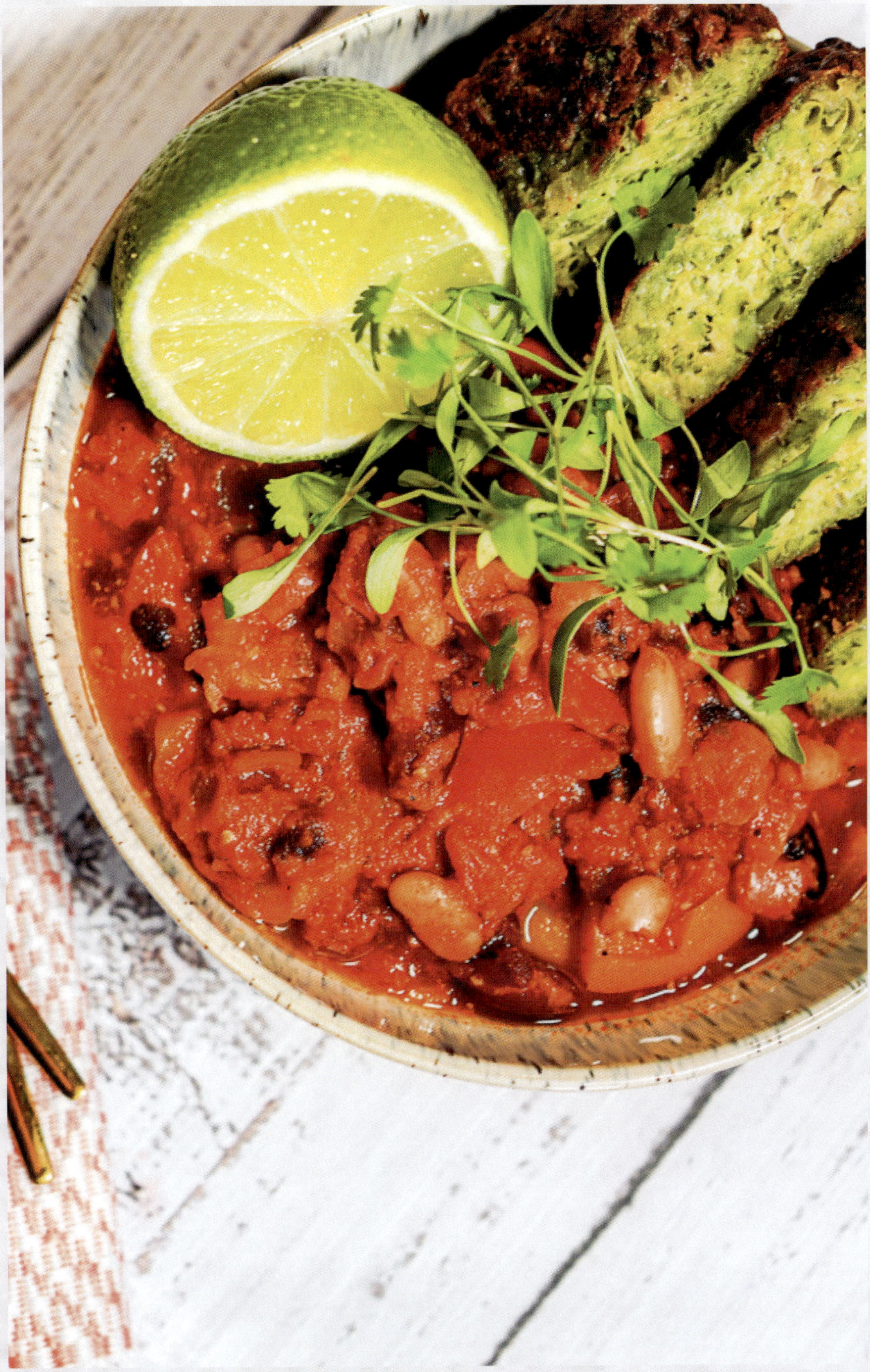

PEA AND MINT FRITTERS

NUTS FREE · SOY FREE · GLUTEN FREE · REFINED SUGAR FREE

These super tasty Fritters are the perfect little addition to our Mexican 3 Bean Chilli, their fresh flavour just lifts the entire dish. The mix is easy to make and goes a long way, so if you have any spare they are a great little snack for lunch the next day.

8 Servings

EQUIPMENT NEEDED:

A chopping board, a sharp knife, box grater or zester, a colander, garlic crusher, a set of measuring cups, a food processor or a bowl and potato masher, a skillet or non-stick frying pan, lemon juicer.

INGREDIENTS:

1 Large Red Onion, Small Diced
3 Large Garlic Cloves, Minced
1.5 Cups Frozen Peas, Thawed
5 Tbs Nutritional Yeast
20 Leaves Fresh Mint, Chopped
1 Lemon, Zested and Juiced
1 Cup Self-Raising Flour, Gluten Free
2 Tsp Baking Powder, Gluten Free
1/2cup Olive Oil for Shallow Frying
Sea Salt, To Taste
Cracked Black Pepper

Store in an airtight container in the fridge for 4-5 days or freeze for 3 months from raw or cooked.

Sauté onions in shallow frying pan with olive oil for 5 minutes on a medium to high heat with some olive oil.

Add the garlic and continue to sauté for another 1-2 minutes, until they are softened and slightly caramelised.

Add them into a food processor (not a blender as the mix is too thick for a jug) along with the rest of the ingredients and pulse until a rough paste is formed. It's quite nice to have some whole peas in for texture so do not over blitz or alternatively mix by hand and mash up peas with a potato masher.

Add olive oil to a non-stick frying pan and place on a medium heat.

When the oil is hot, carefully take 1 heaped tbsp of the mixture and carefully place it into the pan, flattening the mix with the back of the spoon into a 1cm thick circle. Remember the thicker they are the longer they will take to cook right through.

Cook for 3-5 minutes, or until golden and crispy, then flip over to cook for another 3-5 minutes on the other side, don't try to flip them too soon, they're much easier to handle once cooked underneath. Alternatively, preheat the oven on 180c / 350f / Gas Mark 4 and place on a lined baking tray, bake in the oven for 20-25 minuets flipping half way.

Serve and enjoy!!

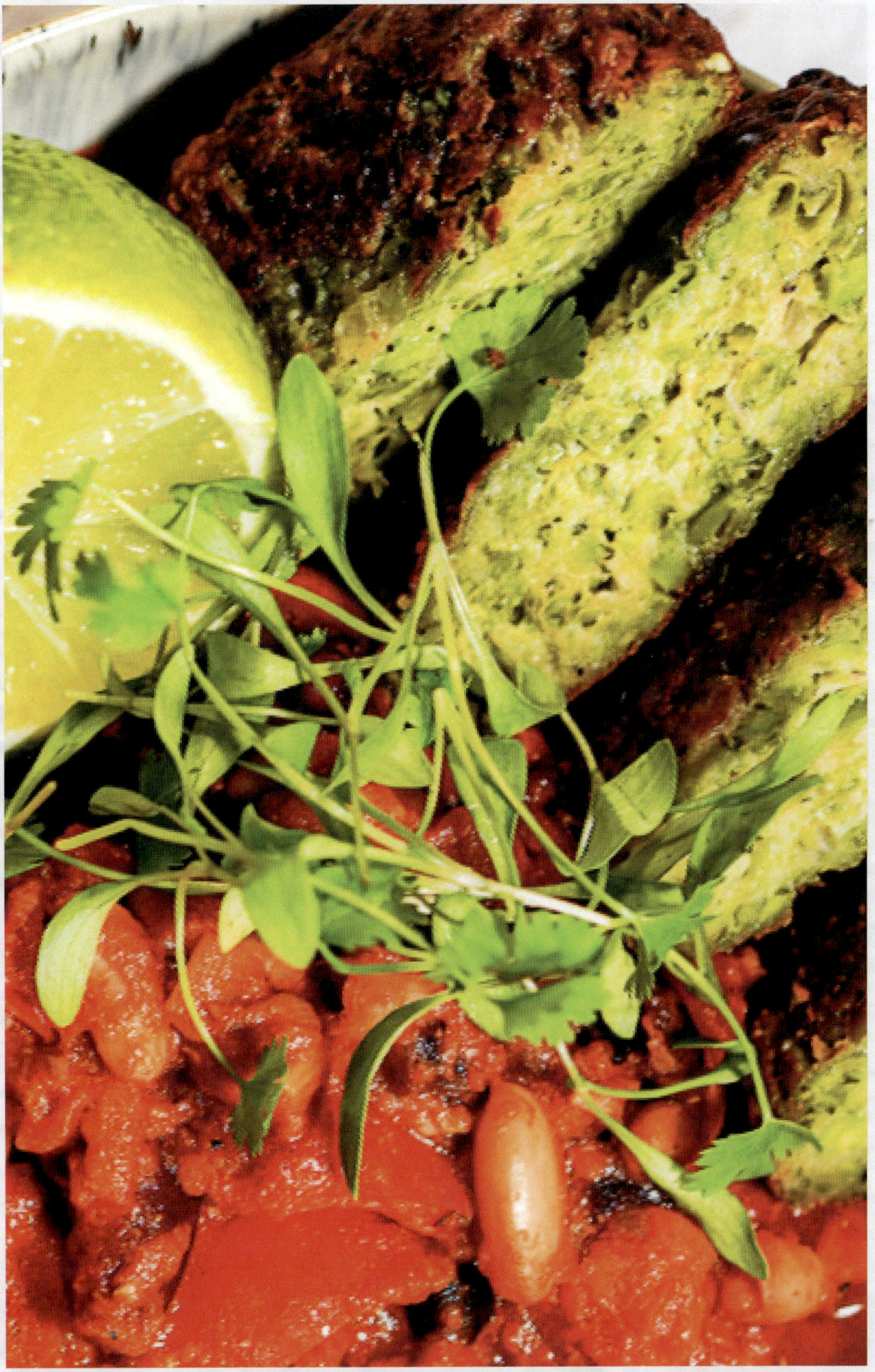

THE ULTIMATE BEYOND BURGER

NUTS FREE | SOY FREE | GLUTEN FREE | REFINED SUGAR FREE

While we pride ourselves on our home-cooked whole foods, we feel that the 'Beyond Meat' Burger is an excellent meat substitute for those dipping their toes in plant-based nutrition. The resemblance this patty has to meat is pretty remarkable. Going plant based for most isn't an easy transition, so having an alternative like this makes that transition much easier and opens the doors to people trying new plant-based options. Having researched the product we found they are an excellent source of protein and fibre which is sourced from peas and mung beans and uses natural colourings like beetroot powder and apple extracts. They also don't contain any vital wheat gluten or soy, like most processed substitutes. Although these burgers are good alternative, they do contain a tad too much sodium - and although we need sodium to survive, we must always be cautious on how much we consume, especially if you are the kind of person who adds salt to everything. It can add up pretty quickly. At Indigo the Ultimate Beyond Burger is loaded with all our homemade natural, juicy, raw food condiments which not only complement it with so much more flavour, but they also add numerous minerals, vitamins and water which help to balance out the sodium levels.

---

1 Serving

EQUIPMENT NEEDED:
A chopping board, a sharp knife, a colander, a baking tray.

INGREDIENTS:
1 Beyond Burger, Thawed
1 Ciabatta Bun Or GF Burger Bun for GF option
1 tbsp Tomato Chutney (see page 98)
3 Leaves Baby Gem Lettuce
1-2 Slices Beef Tomato
3 Slices of Pickled Gherkins
1 tbsp Violife Mozzarella Cheese
1 tbsp Sweet Pickled Cabbage (see page 136)
2 tbsp Spicy Kale Slaw (see page 138)
Fresh Coriander

Allow the beyond burger to completely thaw on a tray, once defrosted flatten down using the palm of your hand or a burger press, until it's around half the thickness and wider in width.

Place the burger under the grill on a high heat for 3-4 minutes on either side.

Meanwhile wash and prepare vegetables.

Once the burgers are cooked on both sides, add the cheese, and return to the grill until nicely melted.

Slice your bun in half evenly, place under the grill and toast until golden brown.

Place the bottom half of the bun on your plate and add the tomato chutney first, followed by baby gem, slice tomato, gherkins, cheesy Beyond patty, kale slaw, pickled cabbage, coriander and top of bun.

Carefully pierce through the burger with the sharp end of skewer, keeping the height.

Serve straight away and enjoy.

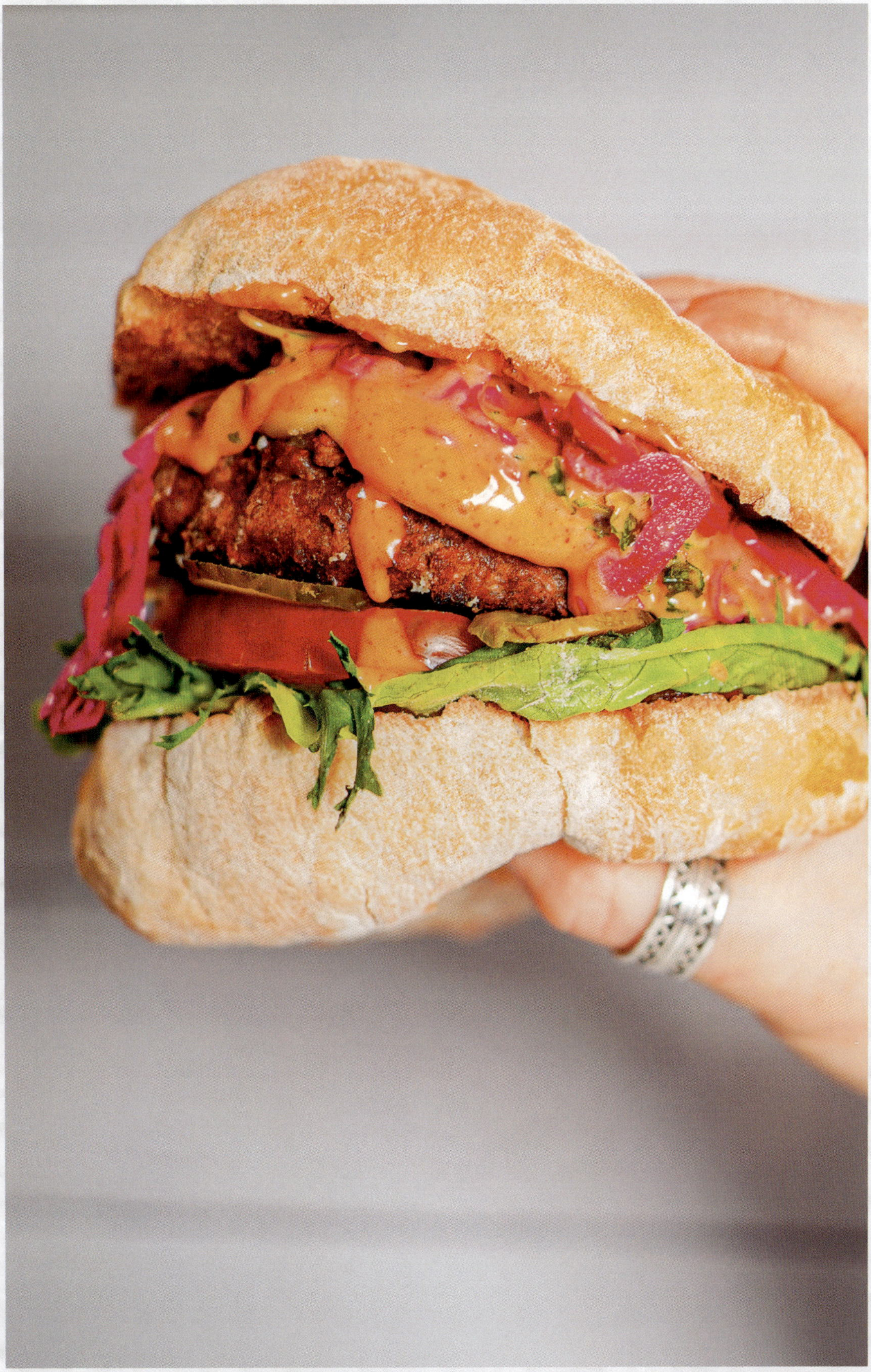

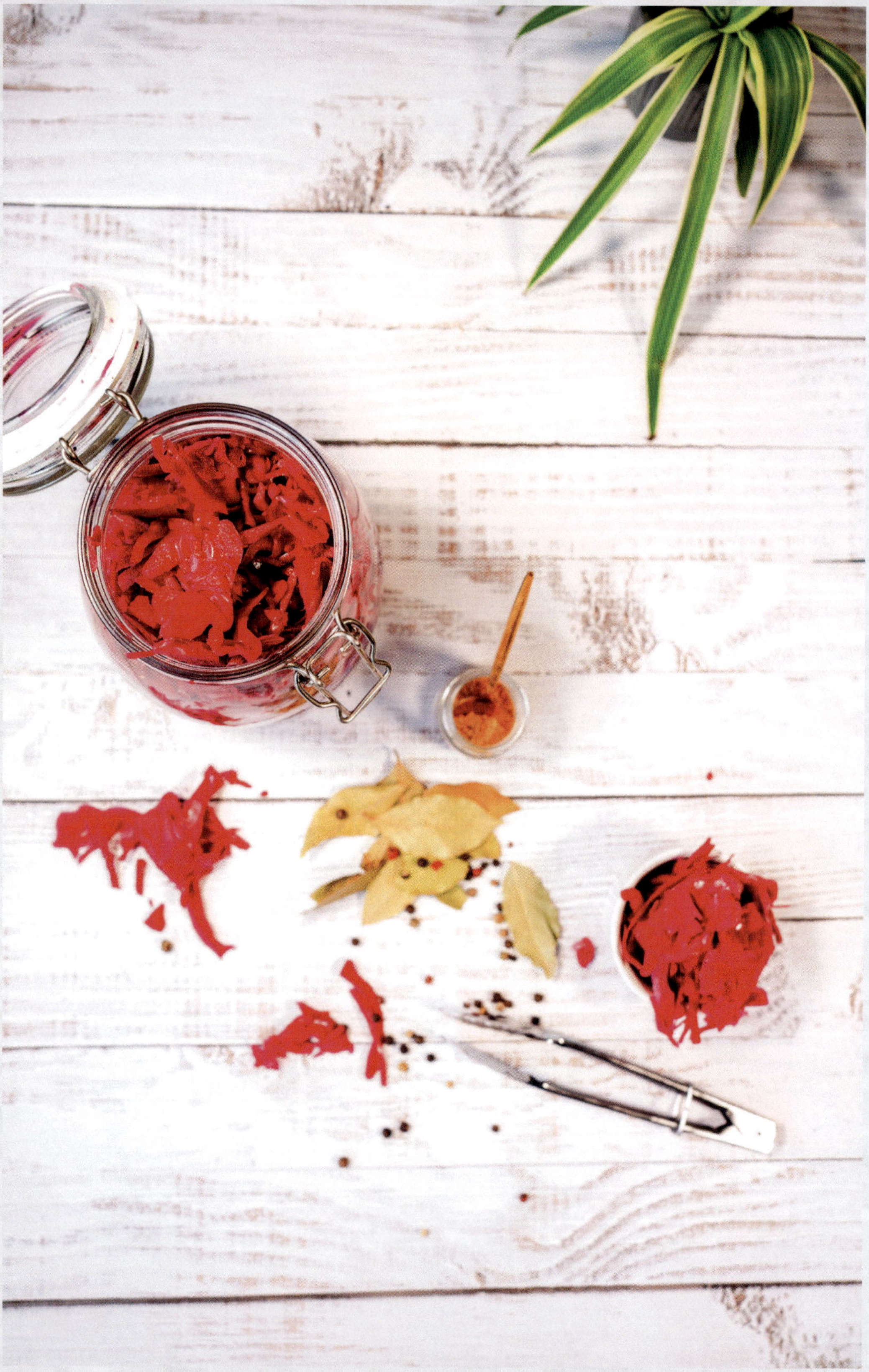

SIDES AND SMALL PLATES

A collection of tantalising small plates, sides and sharers, perfect for parties and family feasts.

CRISPY SALT AND PEPPER TOFU

NUTS FREE · GLUTEN FREE · REFINED SUGAR FREE

A classical Chinese dish that is crispy and golden on the outside, and soft and succulent on the inside, with a magnetic flavour that leaves your mouth watering for more. Tofu can either be a hit or miss, and that all boils down to how it's cooked. So here's a few key tips before we start to make sure you get this recipe just right!! These are steps:

- Always use firm tofu, extra firm may lose ability to absorb flavour while silken tofu may fall apart.
- Remove as much water as possible, removing excess water from the tofu is key, making a salty marinade using tamari will help pull out the moisture from the tofu, as well as firming it up slightly and adding some extra flavour. Also pressing it or patting it with a clean dry cloth helps remove excess water.
- Hot oil, this is key to achieve that crispy coating, allow your tofu to come up to room temperature on a clean kitchen cloth or kitchen roll before shallow frying it. Fridge cold tofu will drop the temperature of the oil resulting in soggy, greasy tofu.
- It's all about the timing, do not dust the tofu in flour until your oil is hot and you're ready to wok!! The flour will absorb the moisture from inside the tofu leading to a tacky, wet coating. This will congeal the tofu together and stick to the pan. Make sure there is plenty of flour in the tray you're dusting from too, this will form a thick coating.
- Lastly, only season the tofu right at the end of cooking with your spices, once it is crispy, crunchy, and ready to eat, if you add the seasoning too soon it will burn in the pan and ruin your lovely golden coating.

4-6 Servings

EQUIPMENT NEEDED:

A chopping board, a sharp knife, a colander, garlic crusher, a set of measuring cups, a large skillet or non-stick frying pan, a large bowl or tub, measuring jug, a deep sided tray or large mixing bowl.

INGREDIENTS:

600g pack Firm Tofu, drained
100ml Tamari Gluten Free Soy Sauce
500ml Water
½ Cup Olive Oil, for Shallow Fry
Corn Flour, for coating
1 Large Red Pepper, Sliced
1 Small Red Onion, Sliced
1 Medium Green Chilli, Sliced
2 Garlic Cloves, Minced Chinese
1-2tsp of Salt & Pepper Seasoning (see page 128)

To Garnish

Spring Onions, sliced on angle
Pickled Cabbage, see page
Fresh Chilli, sliced
Fresh Coriander, sprigs
Sesame Seeds, toasted
Bean Sprouts

Firstly make the brine by mixing the water and tamari together in a bowl deep enough to marinade the tofu in.

Drain the tofu, and rinse from the packet, cut into 1-inch cubes.

Add the tofu to the brine, and let it soak for at least 90 minutes at room temperature.

Meanwhile wash and prepare the vegetables.

Once the tofu is ready, drain well and rest on a sheet of strong kitchen roll or a clean cloth to soak up any excess moisture, patting dry.

When the tofu is room temp, place a shallow non-stick frying pan on a high heat with of olive oil.

Place a thick layer of corn flour into a large tray and gently toss the tofu in it creating a nice coating.

When the oil is hot, in small batches, shake off any excess flour from the tofu and add to the pan, make sure there is room between each piece so they can be flipped occasionally and cook evenly on all sides. Cook for around 8-10 minutes all together making sure each side of the tofu is crispy and golden brown.

Place cooked tofu on a clean cloth or kitchen paper and let rest while cooking the veg.

Add the peppers, onions, chilli, and garlic to the same pan and cook for 2 minutes until nice and brown, and return the tofu to the pan with the Chinese Salt and Pepper Seasoning, cook for 30-45 seconds, just while the flavours infuse.

Serve immediately in a small bowl or plate and garnish with sesame seeds, coriander, spring onions, bean sprouts, pickled cabbage, and fresh chilli.

Follow the same cooking technique and add to curries or stews for additional protein. Store in an airtight container the fridge for 3-4 days.

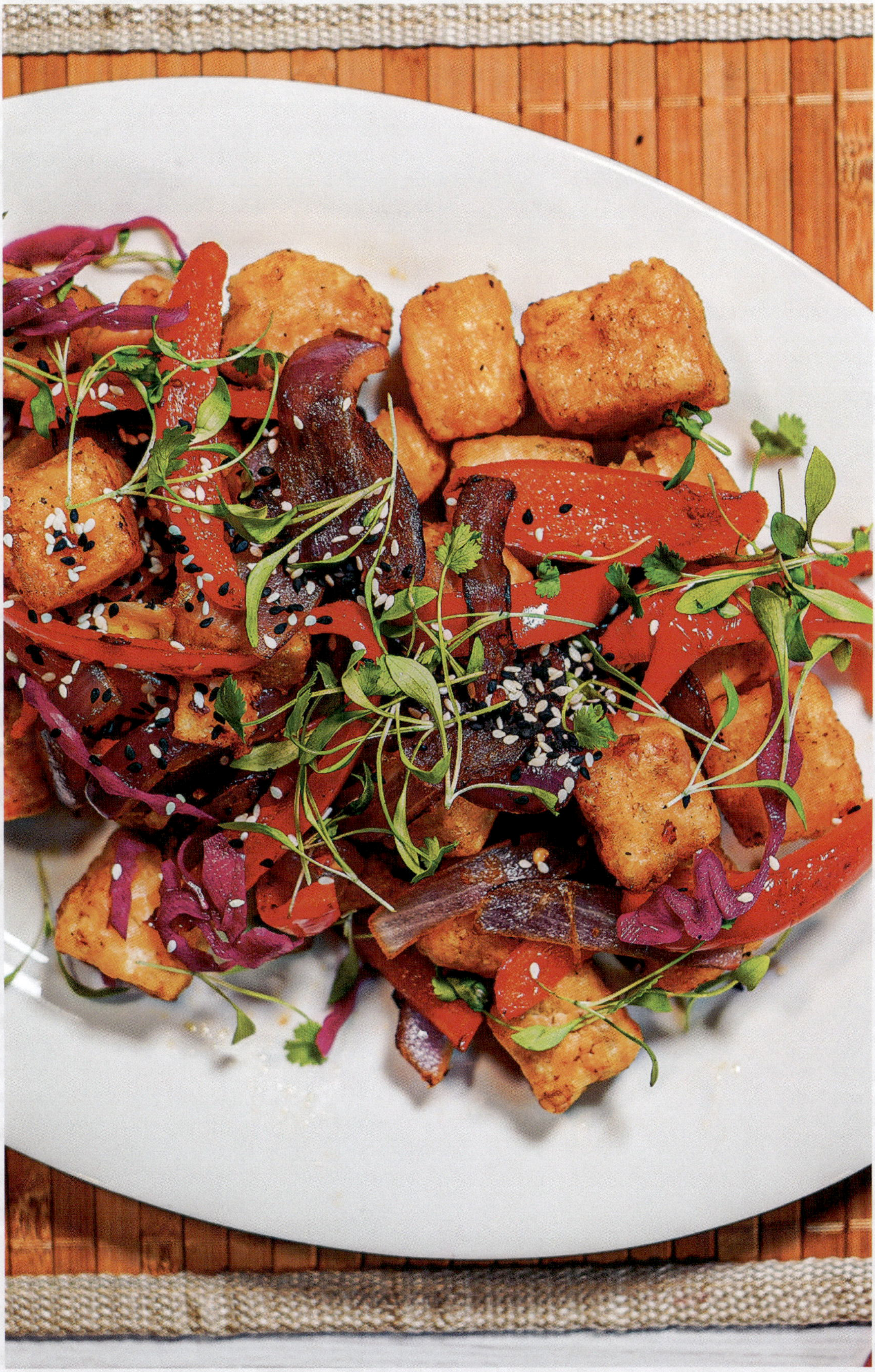

SALT AND PEPPER SWEET POTATO WEDGES

NUTS FREE · SOY FREE · GLUTEN FREE · REFINED SUGAR FREE

Salt and pepper seasoning works on almost anything, but these Salt and Pepper Sweet Potato Wedges are truly addictive. Naturally sweetened and caramelised on the outside, soft and fluffy on the inside, and spiced to perfection with our aromatic Chinese Salt and Pepper Seasoning. I've shared 2 different ways to make these wedges, the healthier way and plant-based junkie way for when you feel a bit naughty!!

3-4 Servings

EQUIPMENT NEEDED:

A chopping board, a sharp knife, a colander, a baking tray or fryer (optional).

INGREDIENTS:

3-4 Medium Sweet Potato, Wedged 3cm Thick
Olive Oil, dash for baking
Rapeseed oil for deep frying
Chinese Salt and Pepper Mix (see page 128)

To Garnish

Beansprouts
Red Chillies, Sliced
Spring Onions, Fine Slice, Half-Moon Angle
Sweet Pickled Cabbage, Drained (see page 136)
Coriander

Store in an airtight container for 4-5 days in the fridge.

The Healthy Way

Preheat the oven at 200c/390f/gas mark 6.

Meanwhile, wash sweet potatoes with a clean scourer to remove any dried soil off the skin.

Nib each end of the sweet potato with a sharp knife and cut into 2-3cm wedges, by cutting the potato in half-length ways and then in to 3-4 wedges either side, depending on size.

Line a medium baking tray and lay the sweet potatoes flat.

Season with salt and pepper and rub the tiniest amount of oil into the wedges.

Place in the oven for 18-20 minutes, flipping halfway.

Remove from the oven and add another good pinch of the seasoning, garnish with beansprouts, spring onions, chillies, pickled cabbage, and coriander.

Served with the Ultimate Beyond and as a side with our mains.

Plant Based Junkie Style

Pre-heat the fryer on 140c/275f to blanch (half cook) on low heat first.

Blanch the prepped wedges in the fryer for 5-6 minutes, take out the oil and allow to cool.

Raise the temperature to 190c/370f, once the oil is up to temperature, return the wedges and cook for a further 4-5 minutes until golden and crispy.

Drain well and place in a bowl or tray with some kitchen roll or a clean cloth to absorb excess oil, season well with Chinese Salt and Pepper Seasoning serve as above.

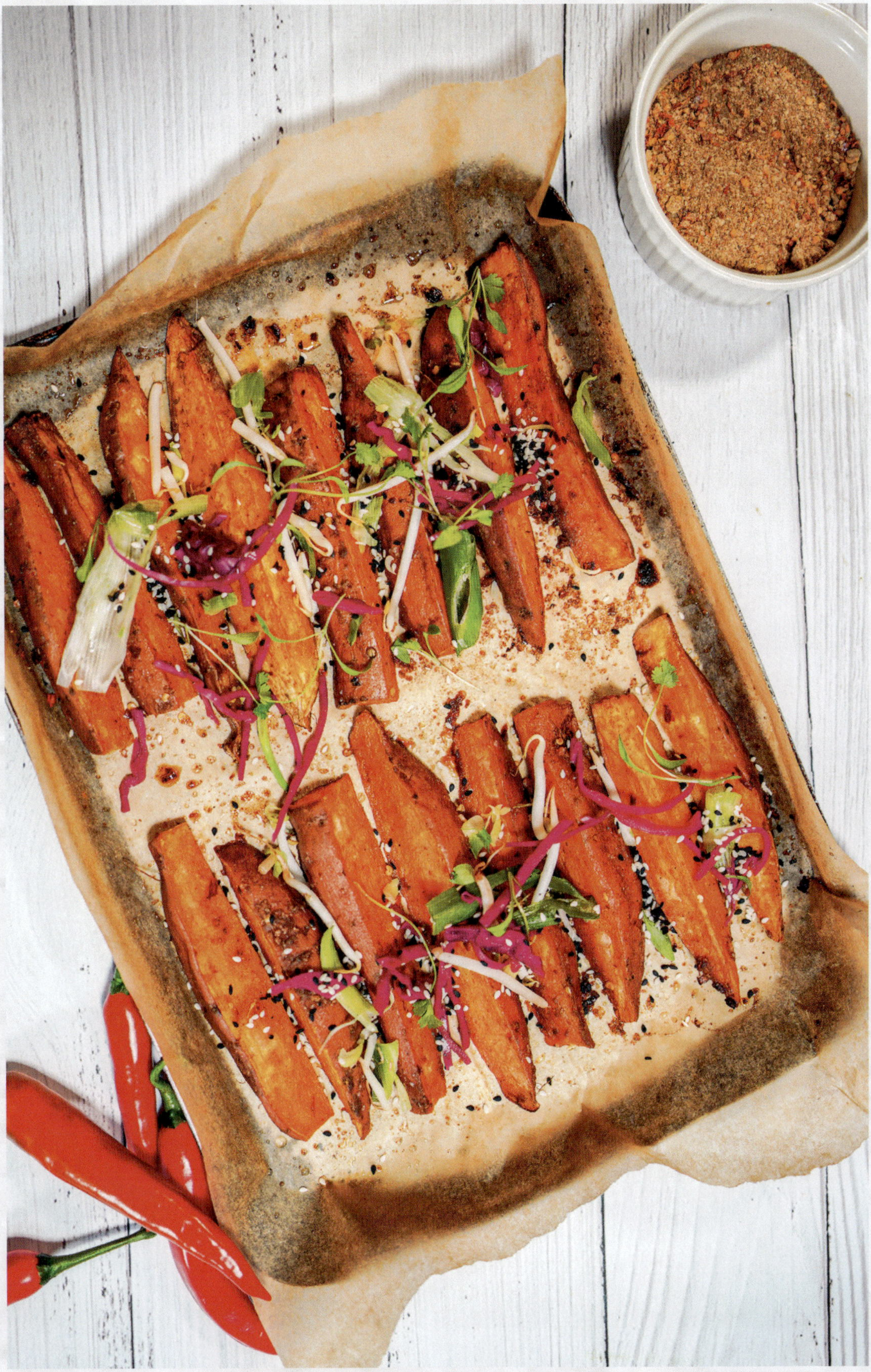

CHINESE SALT AND PEPPER SEASONING

An aromatic blend of chilli, garlic, Chinese 5 spice, salt, and pepper. This spice hit the streets of Liverpool when I was growing up and every chippy jumped on board with the 'Salt and Pepper' craze. It was salt and pepper everything, and still to this day. Liverpool is mad for the spice!

125g Servings

EQUIPMENT NEEDED:

A mixing bowl, a set of measuring cups, a whisk, and airtight jar.

INGREDIENTS:

2 Tbs Chilli Flakes
1 Tsp Mild Chilli Powder
1.5 Tbs Chinese 5 Spice
2 Tbs Garlic Powder
2 Tbs Onion Powder
3.5 Tbs White Pepper
6 Tbs Sea Salt

Mix all ingredients together in a mixing bowl, rubbing out any lump with fingers, you may want to wear gloves to avoid the heat from the chillies stinging your fingers. Wash hands straight away after handling chilli.

Store in an airtight container like a mason jar in a cool dark place for up to 6 months.

GOLDEN BATTER INGREDIENTS

EQUIPMENT NEEDED:
A small whisk, mixing bowl, a set of measuring cups.

INGREDIENTS:
1.5 Cups Gluten Free Self-Raising Flour
2.5 Cups Soda Water
½ Tsp Turmeric
½ Tsp Garlic Powder
½ Tsp Turmeric
½ Tsp Garlic Powder

Place all the dry ingredients into a large bowl and pour in the soda water, whisking until smooth and free from lumps, the batter should be a medium thickness, leaving a ribbon affect when mixing.

Use straight away or store in the fridge in an airtight container for 24 hours.

DUSTING FLOUR INGREDIENTS

EQUIPMENT NEEDED:
small whisk, mixing bowl, a set of measuring cups

INGREDIENTS:
2 Cups Gluten Free Self-Raising Flour
2 Cups Corn Flour
½ Tsp Turmeric
½ Tsp Garlic Powder
Pinch Of Sea Salt
Pinch Of Cracked Black Pepper

Mix all the ingredients together in a bowl making sure there are no lumps and set a side.

LOADED SWEET POTATO WEDGES

NUTS FREE · SOY FREE · GLUTEN FREE · REFINED SUGAR FREE

Sweet potato wedges, topped with all the Indigo favourites. This dish got us rave reviews from Liverpool Confidential back when we first opened and it's no surprise as it's packed with so many flavours, colours, and different textures. The combination of Chinky Pumpkin Seed Pesto, Traditional Hummus and Spicy Chipotle, with fresh herbs, crunchy bean sprouts, and tiny bursts of juicy sweetness from the pomegranate seeds leaves your mouth watering for more!!

3-4 Servings

EQUIPMENT NEEDED:
A chopping board, a sharp knife, a colander, a baking tray, or fryer (optional).

INGREDIENTS:
3-4 Sweet Potatoes
Olive Oil, dash for baking
Rapeseed oil for deep frying
Sea Salt to Taste
Pinch Of Cracked Black Pepper
3-4 Tbs Chipotle Sauce (see page 95)
3-4 Tbs Chunky Sunflower Seed Pesto (see page 90)
3-4 Tbs Creamy Smooth Hummus (see page 92)

To Garnish
Sweet Pickled Cabbage, Drained (see page 136)
Fresh Coriander
Pomegranate, Seeds
Sesame Seeds
Pumpkin Seeds, Toasted
Spring Onions, Fine Slice, Half-Moon Angle
Bean Spouts

Can be stored in fridge for 3-4 days.

Follow the instructions to make Sweet Potato Wedges (see page 118), no need to add the salt and pepper seasoning, unless you want to of course, but at Indigo we keep them plain as there's so many other toppings and flavours being loaded on.

Once the sweet potato wedges are cooked, stack the sweet potatoes on a plate nice and high, add a dollop of hummus to the centre of the wedges, circling the pesto and chipotle sauce around the hummus.

Stack the beansprouts, pickled cabbage, and spring onion in the centre to build height.

Finish with coriander, pomegranates, and seeds.

Serve immediately.

These are great for sharing!!

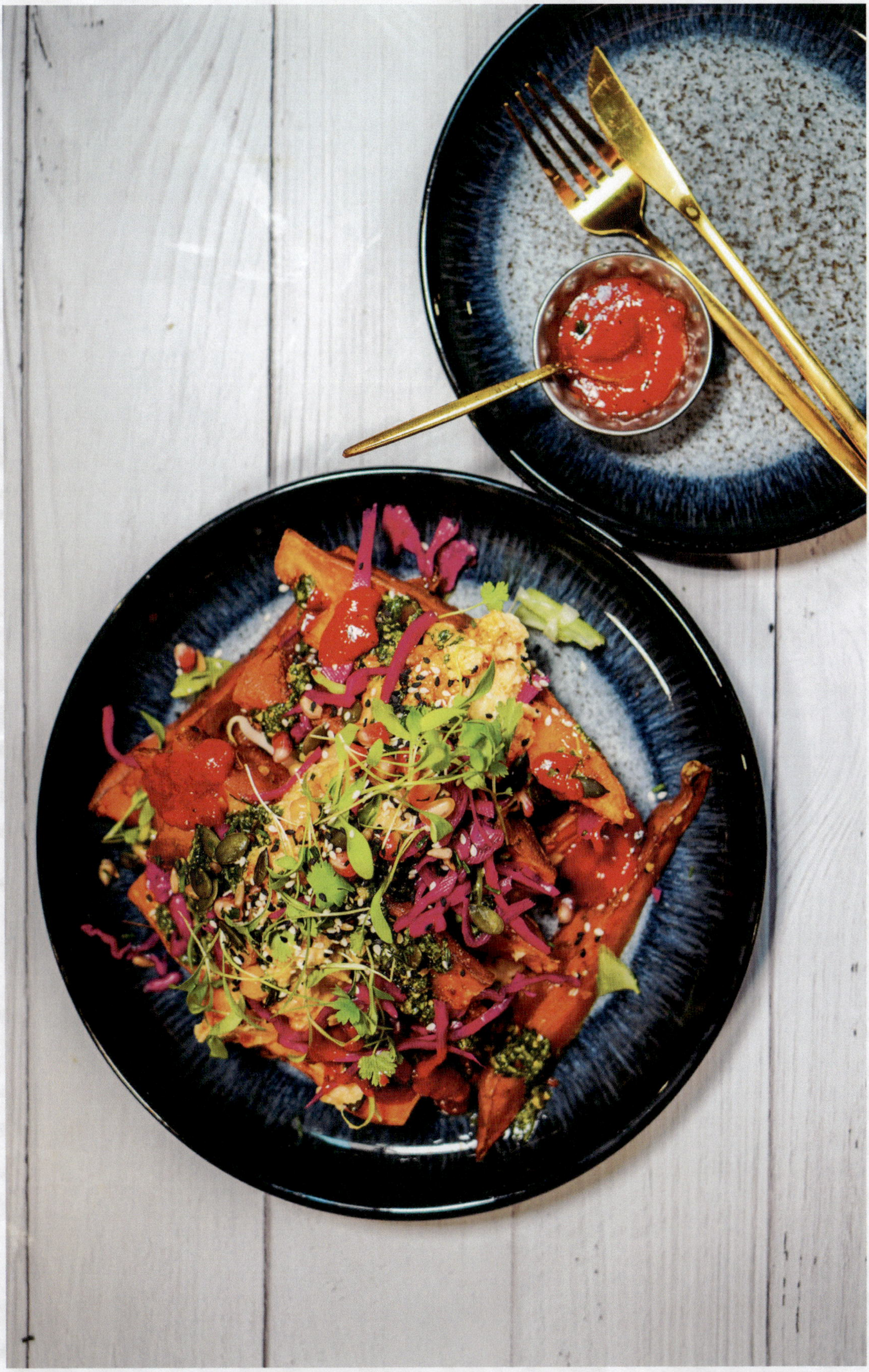

CRISPY KUNG PAO CAULI WINGS

NUTS FREE · GLUTEN FREE · REFINED SUGAR FREE

These sticky chilli wings are the perfect treat when you're trying to convert your meat-eating friends over to the vegan side, the right texture and flavour is all you need to entice them, and these wings have got it all. Tossed in our famous Kung Pao Sauce and topped with crunchy bean sprouts, spring onions, fresh coriander, pickled cabbage and chilli. This concoction of Asian ingredients makes these wings totally irresistible. I've given a couple of alternative ways to cook this recipe, the healthy way, the plant-based junkie way, and an even crunchier way! It's a little bit messy so roll your sleeves up and get your pinny on!

This recipe makes enough to share which is great as they are incredibly moreish!!

6-8 Servings

EQUIPMENT NEEDED:

A chopping board, a sharp knife, a colander, a baking tray, fryer (optional), 3-4 medium mixing bowls or deep trays, 2 sets of tongs, a set of measuring cups.

INGREDIENTS:

1 Medium Cauliflower, 2inch Florets
1 Batch Golden Batter (see page 129)
1 Batch Dusting Flour (see page 129)
Breadcrumbs, Gluten Free (optional for extra crunch)
1 Bunch Spring Onion, Thin Sliced on Angle
1 Small Bag Bean Sprouts
½ Cup Sweet Pickled Cabbage, Drained (see page 136)
1 Tbs Sesame Seeds
Olive Oil for baking
Rapeseed oil for deep frying
2 Red Chillies, Thinly Sliced on An Angle
1 Cup Kung Pao Sauce (see page 100)

Store in the fridge in an airtight jar for 3-4 days.

Method

Wash and prepare the cauliflower into small florets using knife, keeping as much as the stalk as possible.

Make the golden batter in a mixing bowl and toss in the cauliflower.

If you're choosing to bake, you can make the dusting flour or alternatively, if you want to take these wings up another notch and coat them in breadcrumbs for an even crunchier texture, prepare a bowl of breadcrumbs instead.

TIP - Always keep one hand exclusively for wet ingredients and the other hand for dry ingredients. That way, the ingredients won't mix and form a sticky paste around your fingers. Alternatively use 2 sets of tongs to avoid the mess.

The healthier way

Preheat the oven to 180c/350f/gas mark 4.

With one hand pick the cauliflower out of the batter, shaking off any excess, then toss the battered cauliflower into the bowl of dusting flour or breadcrumbs and use the other hand to scoop over the dry ingredients. When the cauliflower is fully coated place the cauliflower onto a lined baking tray using the dry hand, repeat until all cauliflower is done.

Drizzle with a small amount of oil and bake for 18-22 minutes, flipping halfway.

Plant Based Junkie Style

Set the fryer to 190c or 375f.

With one hand pick the cauliflower out of the batter, shake off any excess and carefully dip each piece of cauliflower halfway into the oil for 5 seconds before letting go, this will avoid the battered cauliflower getting stuck to the baskets. When repeating this step be careful not to overload the basket as they will stick together in one big clump.

Or alternately toss the battered cauliflower into the bowl of breadcrumbs and coat well.

Place directly in the basket with a small gap between each wing and cook for 5-6 minutes until golden brown and start to float.

Lift the basket and allow to drain well and then place them on a clean cloth or some kitchen roll to absorb any excess oil.

Once the cauliflowers are cooked either way, toss them in a mixing bowl with the Kung Poa Sauce and Sesame.

Dish out and garnish with spring onions, pickled red cabbage, coriander, and chilli.

Serve straight away and enjoy.

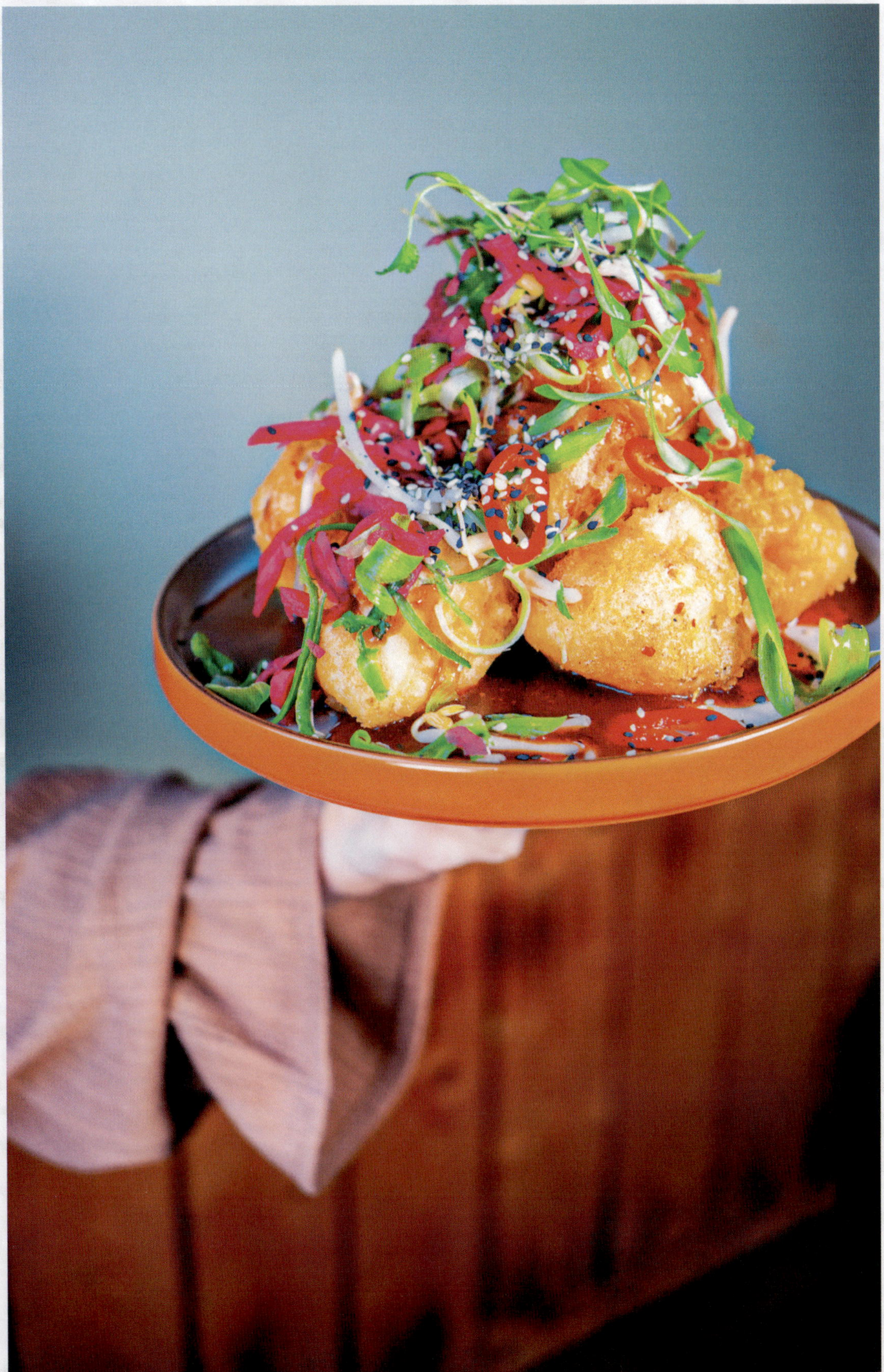

CASHEW MAC AND CHEESE

From one ex cheese lover to another, this macaroni will blow any dairy indulged mac and cheese out of the dairy farm with our famous Smoked Cashew Cheese recipe. Did you know that cheese/dairy is one of hardest animal-based products to give up for almost everyone trying to go vegan, that's due an addictive hormone in cow's milk, which entices the calf back to the udder. This is a clever hormone that helps the baby cow grow from a 60 lb pound calf to a 450 lb cow in just a couple of months? No wonder obesity and heart disease are the number one killers in the world today. Cows stop drinking milk after 2-3 months of age as it's extremely hard to digest, they naturally move on to feed from graze and water. So, why are we, as humans, conditioned to keep consuming milk and other dairy products throughout adulthood?

4 Servings

EQUIPMENT NEEDED:

A medium saucepan, a set of measuring cups, chopping board, sharp knife.

INGREDIENTS:

4 Cups Macaroni Pasta, Cooked
8 Tbs Smoked Cashew Cheese (see page 101)
2 Cups Water or Plant Based Milk
Sea Salt to Taste
Pinch of Cracked Black Pepper
Chives, Fine Sliced
Crispy Onions

Firstly, cook your pasta for the required cooking time and drain, add a dash of oil to stop the pasta sticking.

Place the pasta back into the pan with the cashew cheese and the liquid, cook on a medium to high heat and bring to the boil, keep stirring until you reach a creamy consistency.

If it becomes too thick add a dash of liquid to loosen.

Season and serve straight away, garnishing with chives and crispy onions.

Allow proper cooling before storing.

Store in an airtight container in the fridge for 3-4 days.

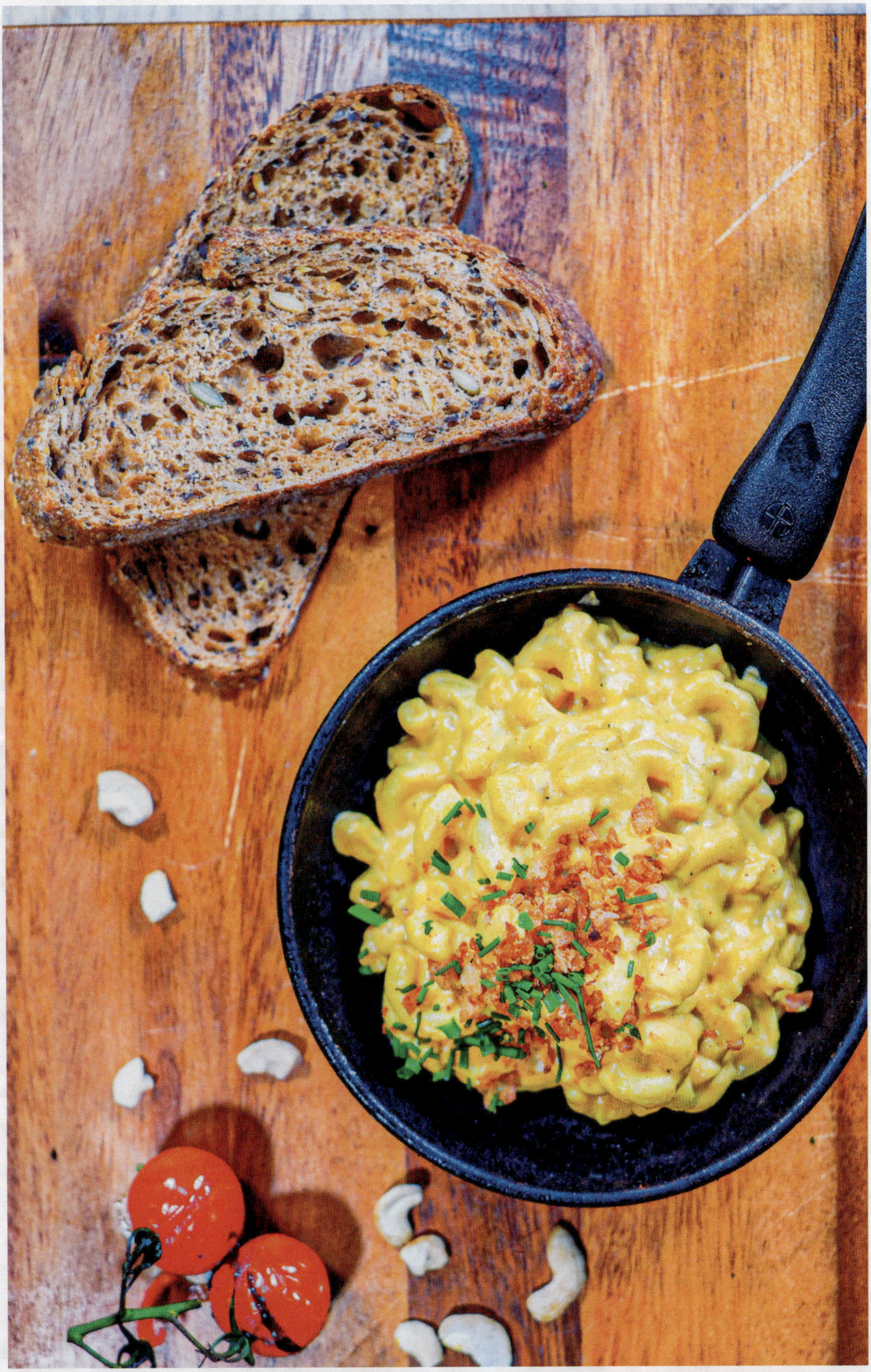

SWEET PICKLED CABBAGE

NUTS FREE *SOY FREE* *GLUTEN FREE* *REFINED SUGAR FREE*

Don't be put off by the word pickled, so many people avert if something's pickled, but our sweet and lightly spiced liquor brings our cabbage to life - adding so much more crunch, colour, and depth to any dish. Pickling food has been around for centuries and was a clever way to preserve food in the olden days. Our ancestors were onto something for sure as pickling food wards off harmful bacteria, not only in the food but in our gut too.

800g Servings

EQUIPMENT NEEDED:

A chopping board, sharp knife, or mandolin, strainer, large saucepan, a 1 litre airtight jar for storing, measuring jug.

INGREDIENTS:

1 Small Red Cabbage Red, Fine Sliced
5 Dried Bay Leaves
1 Tbs Peppercorns
2 Tbs Mustard Seeds
3 Tbs Fennel Seeds
600ml Water
300ml White Wine Vinegar
300ml Rice Wine Vinegar
100ml Maple Syrup

Store in an airtight jar for 1 month in the fridge.

Place the seeds in a large saucepan on medium heat and toast for 10-20 seconds allowing aromas to release. Add the water first to the pan, and then the rest of the ingredients, bring to boil and simmer for 20 mins. Take off heat and allow it to fully cool.

Meanwhile, peel the outer layers of the cabbage, and discard.

Carefully cut the cabbage into quarters and discard the thick white core and fine slice using a mandolin or a very sharp knife, the finer the cabbage the better.

Once complete squeeze the cabbage into a 1 litre mason jar or alternatively a large bowl and push down tightly.

Once the pickled liquor is completely cold, strain out most of the seeds and leaves and carefully pour the liquor over the cabbage making sure it's completely submerged for 12-24 hours before eating.

You may reuse the pickling liquor once again if you wish to save time in future.

Served with our Blind Scouse (see page 106), Rainbow Earth Bowl (112), The Ultimate Beyond Burger (see page 120) or just as a side dish.

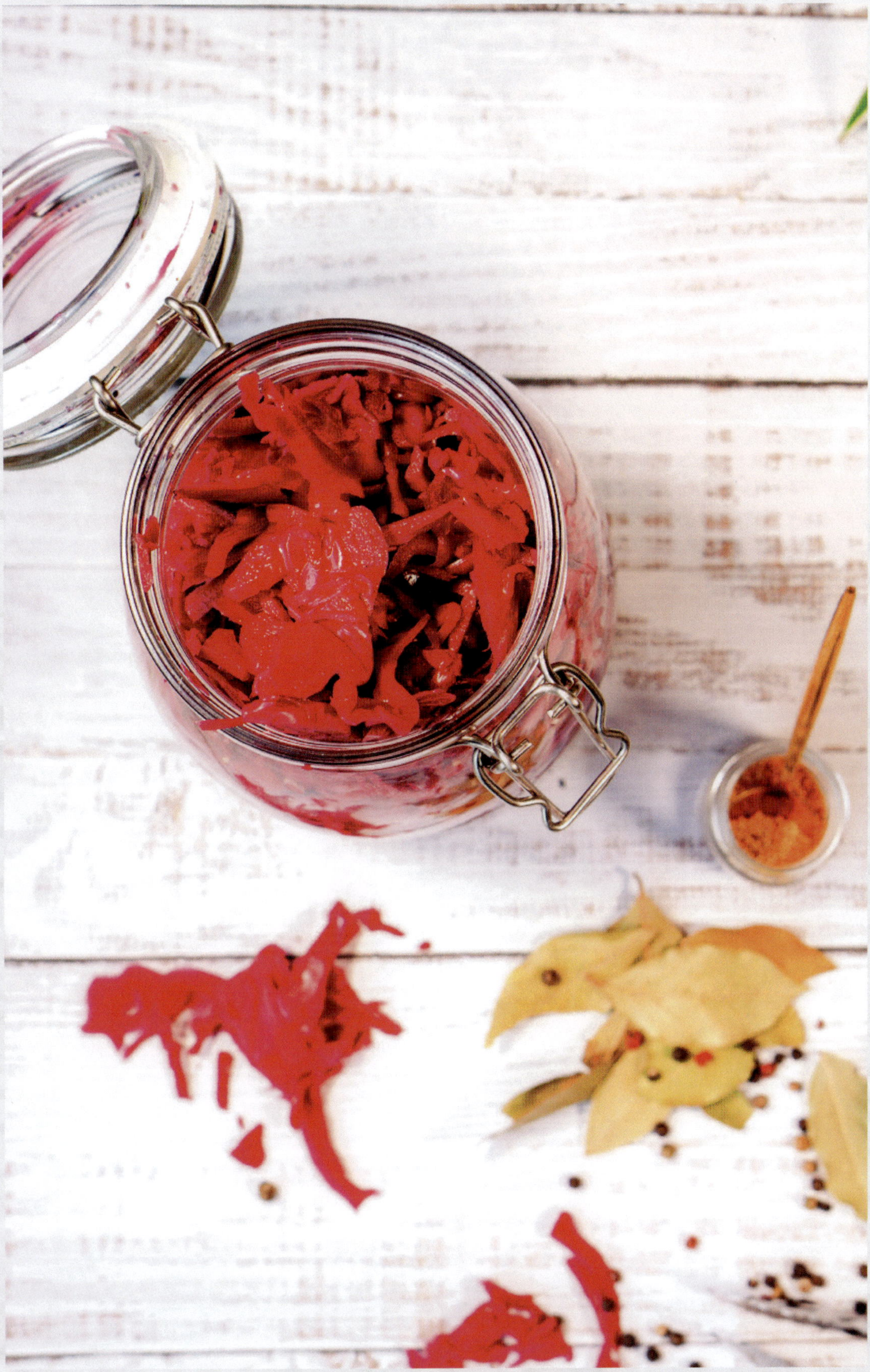

SPICY KALE SLAW

NUTS FREE · SOY FREE · GLUTEN FREE · REFINED SUGAR FREE

An Indigo twist on the traditional, shop bought, coleslaw that made its way into many homes. Swapping out the cabbage for kale in this recipe sends the health benefits through the roof due to kale's high concentration of vitamins and minerals. But, did you know that this popular dark, leafy, green is extremely hard to digest raw? The cellular structure is quite tough for the body to break down, so be sure to give it some love and literally massage the leaves before eating them. By rubbing the leaves, this breaks down its resilient fabrication and you will see the matt looking surface soften and turn glossy once they're ready to consume.

800g Servings

EQUIPMENT NEEDED:

A chopping board, sharp knife, box grater, mixing bowl, colander, peeler.

INGREDIENTS:

100g (1 bag) Curly Kale, Pulled, Massaged, Fine Sliced
3 Large Carrots, Grated
1 Large Red Onion, Fine Sliced
8-10 Tbs Burger Sauce (see page 95)
Sea Salt to Taste
Pinch Of Cracked Black Pepper

Wash and prepare all ingredients.

To prepare the kale, pull the leaves off the stalk, and massage vigorously, rubbing the leaves for around 2-3 mins between your fingers until the leaves soften.

Carefully slice the kale as fine as possible using a sharp knife.

Mix the kale and burger sauce together in a mixing bowl and season.

Serve and Enjoy.

Served on our Rainbow Earth Bowl (see page 112) and The Ultimate Beyond Burger (see page 120).

Store in the fridge in an airtight jar for 4-5 days.

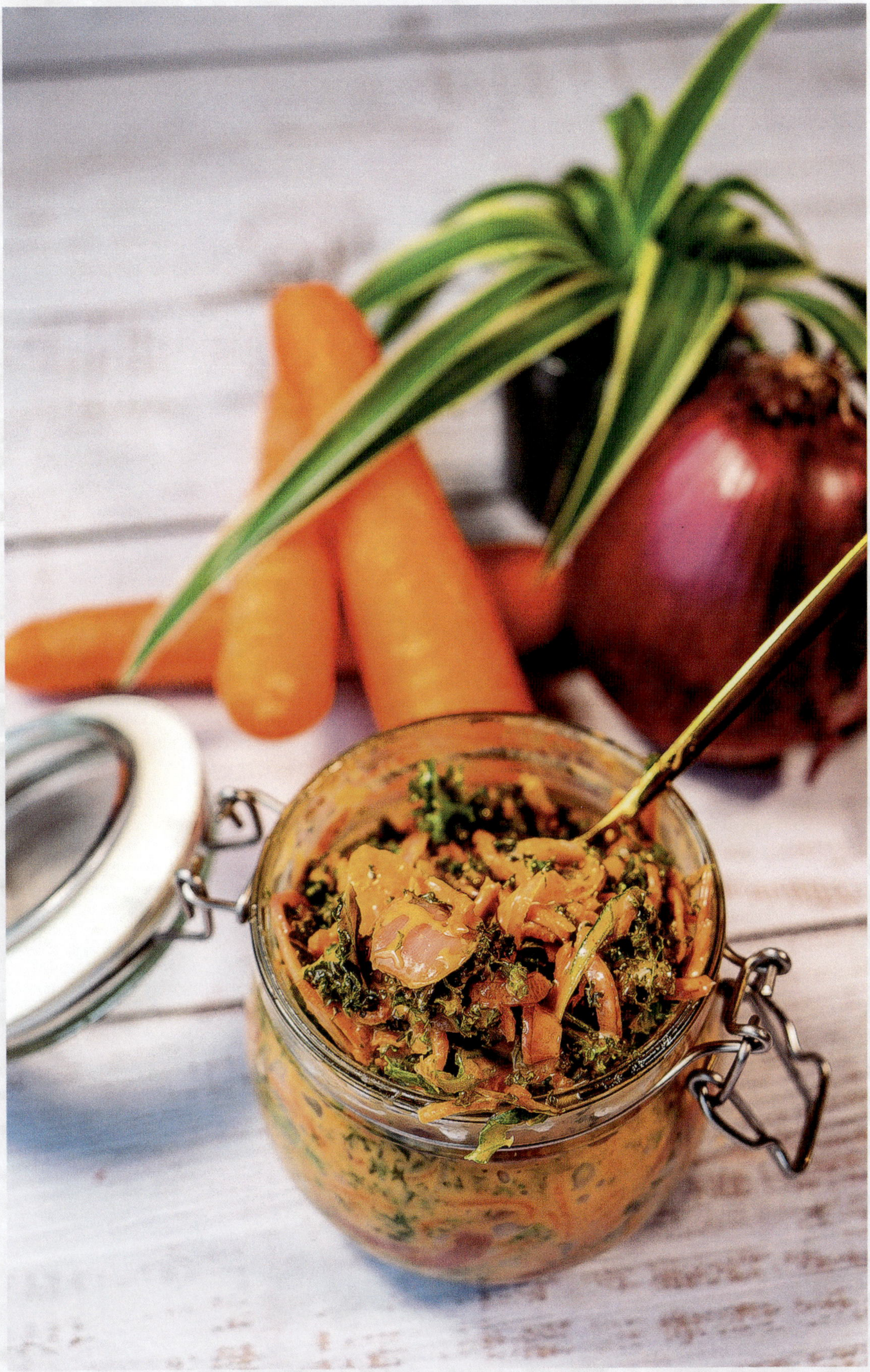

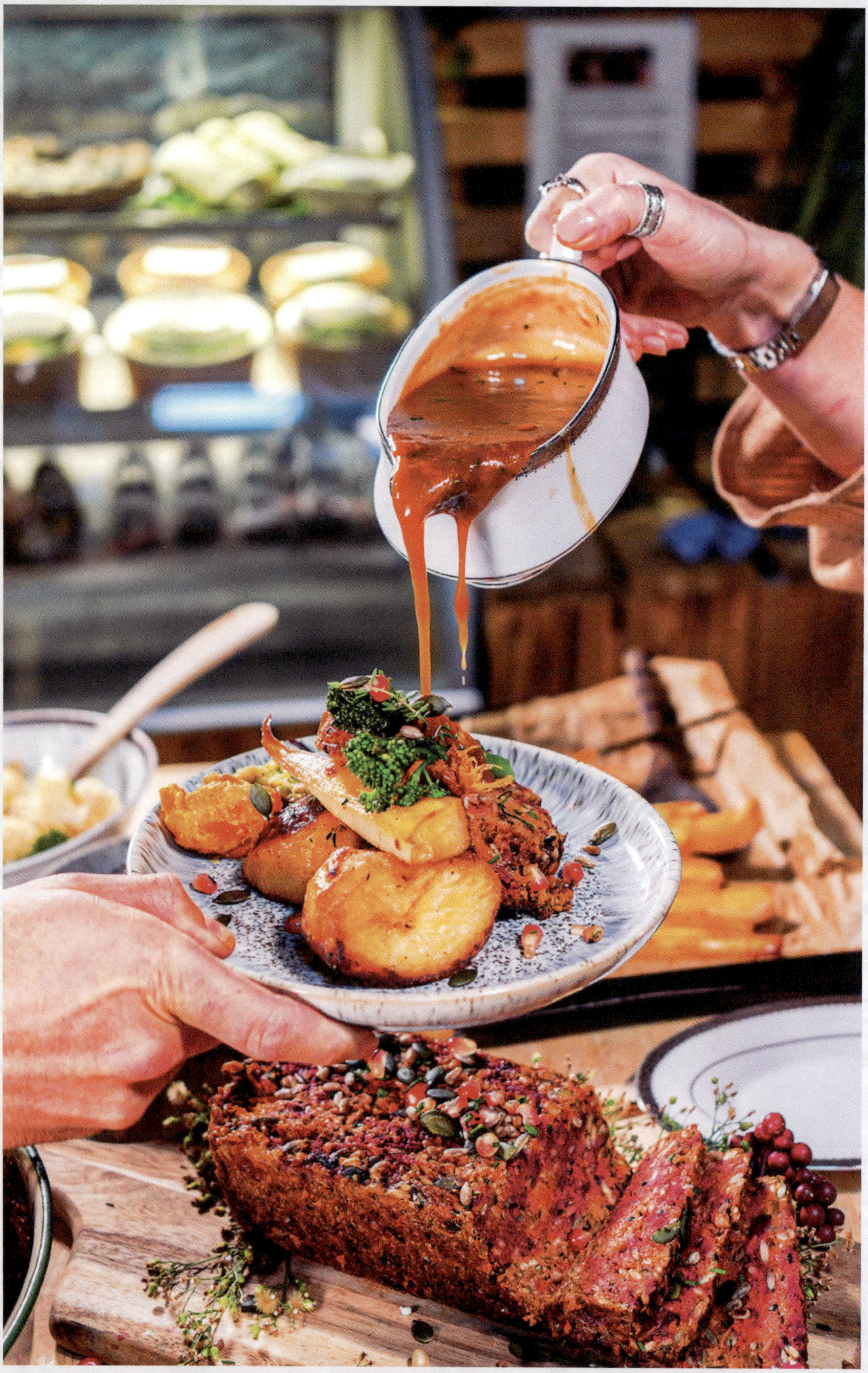

RAINBOW ROAST DINNER

When the Autumn months sneak in, there's nothing more consoling than a good old Sunday Roast Dinner with loved ones. Traditionally 'Roast Dinners' are completely based around the meat component, and quite often people say 'a Roast Dinner without meat, what do you have then?' with a confused look. Sadly, people don't realise that everything on a Roast Dinner is pretty much plant based apart from the dead animal in the middle of the table, and it is often thought the vegetables are just there to fill the plate.

But when it comes to our Rainbow Roast, every single component plays a perfect role in bringing the sensational flavours of Autumn and Winter together. The colours showcase high vibe nutrition, the flavours reveal real food made with love and the heart of our dinner table presents a karma free feast that goes against most family traditions.

LENTIL, CRANBERRY AND ORANGE NUT-LESS ROAST

NUTS FREE · SOY FREE · GLUTEN FREE · REFINED SUGAR FREE

This show stopping centrepiece strikes a delicious balance of sweet and savoury notes, a fantastic blend of fruits, herbs, veggies, lentils, and seeds. Originally, we made this recipe with cashew and peanuts, but with allergies on the rise, we decided to swap them out and replace them with lots of essential super seeds. This way so no one was ever left out. In this recipe we have used a perfect combination of seeds, grains and vegetables to create an ideal ratio of protein, carbs and fibres. Which, shape and slice into the most perfect plant-based roast that will certainly turn heads at the dinner table.

Tip: The foundations of this recipe must remain the same to ensure the right consistency is achieved when baking, but the seeds, spices and fruits can be mixed and matched to whatever is in your pantry.

2 loaves

EQUIPMENT NEEDED:

A chopping board, sharp knife, strainer, 2 medium saucepans, bowls to soak, a set of measuring cups, 2 x bread tins, a box grater, a measuring jug, a large deep sided tray, or large mixing bowl.

INGREDIENTS:

1 Medium Sweet Potato, Peeled, Small Diced,

1 Medium Beetroot, Peeled, Fine Grated,

1 Cup Puy Lentils

4 Cups Rolled Oats, Gluten Free

500ml Orange Juice, Not from Concentrate

½ Cup Dried Cranberries

2 Tbs Garlic Powder

½ Smoked Paprika

3 Tsp Oregano

1 Tbs Wholegrain Mustard

2 Tsp Sesame Seeds

¼ Tsp Nutmeg

½ Tsp Cinnamon

8 Tbs Hemp Seeds, shelled

8 Tbs Pumpkin Seeds

8 Tbs Sunflower Seeds

Sea Salt To Taste

Pinch Of Cracked Black Pepper

Pre-soak the pumpkin seeds in cold water for a minimum of 8 hours in the fridge or simply overnight before starting this recipe, rinse well once soaked. Also, pre-soak the lentils and sunflower seeds in separate bowls in cold water for 2 hours and rinse well before use. Optional but advised (see page 20 for information on the benefits of soaking).

Pre-heat the oven 180c/350f/ gas mark 4.

Wash and prepare the vegetables as stated.

Place the sweet potatoes in a small saucepan, fill with just enough cold water to cover and bring to the boil for 12-15 minutes until soft but retaining a bite, and allow to cool.

Once the lentils are soaked, rinse well and place in a small saucepan, fill with just enough cold water to cover and boil for 15-20 minutes, until soft but with a bite and allow to cool.

Meanwhile measure out the rest of your ingredients into a large mixing bowl.

Add the cooked lentils, sweet potato, grated beetroot, orange juice and soaked seeds to the mixing bowl and mix until all the ingredients are combined, leave for half an hour whilst the oats soak up all the moisture.

Line a bread tin with parchment paper, rubbing some coconut oil on the tin to hold the paper in place and add the mix, pack down tightly, cover with foil ensuring the foil is not directly touching the mix, use grease-proof paper as a barrier and place in in the oven for 90 minutes on the middle shelf.

After 45 minutes carefully remove paper and foil, cook for a further 45 minutes.

Remove from the oven, and allow to rest for 15-20 minutes before slicing to prevent crumbling.

At Indigo we then grill the slices on either side for 4 minutes until golden and crisp before serving but it can be served after resting.

Serve and enjoy!

This mix can also be used to make burgers, or if you have any left-over slices of Nut Roast try wrapping them in a tortilla with some of our Traditional Hummus (see page 92), Chunky Pumpkin Seeds Pesto (see page 90), and Caramelised Onion Chutney (86) it's a treat!

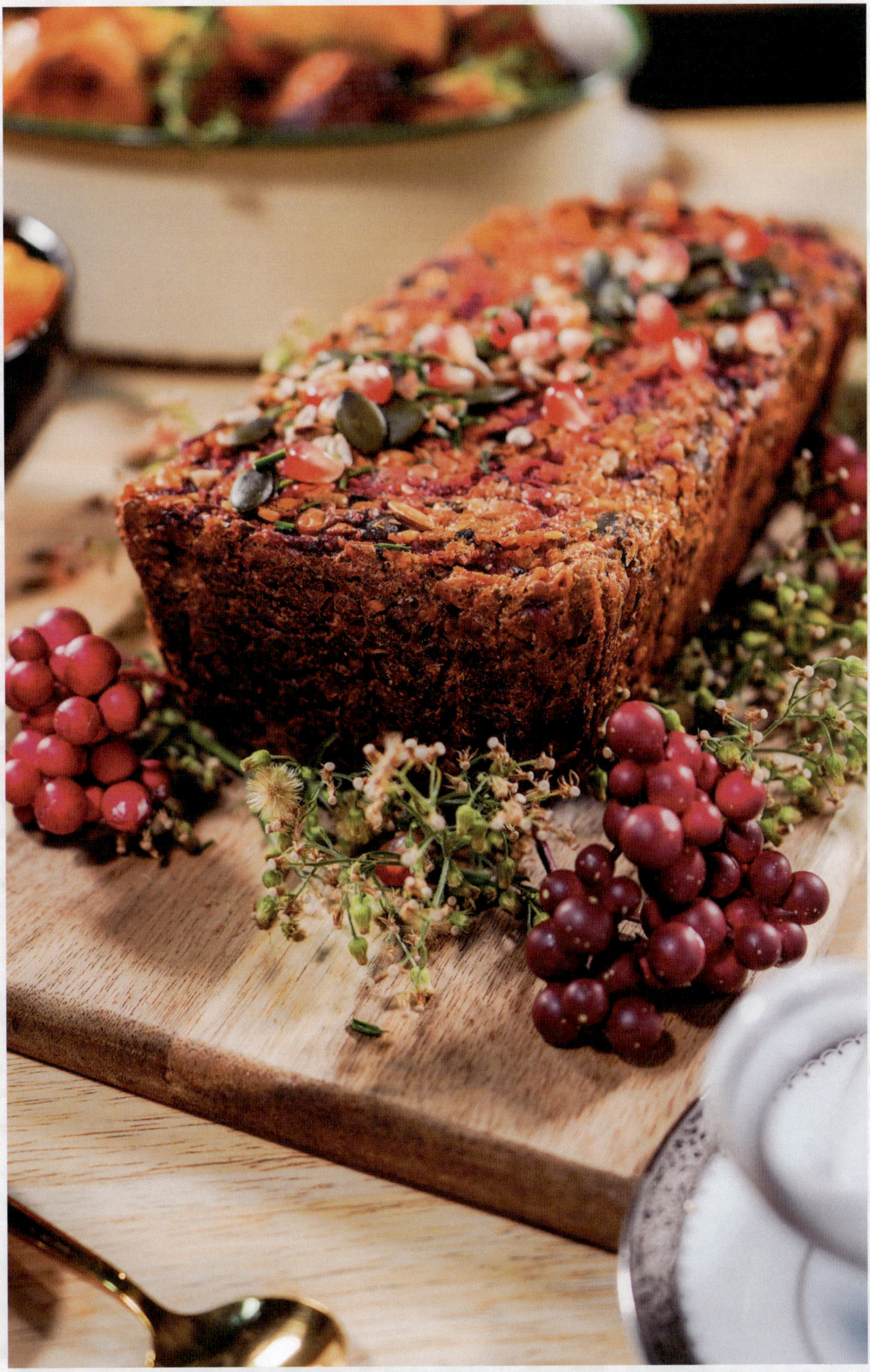

GARLIC, LEMON AND HERB ROAST POTATOES

NUTS FREE — SOY FREE — GLUTEN FREE — REFINED SUGAR FREE

Roast potatoes, it's all about the roast potatoes! Soft and fluffy on the inside, golden, crispy, and crunchy on the outside. We boil ours just until they are about good enough to mash, this is key for the rustle. Rubbed and marinated in fresh garlic, lemon, rosemary, and thyme. Now I know you may be questioning the use of lemon on a Roast Dinner, but the infusion of the citrus fruit flavours is just sensational.

6-8 Servings

EQUIPMENT NEEDED:

A chopping board, sharp knife, colander, large pan, large deep sided baking tray, a garlic crusher, a peeler.

INGREDIENTS:

2.5kg Red Rooster Potatoes, Peeled, Quartered
½ Lemon
10 Stalks Thyme, Roughly Chopped
5 Stalks Rosemary, Roughly Chopped
6-8 Cloves Garlic, Minced
1 Cup of Olive Oil
Sea Salt to Taste
Pinch Of Cracked Black Pepper

Can be stored in an airtight container in the fridge for 4-5 days.

Wash and peel the potatoes, cut into large even sized pieces, and rinse away any starch.

Place the potatoes into a large pan with enough water in to cover them 2 inches, add a generous pinch of salt, 1 sprig of rosemary and a smashed garlic clove or 2 to infuse while cooking.

Bring the water up to the boil, boil rapidly for about 3 minutes, then lower to a gentle simmer for around 15-20 minutes or until potatoes are falling off a sharp knife.

Preheat the oven at 200c/400c/gas 6 and place a large roasting tray in the oven with the oil, make sure the tray is big enough to spread the potatoes out in a single layer.

Once the potatoes are cooked, drain in a colander, and let them air dry for a few minutes, gently shaking the colander back and forth a few times to get them nice and fluffy.

Carefully rub the minced garlic into the potatoes using your hands.

Take the tray with the hot oil out the oven and carefully place in the potatoes, spooning over the hot oil so they are fully covered and start to bubble all over.

Add the herbs, and squeeze the juice from half a lemon evenly over the potatoes, toss the skin in the tray too, season well.

Make sure to spread the potatoes evenly in a single layer with plenty of room between them so they can cook evenly.

Place in the oven for 60 minutes on the middle shelf to start with, the carefully flip them over and roast again for a further 30-60 minutes or however long it takes to get them to reach a crunchy golden-brown texture or your desired colour and crispness.

Serve with all our Sunday roast trimmings and enjoy.

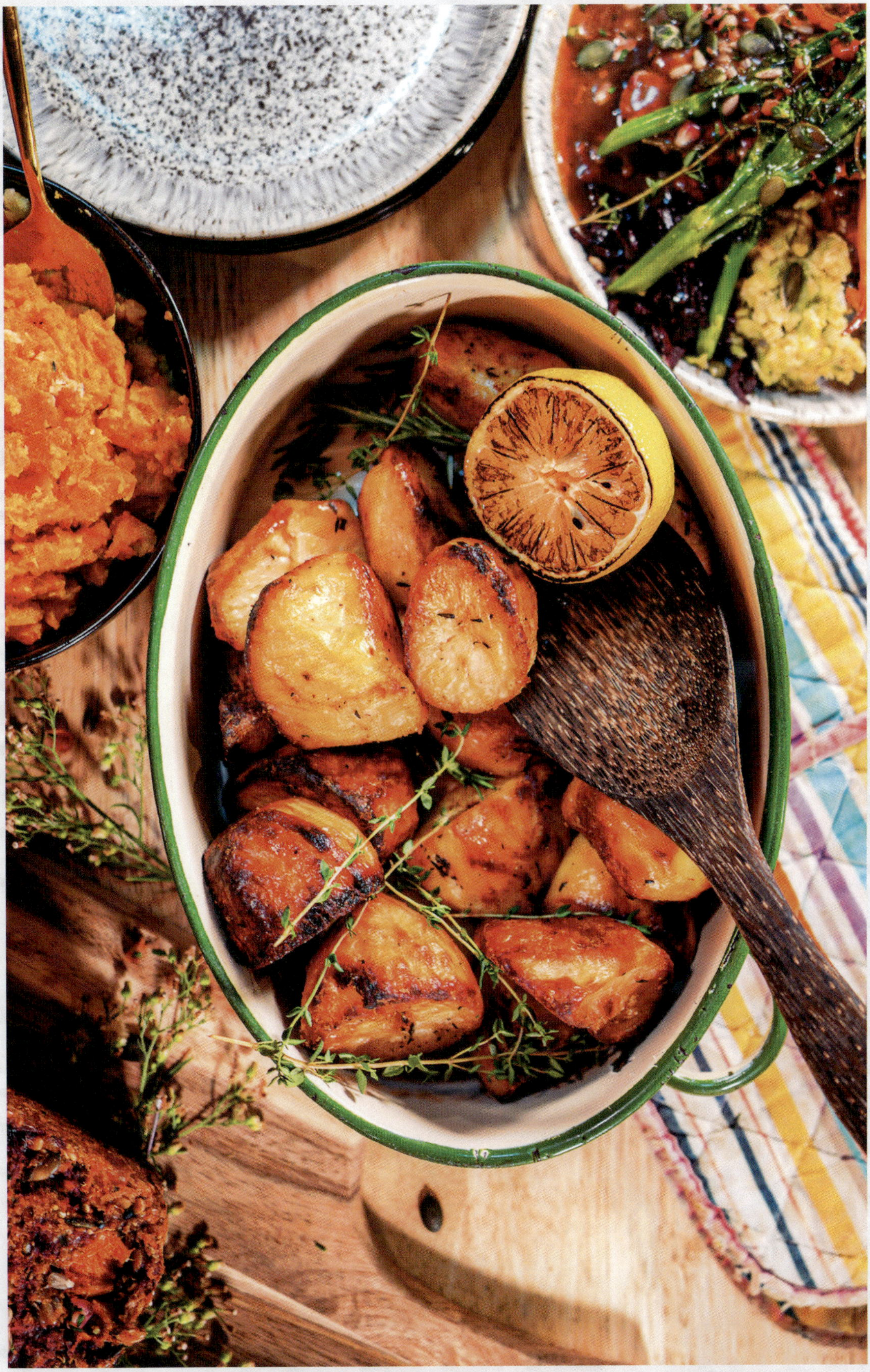

BUTTERY CARROT AND SWEDE MASH

Carrot and Swede mash takes me right back to my family kitchen, it was always my favourite side veg growing up, along with sprouts, believe it or not. When my mum made it, she spiced it with freshly grated nutmeg, which just gave the dish so much more depth. Nutmeg is one of those spices that have been found to increase mood and the link between food and mood is becoming so much more apparent now. Nutmeg, like most herbs and spices, contain high amounts of anti-inflammatory properties which help relieve stress, anxiety, and depression.

125g Servings

EQUIPMENT NEEDED:

A chopping board, sharp knife, colander, large pan.

INGREDIENTS:

5 Large Carrots, Sliced 1-2cm Chunks
½ Swede, Chopped 2-3cm Chunks
5 Tbs Plant Butter
Pinch Of Fresh or Dried Nutmeg
Sea Salt to Taste
Pinch Of Cracked Black Pepper

Store in an airtight container in the fridge for 4-5 days or freeze for up to 3months.

Wash and prepare vegetables, chopping the carrots a little bit smaller than the swede as they are more dense.

Place carrot and swede in a pot and add enough cold water to cover them by 2 inches, add a pinch of salt to the water and place on a high heat.

Bring to the boil and cook for 40-50-minutes until both vegetables fall from a sharp knife easily.

Carefully drain into a colander and let them air dry for a couple of minutes. Place them back in the pan on a low heat, add the butter and nutmeg, season well.

Using a masher, start to mash your vegetables right down, making sure the pan doesn't catch on the heat (this is a technique to remove any excess moisture from the vegetables).

Serve straight away and enjoy or allow proper cooling before storing.

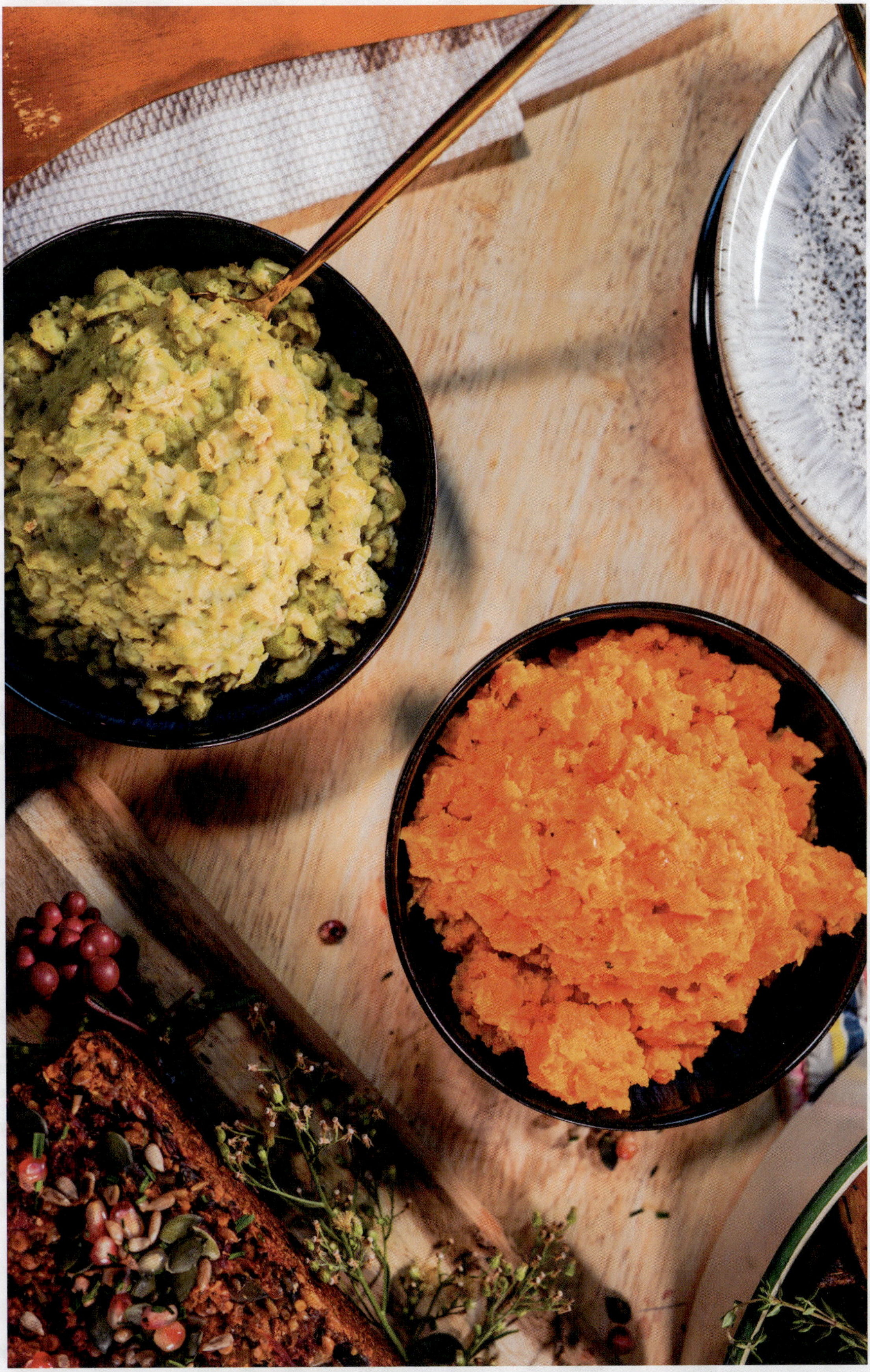

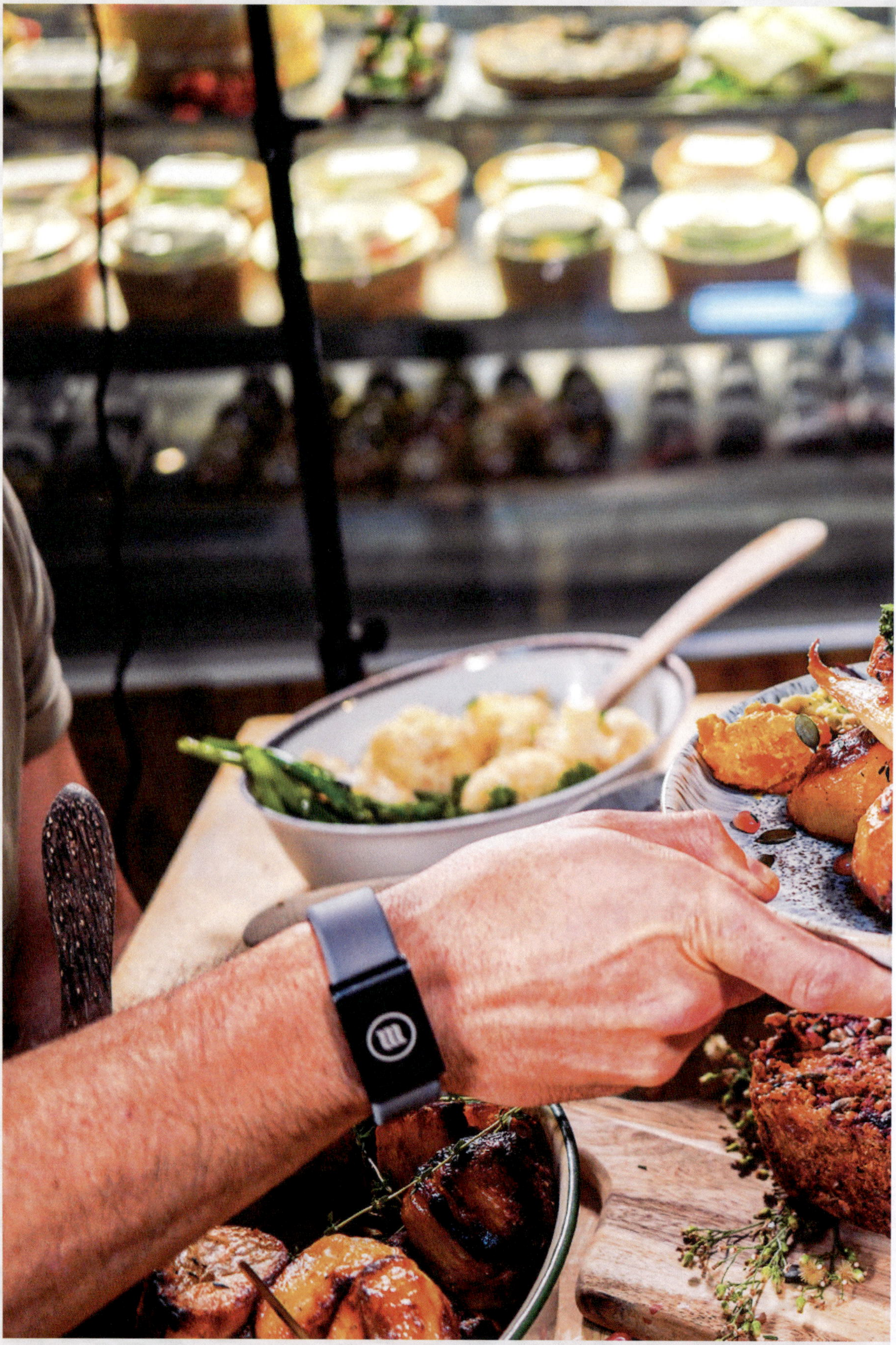

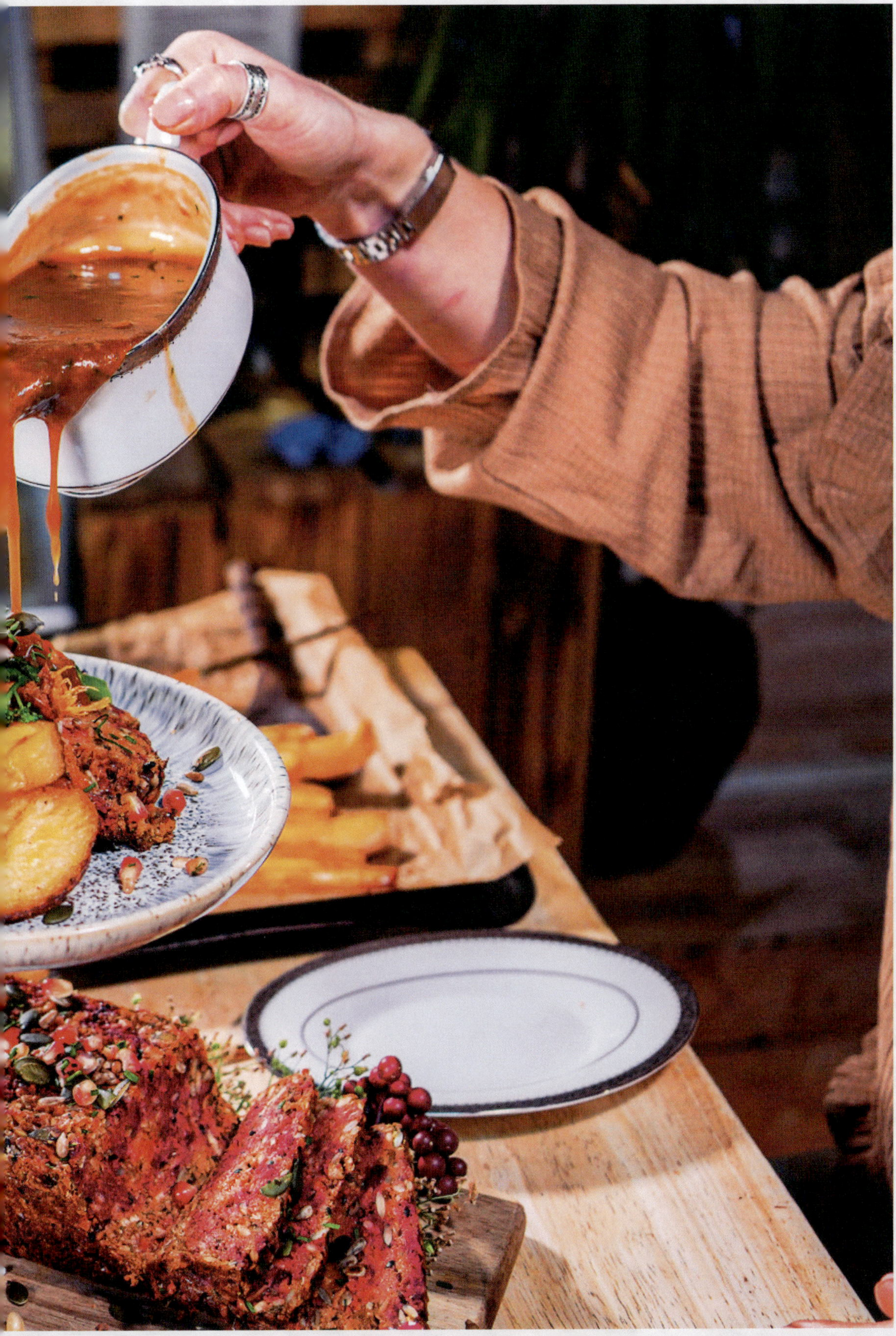

SWEET CUMIN ROASTED PARSNIPS

NUTS FREE · SOY FREE · GLUTEN FREE · REFINED SUGAR FREE

These golden roasted parsnips are the perfect earthy treat and most definitely a must on your Sunday Roast Dinner! Sweet and nutty with a hint of warmth coming through from the cumin. Cumin seeds are an extremely dense source of iron which many adults are lacking, it also promotes a healthy gut by increasing the activity of digestive enzymes which speed up digestion.

6-8 Servings

EQUIPMENT NEEDED:

A chopping board, sharp knife, colander, large pan, medium baking tray.

INGREDIENTS:

4 Medium Parsnips, Sliced Length Ways
1 Tsp Cumin Seeds
4 Tbs Maple Syrup
Water, Splash
Olive Oil
Sea Salt to Taste
Pinch Of Cracked Black Pepper

Store in an airtight container in the fridge for 4-5 days.

Wash and prepare parsnips, no need to peel, just cut lengthways into 1/4s or 1/6s depending on their size.

Place in a pan and add enough water to cover them by 1 inch, add a pinch of salt and bring to the boil, once boiling, reduce to a simmer and cook for 15 minutes or until they fall from a sharp knife.

Meanwhile preheat the oven on 180c/350f/gas mark 4.

Once cooked, carefully drain the parsnips into a colander and let them air dry for a couple of minutes.

Place on to a lined baking tray, drizzle with maple, olive oil, cumin seeds, salt and pepper and add a dash of water to stop the maple syrup burning.

Place in the oven for 15-20 minutes, on the middle shelf, until golden brown.

Serve straight away and enjoy, or allow proper cooling before storing.

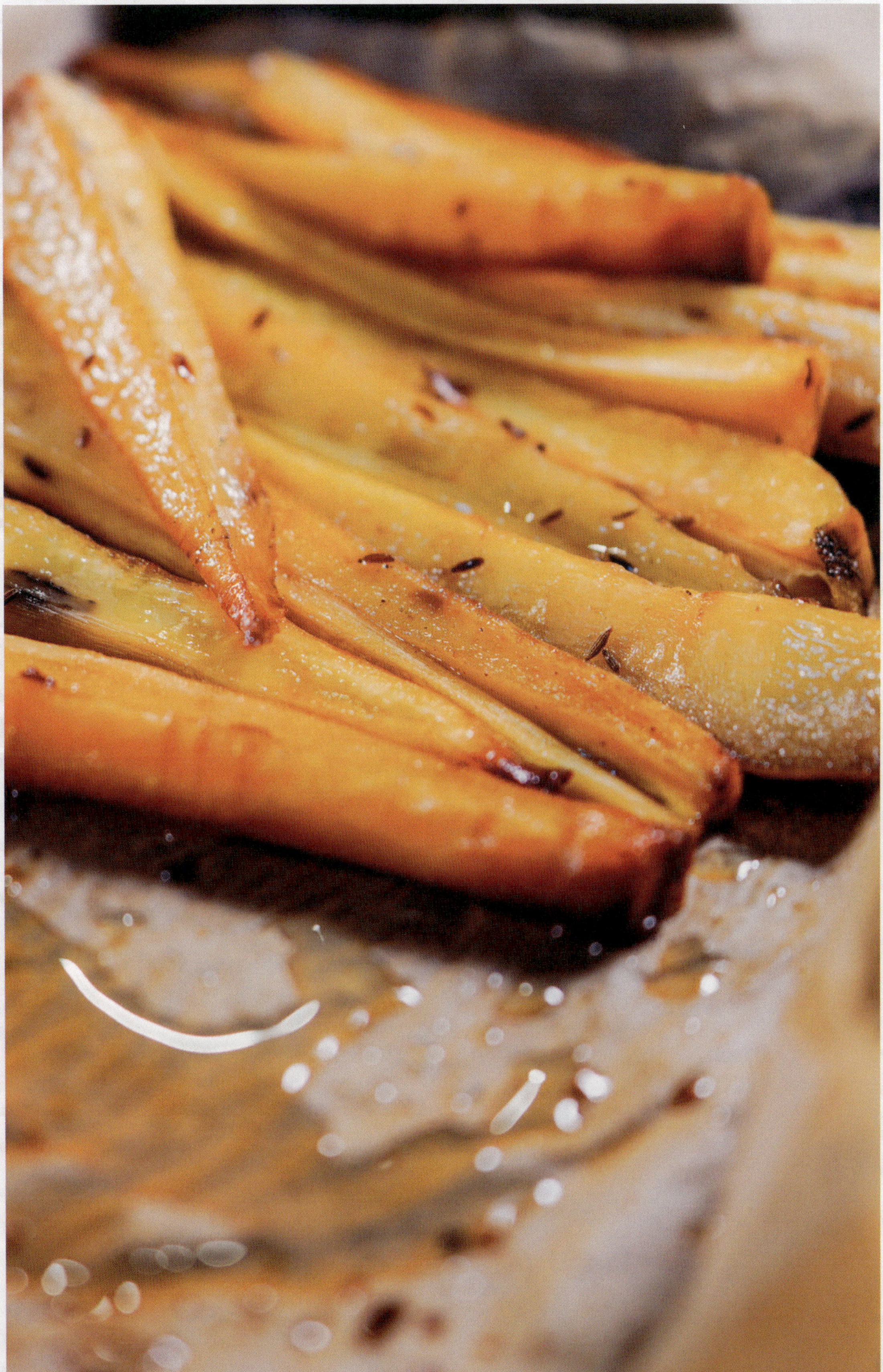

SWEET BRAISED RED CABBAGE

NUTS FREE | SOY FREE | GLUTEN FREE | REFINED SUGAR FREE

A wonderful sweet and savoury blend of flavours with just the right amount of tanginess, lifting any dish it's paired with. A light and fruity concoction that not only looks and tastes sensational, but it also takes very little effort to make. It is cost effective and is super high in essential minerals and vitamins.

7-8 Servings

EQUIPMENT NEEDED:

A chopping board, sharp knife or mandolin, large heavy based pan, measuring jug.

INGREDIENTS:

1 Small Red Cabbage, Quartered, Fine Sliced
200ml Balsamic Vinegar
200ml Orange Juice
1 Cinnamon Stick
Pinch Nutmeg
1 Tbs Plant Butter
¼ Cup Maple Syrup
Sea Salt to Taste
Pinch Of Cracked Black Pepper

Peel the outer layers of the cabbage, discard and rinse the remainder.

Carefully cut the cabbage in to quarters with a sharp knife and remove the white chunky core.

Finely slice the cabbage on a mandolin or with a very sharp knife and add to a medium sized, heavy based pan with the rest of the ingredients except the butter, the liquid should be halfway below cabbage level, place a piece of grease proof over the cabbage and then foil tightly.

Place the pan on a medium heat and cook for 35-45 minutes until all the liquid has reduced, checking regularly after 30mins.

Once all the liquid has evaporated, you should be left with a sticky cabbage, season and stir in the butter, this will make the cabbage nice and glossy

Serve and enjoy or allow proper cooling before storing.

Store in an airtight container in the fridge for 4-5 days or freeze for up to 3months.

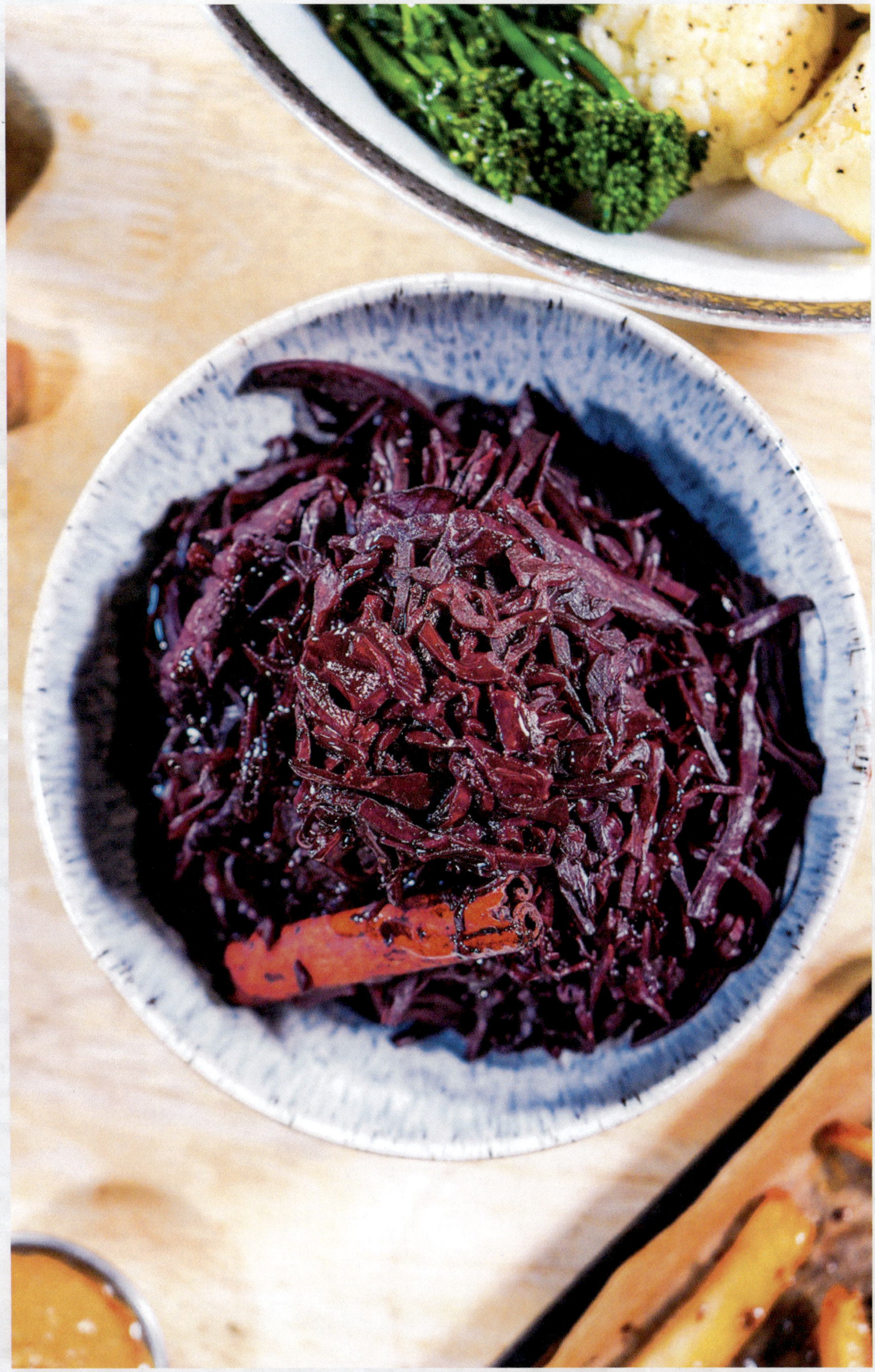

MINTED MUSHY PEAS

Nuts Free, Soy Free, Gluten Free, Refined Sugar Free

Proper mushy peas, made from scratch. Soaked, boiled, and cooked until these hard little bullets soften and swell releasing their characteristic flavour as they turn into the mush you love. No roast dinner is complete without these peas, they are high in iron, potassium, fibre and contain vitamins A, C, B1 and B5.

8 Servings

EQUIPMENT NEEDED:

A bowl to soak, colander, large heavy based pan, measuring jug, scales.

INGREDIENTS:

250g Dried Marrow Fat Peas, Soaked
2 Tbs Baking Powder
900ml Water
2 Tbs Butter
1 Tsp Garlic Powder
1 Tsp Dried Mint
Squeeze Of Lemon
Sea Salt to Taste
Pinch Of Cracked Black Pepper

Store in an airtight container in the fridge for 4-5 days or freeze for up to 3months.

Soak the marrow fat peas overnight in room temp water with the baking powder (see page 20 for benefits of soaking)

Once fully soaked, drain and rinse well.

Place the rinsed peas in a saucepan and cover with water, over a medium-high heat bring the peas to a boil, then reduce the heat to low and simmer for 45-55 minutes until soft, tender, and mushy.

Keep checking after 30 minutes to avoid the peas catching to the pan, especially towards the end, adding more water if necessary. If some of the peas are still hard, cook for slightly longer and just keep adding water until they are soft and mushy to avoid the pan burning.

Once all the peas are softened, mash in the butter, garlic, mint, lemon, and season well.

Serve and enjoy or allow proper cooling before storing.

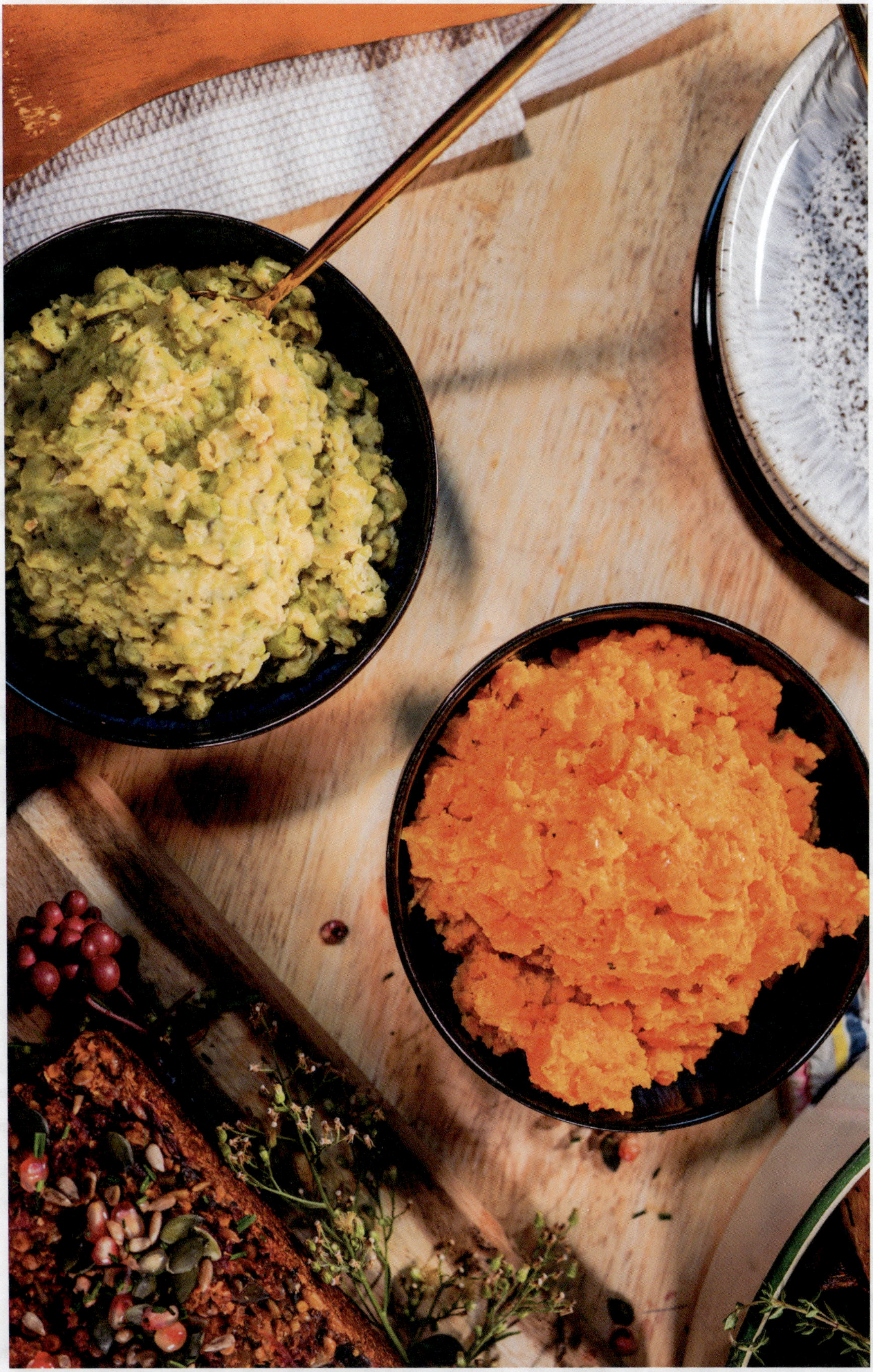

TRADITIONAL RICH GRAVY

NUTS FREE · SOY FREE · GLUTEN FREE · REFINED SUGAR FREE

Gravy made the right way; Gravy made my Nan's way... without the beef dripping of course!!

It's so easy these days to simply boil the kettle and scoop a spoon of gravy granules into some hot water for an instant thick and luxurious gravy, but where's the fun in that?

Adding homemade stock, to a homemade gluten free roux with some of my Nan's secret crumb, is much more appealing. This makes the most flavoursome, rich home-made gravy that saves on waist and costs pennies to make.

So, let's go back to basics and start from scratch by simply roasting off all the veg offcuts - (which realistically would have gone in the bin) with garlic and herbs to make a nice stock. Roasting vegetables first will deepen the flavour of a stock because of the caramelisation that takes place from the browning of the natural sugars in the veg. Then boiling up all the roasted veg for an hour literally makes the perfect base for a gravy.

8 Servings

EQUIPMENT NEEDED:

A medium heavy based saucepan, whisk, measuring jug, a set measuring cups, a spatula ladel.

INGREDIENTS:

1/2 Cup Plant-Based Butter
½ Cup Gluten Free Plain Flour
3 Garlic Cloves, Minced
5 Sprigs Thyme, Rough Chopped
2 Sprigs Rosemary, Rough Chopped
1/2 Cup Tomato Juice from Can
1 Tbs Gravy Salt Crumb
1 Tbs Veg Stock
1 Tbs Mushroom Stock
2 Litres Water or Home-Made Stock
Cracked Black Pepper

Melt the butter and garlic on low heat in the saucepan and add the flour to make a roux, cook out the roux for 3-5 minutes using a spatula too press out any lumps.

Crumble in the gravy salt and add stock powders into the roux, again pressing out any lumps with the spatula.

Add the rosemary and begin to whisk in the stock or water 1 ladle at time, as the liquid is added, the roux will thicken, make sure any lumps are whisked or pressed out at this point.

Add the tomato juice and bring to the boil, simmer for 20-25 minutes to let all the flavours infuse, roux cook out as the gravy thickens, add the thyme for the last 5 minutes.

Serve and enjoy smothered over our roast or allow proper cooling before storage.

Store in the fridge in an airtight container for 4-5 days or freeze for 3 months.

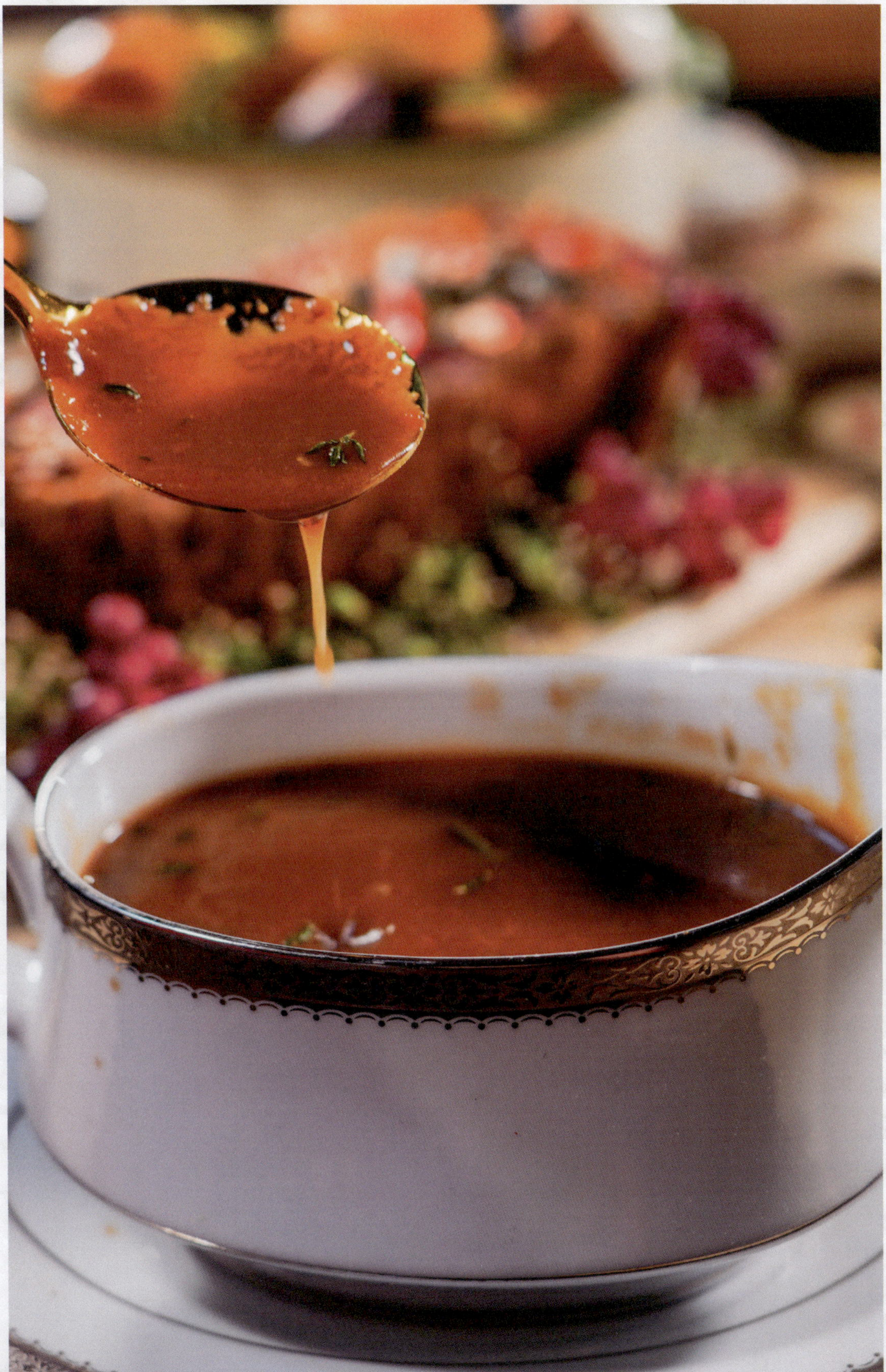

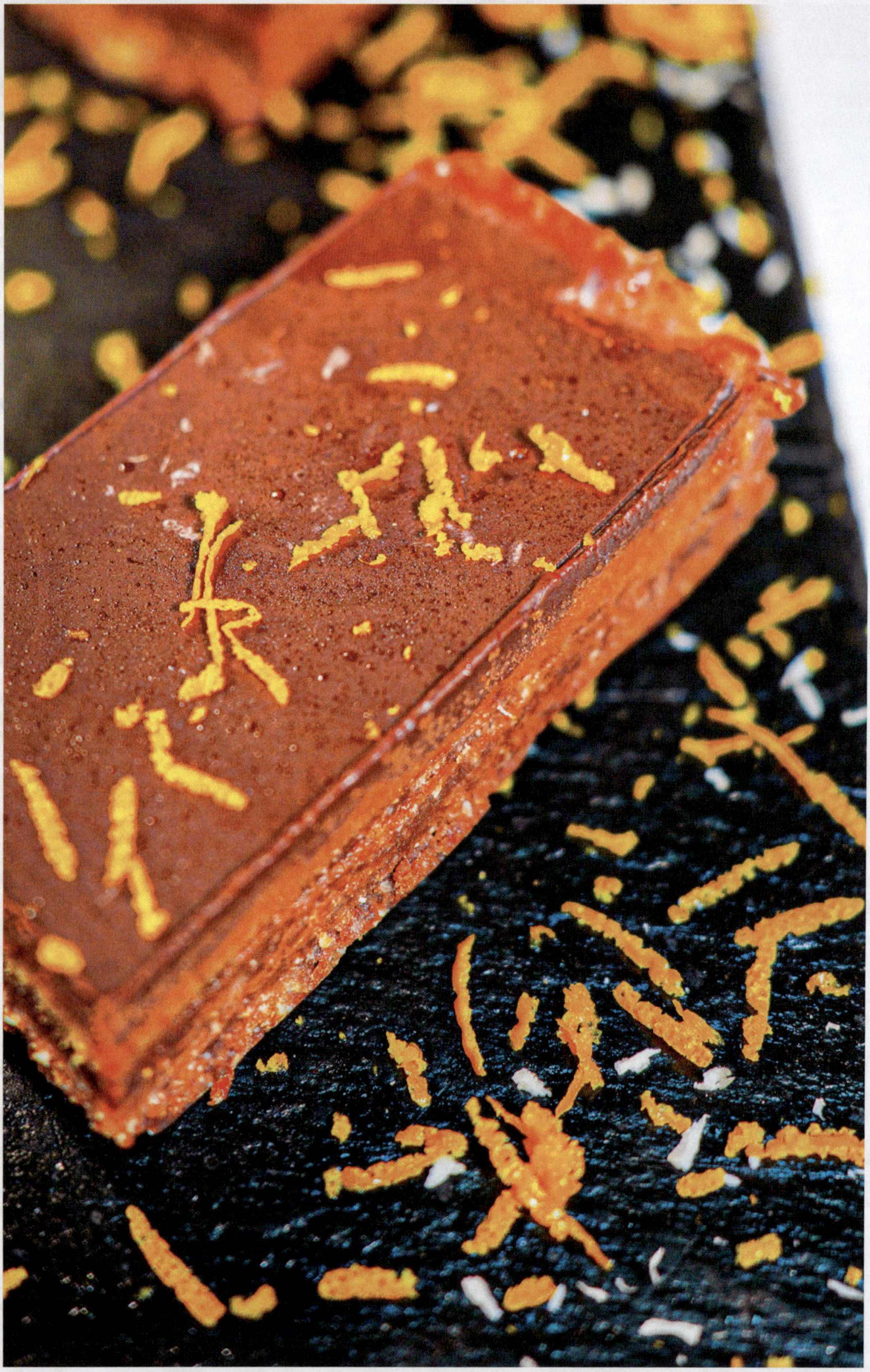

DESSERTS

When it came to offering desserts at Indigo Greens, we never planned to make our own - why would we when we have so many talented local independents who specialise in vegan desserts in our city. As a small business ourselves, we wanted to create a space that supported other vegan businesses too, bringing together the individual talents of our community and work side by side. We also thought it would be a great collaboration to feature their recipes in our cookbook, as our customers love their treats as much as they love our food.

We have been given permission to use the following recipes in our book.

Please note: A high-powered food processor like a Magi-mix is needed. If you don't have one then it is possible to use a food processor with less power, but it may take longer for everything to blend and come together

CHOCOLATE ORANGE COOKIE DOUGH SLABS - THE NAKERY RECIPE

NUTS FREE • SOY FREE • GLUTEN FREE • REFINED SUGAR FREE

These super rich Chocolate Orange Cookie Dough Slabs are one of 'The Nakerys' most popular treats. Not only do they taste sensational with that citrus note, but they are also highly nutritious and filled with plenty of fibre, protein, heart healthy fats, vitamins and minerals - including magnesium, which so many of us are often deficient in. Magnesium has been proven to be a key part of over 300 cellular roles in the body and it's the cacao in this recipe that offers so much of it. The cacao plant has also been used for thousands of years as a sacred heart-opening, healing medicine in the indigenous tribes. If you're not a fan of chocolate orange try swapping out the flavour for peppermint, rose or lemon.

8-10 Servings

EQUIPMENT NEEDED:

A food processor, spring form tin, chopping board, sharp knife.

INGREDIENTS:

Cookie Dough Layer:

275g Oats
225g Ground Almonds
200g Maple Syrup
80g Raw Chocolate Chips
60g Coconut Oil
3 Tbs Cacao Powder (either regular or ceremonial grade)
2 Tsp Orange Extract
Himalayan Pink Salt

Raw Caramel Layer:

140g Pre-Soaked Dates (soak in boiled water for 15 minutes)
100g Almond Butter
75g Coconut Oil
Orange Extract (to taste)

Raw Chocolate Layer:

200g Raw Vegan Chocolate of your choice
Small amount of coconut oil

Firstly, add oats into a food processor until a flour forms. Then, add almond flour until well mixed.

Next add coconut oil, orange extract and maple and blitz again until it reaches a dough-like consistency.

Then add your chocolate chips, cacao powder and pinch of salt. Blend until well combined but try not to overbend so that the chocolate chips remain intact. You want the different textures to stand out here.

Press this into a pre-greased springform tin and set aside. Sometimes it's also best to line the tin with parchment paper too, to avoid sticking.

For the caramel layer, add the pre-soaked dates into the food processor along with the coconut oil, almond butter, and orange extract.

Blend until smooth and then spread evenly onto the cookie dough base.

Set the slab aside in the freezer for about one hour.

After one hour, melt your raw vegan chocolate using the double boiler method. Add a few tbs of melted coconut oil to thin out the chocolate slightly. (You want to be able to pour this on to the cookie dough slab).

Pour on to cookie dough and set for a further 15 minutes in the freezer.

Cut into size of your choice and serve.

Keep in fridge for one week or in the freezer for one month in an airtight container.

Instagram – thenakery

Mission: "To re-connect people back to nature. By using healing ingredients with intention, that have been used for thousands of years, we can bring the sacredness back into food."

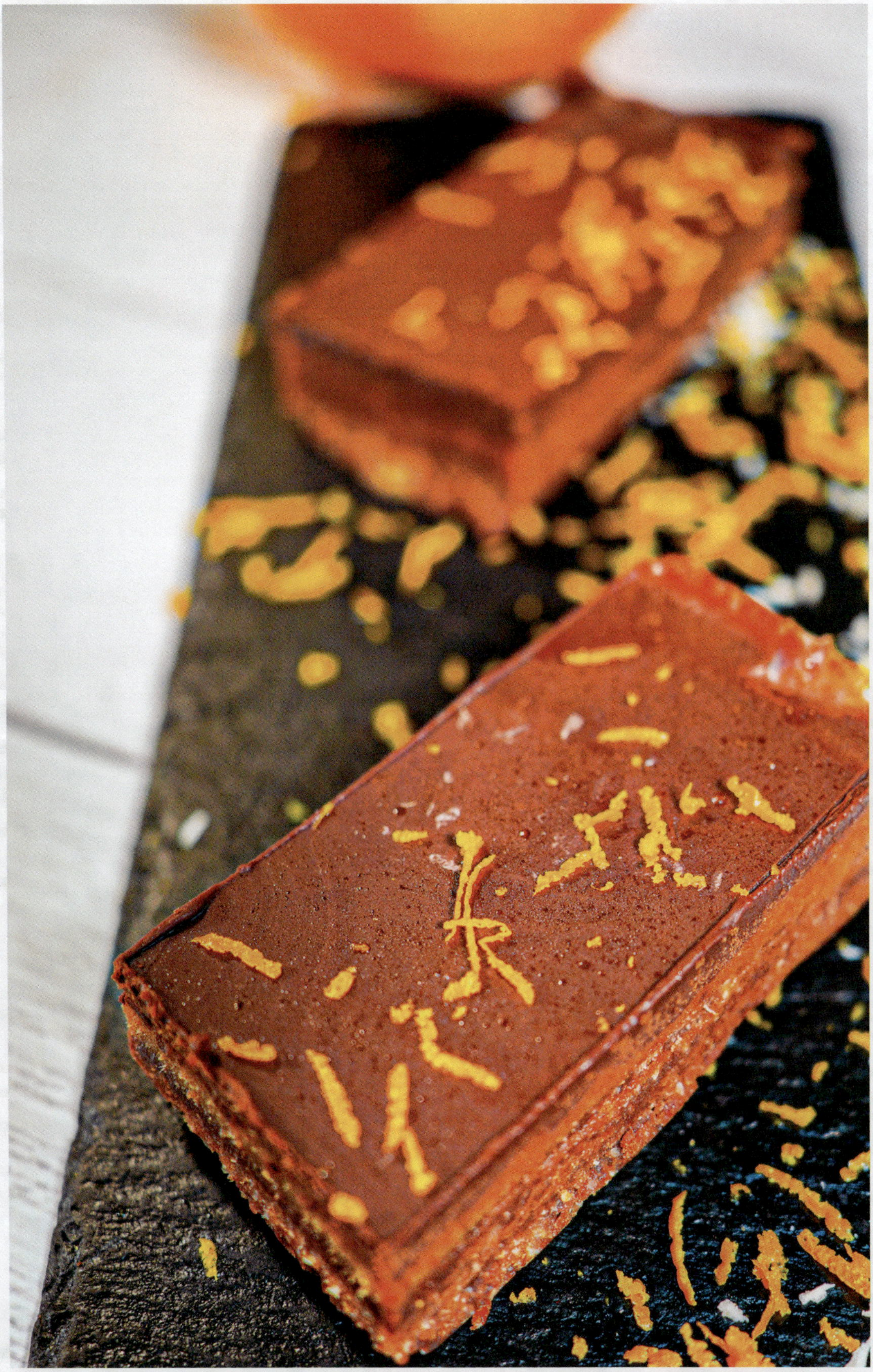

TAHINI ENERGY BALLS
– HI VIBE NUTRITION RECIPE

Who doesn't love a good healthy easy to make treat? With only 5 natural ingredients you can make these delicious Tahini Energy balls from Hi Vibe Nutrition in just 10 minutes. These super nutritious snacks are high in fibre, minerals, and good fats so they are good for the heart health, brain function and thyroid health. Cashew nuts are a great source of plant-based protein, low in sugar and rich in fibre making these a great addition to your daily diet. Tahini is one of the main ingredients in this recipe which can help lower cholesterol and coconut is high in selenium, manganese and copper, so combining these ingredients together is not only a delicious treat but also offers lots of health benefits too.

10-12 Servings

EQUIPMENT NEEDED:
A food processor, baking tray.

INGREDIENTS:
1 ½ Cups of Desiccated Coconut
½ Cup Cashew Nuts
½ Cup Raisins
¼ Cup Agave
½ Cup Tahini

To make these Tahini Energy Balls simply put all ingredients into a food processor and blend until the mixture becomes sticky.

Once you can squeeze the mixture together and it sticks, they are ready to roll into Energy balls, I recommend rolling 1-inch sizes balls, but you can make them as big or small as you like.

Then place them onto a tray with grease proof paper and leave them in the fridge for 1 hour. Your Energy Balls are now ready to eat.

Store in an airtight container in the fridge for up to 1 month or in the freezer for 3 months.

Instagram – hi_vibenutrition

Hi Vibe nutrition offer 100% plant based healthy fresh home-cooked food made consciously with love, for your nourishment and dietary needs.

Mission: "To help you love life to the Fullest and live life to the Fullest, the closer we get back to mother earth the more we thrive."

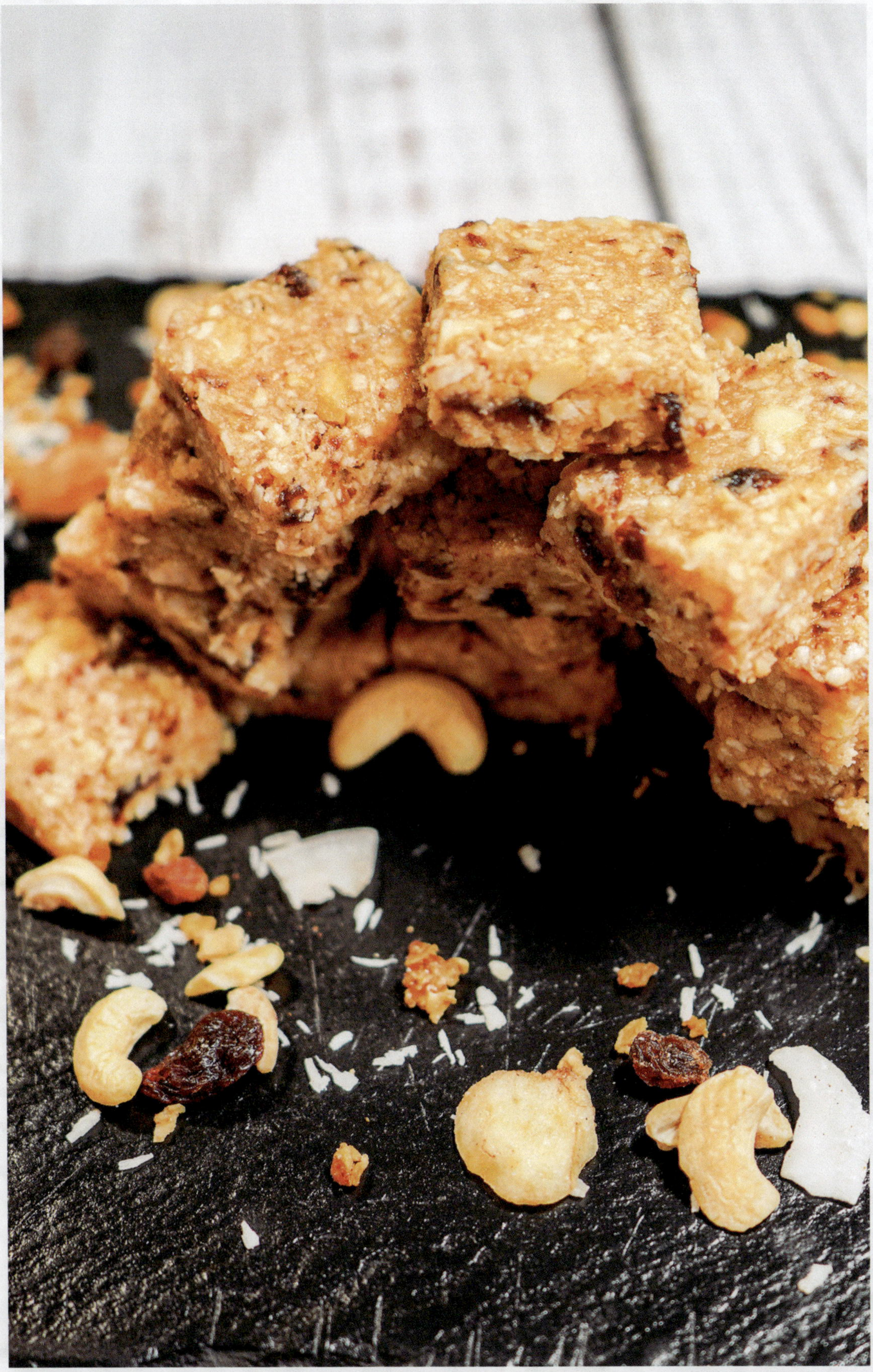

POWER HEALING BALLS
– CELL FUEL RECIPE

A succulent and moist mixture of adaptogenic ingredients that provide an instant hit of energy and an abundance of essential nutrients from protein, fibre, zinc, magnesium, selenium, iron, omega 3 and amino acids. Cell-Fuel focuses on creating natural organic whole food treats that help heal the gut, the mind and of course, repair the cells.

Try splitting this batch into 3 before balling and adding different flavours to each batch so you have yourself a selection of yummy healthy treats for the weeks ahead.

---

20 Servings

EQUIPMENT NEEDED:

A chopping board, sharp knife, box grater, mixing bowl, colander, peeler.

INGREDIENTS:

1kg date, pitted
150g each Brazil, almond, cashew and walnut
150g hemp seeds, shelled
300g oats, gluten free
150g sunflower and pumpkin seeds
2 tbs Sea Moss (optional)
2 tbs Maca powder (optional)
2 tsp Mint/Orange/ Rose Essence (optional for flavour)

Decoration

Cacao Powder
Coconut, desiccated
Orange zest
Lemon zest
Rose petals

Soak the pitted dates in warm water for 30minuites until soft.

Take the dates from the water and blend into a paste.

Add the rest of the ingredients to the blender, including your choice of natural flavouring (optional), whizz up until all the ingredients are combined forming a thick sticky dough.

Remove from the blender and shape into even sized balls on to a lined baking tray or use an ice cream scoop to save you time, dipping in boiling hot water after each ball.

Roll the balls in-between your palms and then roll them in a decoration of your choice.

Place balls in freezer to set.

Allow an hour to thaw before eating.

Store in an airtight container in the fridge for 4-5 days or freeze for up to 3months.

Instagram – iam.nutritional.guru

Mission: "To unlock humanity's potential by improving quality of life through Healing of CELLf with plant powered fuel - CELLfUEL."

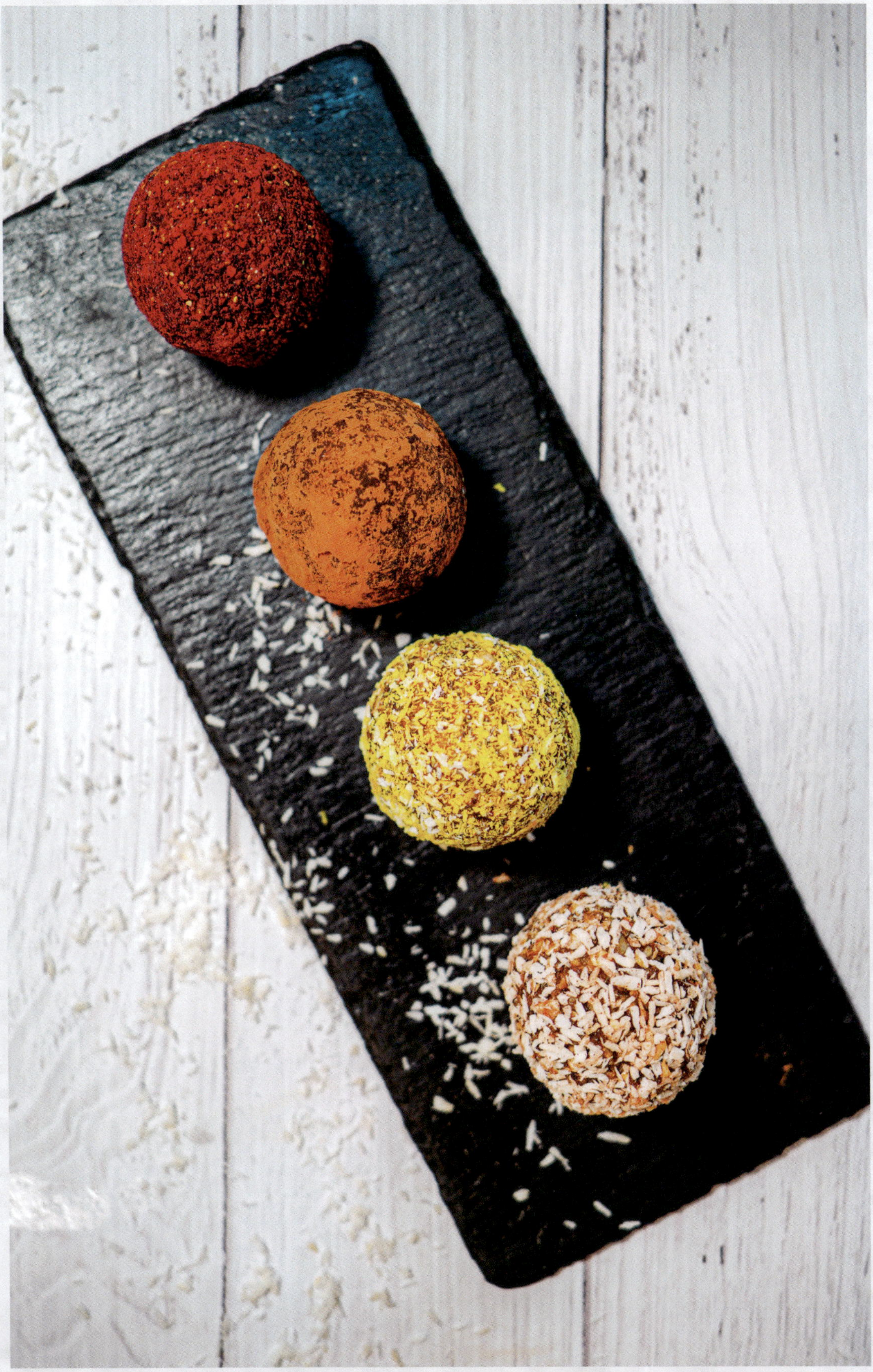

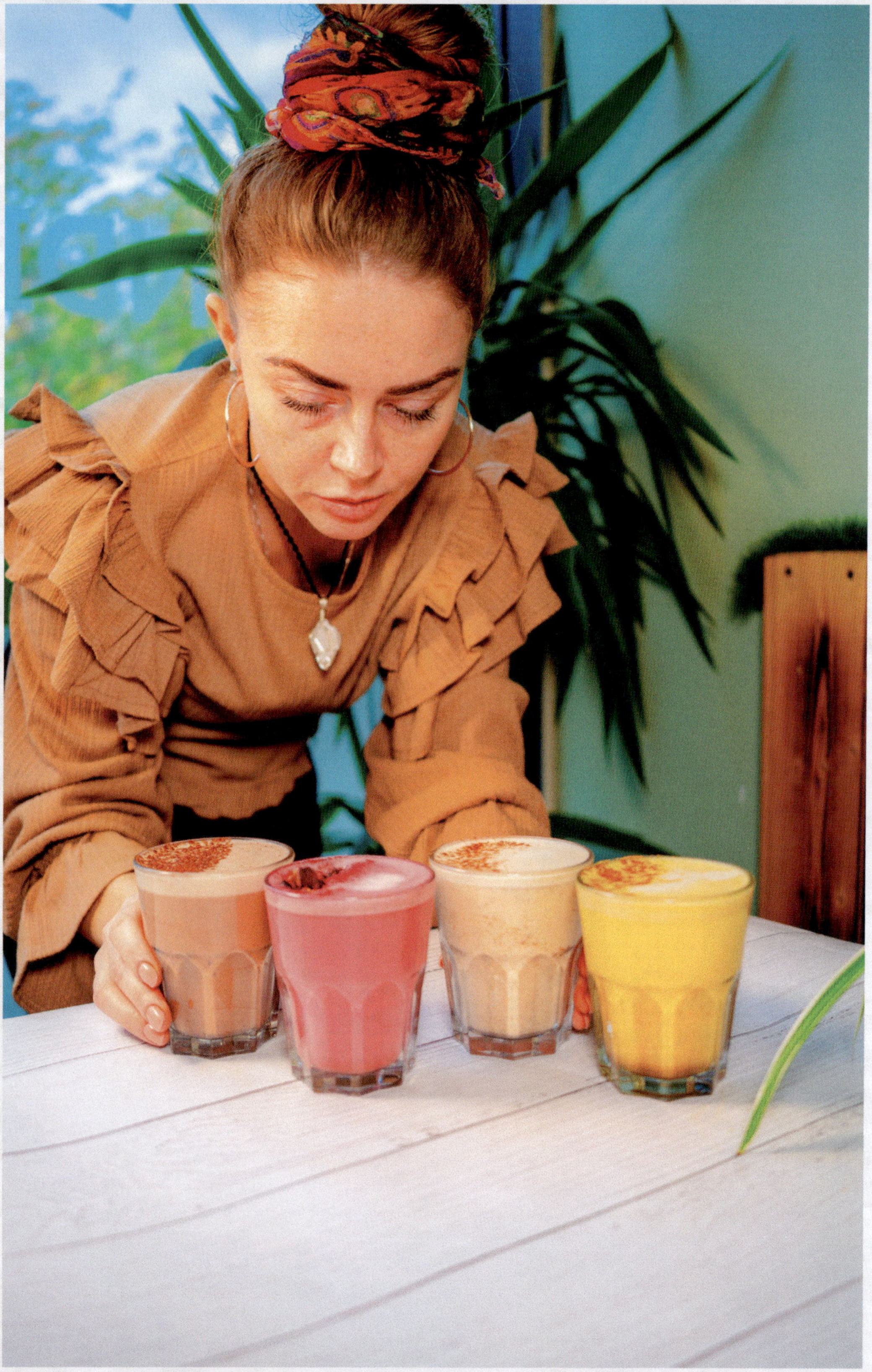

SUPERFOOD LATTE BLENDS

Superfood Lattes have recently made a name for themselves in the world of health and wellness. These vibrant and colourful, healthy alternatives to espresso-based beverages offer a host of health benefits and caffeine-free energy boosts. A warm frothy milk-based drink steamed with a special blend of adaptogenic ingredients high in minerals and vitamins, that taste as good as they look!

TURMERIC LATTE BLEND

An aromatic blend of inflammatory relieving ingredients. Turmeric has been used in India for thousands of years as both a spice and medicinal herb. Recently, science has started to back up traditional claims that turmeric contains compounds with medicinal properties called curcuminoids. Curcumin is the main active ingredient in turmeric, adding black pepper (piperine) enhances the curcumin absorption in the body by 2000% magnifying the healing effects of turmeric.

16 Servings
INGREDIENTS: 5 Tsp Ground Turmeric, 5 Tsp Ground Ginger, 5 Tsp Ground Cinnamon, 1 Tsp Black Pepper
Store in an airtight jar in a cool dark place for up to 6 months.

MUSHY MACA CHOCO LATTE BLEND

An original adaptogenic blend created in house containing the now well-known Reishi Mushroom which has its primary immune-boosting properties, this special complex supports everything from cognitive function, mental wellbeing and energy levels, to healthy digestion, lower levels of inflammation, protection from oxidative stress and general wellness.

10 Servings
INGREDIENTS: 4 Tsp Cacao Powder, 2 Tsp Reishi Mushroom Powder, 2 Tsp Gelatinised Macca Powder, 1 Tsp Nutmeg, 1 Tsp Cinnamon
Store in an airtight jar in a cool dark place for up to 6 months.

BEETROOT AND GINGER LATTE BLEND

Beetroot powder is concentrated form of the blood producing vegetable that's has been known to help people with heart failure, heart disease, blood pressure and cardiovascular problems. This blend of beetroot and immune boosting ginger makes the perfect heart healing elixir that heats and warms up our vital organs from within.

20 Servings
INGREDIENTS: 10 Tsp Beetroot Powder, 10 Tsp Ginger Powder
Store in an airtight jar in a cool dark place for up to 6months.

SPICED CHAI LATTE BLEND

With such a potent mix of spices including cardamom, cinnamon, ginger, and cloves. Our Chai Latte is a powerhouse latte and benefits relating to each spice - cinnamon, one of the main ingredients of our blend, has been found to lower blood pressure, the cinnamon and ginger help increase insulin sensitivity and reduce blood sugar levels. Ginger and cloves are known to reduce nausea and cardamon to prevent bacterial infections and support proper digestion.

6-8 Servings
INGREDIENTS: 3tsp Ground All Spice, 3 tsp Ground Cinnamon, 3tsp Ground Ginger, 1 ½ Tsp Ground Nutmeg, 1½ tsp Ground Cloves, 1½ Ground Cardamon
Store in an airtight jar in a cool dark place for up to 6 months.

TO MAKE A SUPER FOOD LATTE

EQUIPMENT NEEDED:

A mixing bowl, small whisk, an airtight jar for storage.

METHOD

Mix 1 tsp of the superfood blend with a dash of hot water and stir into your preferred cup.

Either steam or boil enough milk fill the cup.

Once hot, slowly pour the milk into the blend, keeping the foam back with a spoon till the very end, creating a frothy layer.

Sprinkle with some of the blend for decoration.

Add a dash of maple syrup to sweeten (optional).

RESOURCES

This section has been added in the hope that this book has opened your eyes and heart to a whole new world of plant-based living. I wish that each reader takes it upon themselves to study the importance of natural whole foods, sustainable living, and animal welfare further, for the future of humanity.

We live in an age where information is just a click of a button away, so there is no longer any excuse to turn a blind eye. Do not let ignorance overrule what you know deep down in your heart is right!

We all have a choice....

Links:

- https://www.webmd.com
- https://www.healthline.com
- https://ourworldindata.org
- https://www.everydayhealth.com
- https://www.nationalgeographic.co.uk

Documentaries:

- A Life on Our Planet – David Attenborough
- What The Health
- Forks Over Knives
- Seaspiracy
- Cowspiracy
- The Game Changes
- Earthlings
- Fat, Sick and Nearly Dead

Printed in Poland
by Amazon Fulfillment
Poland Sp. z o.o., Wrocław
06 June 2022